Quality
Management
for Government

Also available from ASQC Quality Press

Recovering Prosperity Through Quality:
The Midland City Story
Robert A. Schwarz

Government Quality and Productivity: Success Stories
Henry L. Lefevre, editor

Incredibly American: Releasing the Heart of Quality
Marilyn R. Zuckerman and Lewis J. Hatala

A Quality System for Education
Stanley J. Spanbauer

ASQC Total Quality Management Series
Richard S. Johnson

Principles and Practices of TQM
Thomas J. Cartin

Benchmarking: The Search for Industry Best Practices
that Lead to Superior Performance
Robert C. Camp

The Whats, Whys, and Hows of Quality Improvement
George L. Miller and LaRue L. Krumm

Root Cause Analysis: A Tool for Total Quality Management
Paul F. Wilson, Larry D. Dell, and Gaylord F. Anderson

To receive a complimentary catalog of publications,
call 800-248-1946.

Quality Management for Government

A Guide to Federal, State, and Local Implementation

V. Daniel Hunt

ASQC Quality Press
Milwaukee, Wisconsin

Quality Management for Government:
A Guide to Federal, State, and Local Implementation
V. Daniel Hunt

Library of Congress Cataloging-in-Publication Data
Hunt, V. Daniel
    Quality management for government: a guide to federal, state, and
local implementation / V. Daniel Hunt.
        p. cm.
    Includes bibliographical references and index.
    ISBN 0-87389 239-9 (acid-free paper)
    1. Total quality management.   2. Public administration.   3. United
States—Politics and government.   4. State governments—United
States.   5. Local government—United States.   I. Title.
JF1525.T67H86   1993
350.007'8'0973—dc20   93-6397
                                                           CIP

10 9 8 7 6 5 4 3 2 1

ISBN 0-87389-239-9

Acquisitions Editor: Susan Westergard
Production Editor: Annette Wall
Marketing Administrator: Mark Olson
Set in Galliard and Avant Garde by Linda J. Shepherd.
Cover design by Daryl Poulin.
Printed and bound by BookCrafters, Inc.

ASQC Mission: To facilitate continuous improvement and increase customer satisfaction by identifying, communicating, and promoting the use of quality principles, concepts, and technologies; and
thereby be recognized throughout the world as the leading authority on, and champion for, quality.

For a free copy of the ASQC Quality Press Publications Catalog, including ASQC membership information, call 800-248-1946.

Printed in the United States of America

 Printed on acid-free recycled paper

 ASQC
Quality Press
611 East Wisconsin Avenue
Milwaukee, Wisconsin 53202

To Janet Claire Hunt,
the co-producer of this book.

Contents

Foreword

Americans have long enjoyed a love-hate relationship with their government. We hate big government and red tape. We never seem to tire, on the other hand, of praising economy in government, stressing our desire for a more responsive government, and seeking one that operates on a human scale. In short, Americans hate all the negative images usually associated with the term *bureaucracy* and love the ideal images associated with *good government*.

As a nation, our long-standing historical goal is to stem the downward slide into an unproductive welfare state and, at the same time, increase government productivity. Government, most Americans now agree, cannot continue on its present inefficient and expensive course much longer. With the rising federal deficit, pressure is mounting to quickly find a way to fulfill our long-standing vision of good government.

On top of these domestic factors comes a new incentive for change. As the private sector shifts from bureaucratic to customer-responsive management methods in order to compete successfully in the emerging global marketplace, American government at federal, state, and local levels must follow suit. It makes no sense whatsoever for America to build a world-class private sector while our public sector remains bogged down in a bureaucratic quagmire.

To compete in the global economy, we need a productive public sector just as much as we need a productive private sector. If American companies are to compete head-to-head with European and Asian challengers, and come out on top, government enterprises must be far more responsive and ready than they are today to train and educate our workers to meet changing labor demands. And the public infrastructure upon which a modern private sector prospers is also largely under the control of public institutions. But, if this goal is to be met, business as usual in Washington, Sacramento, and Allentown will not do. A new way of managing the public's business must be adopted now.

The *good news* is that the total quality revolution that got its start in American firms in the mid-1980s is doing well. It has led to great strides in productivity, competitiveness, and cost reductions in both large and small manufacturing and service firms. The *great news* is that these proven management techniques can also work to boost government productivity.

What I have in mind is the widespread empowerment of public employees to do their jobs better and at less cost. This can be done by giving all workers the right education, training, and leadership; by giving them sufficient responsibility and the authority to do their jobs right, the first time; and by organizing work along the team approach— the very heart of total quality management. Public managers need not reinvent quality management. Public managers need only take a commonsense approach as they adapt a proven set of management tools for use in public agencies.

I realize that the public sector's work environment is not the same as that found in the private sector. But recent experience has clearly shown that as quality management practices in public agencies are implemented, costs come down—just as in the private sector. The reason is simple: the payoff of total quality management in *both* sectors is rooted in how the workers are treated. Depending on the management system in use, the very same workers can be taught to act like wasteful bureaucrats or efficiency-minded team members. In fact, studies show that workers actually prefer the quality approach to the bureaucratic approach. The choice of which system best serves the interests of America in the 1990s is ours to make—as individuals, as public leaders, and as a nation struggling to preserve our place among world-class competitors.

If Japan can rise from the ashes and prosper using the total quality management revolution and if Ford Motor Company, Xerox, Motorola—and thousands of other Americans companies—can turn from near extinction to some of the best-run companies in the world, so can our government agencies.

The *best news of all*, however, is that a handful of brave public pioneers has already introduced total quality management into the federal workplace. Unfortunately, top executive-branch leadership and members of Congress in Washington are hardly aware of the budding revolution that is taking place right under their noses.

All we need to do to ensure that this workplace revolution does, in fact, transform a listless American bureaucracy into a responsive government of the people, for the people, and by the people is to nurture and spread the work of these quality pioneers. We need only support these brave souls in the Department of Defense, Department of Interior, Social Security Administration, General Services Administration, Veterans Administration—even the Internal Revenue Service—where they have already established quality beachheads.

Support comes in different sizes and shapes. In the U.S. Congress, the kind of support I have in mind includes a new willingness to change the way we legislate, regulate, tax, and spend, and most of all, the way we go about serving the ultimate customer—the American people. At the federal-agency level, support means training all workers in quality management principles and practices and kicking the bureaucratic habit. Total quality management promises to transform American public managers from old-fashioned, hierarchical bosses into leaders who empower their team members to take responsibility for themselves and for fulfilling their human potential on the job.

At the individual level, support means that every public employee from coast to coast should read V. Daniel Hunt's book *Quality Management for Government*. In the chapters that follow is a step-by-step road map to quality management *and*, equally important, to quality leadership in the public workplace. This is not, I stress, a book to be read only by managers, bosses, and executives. The total quality workplace of the future will demand a team approach in which all workers identify and solve problems.

V. Daniel Hunt's clearly written book should be treated as the public foot soldier's guerrilla-warfare manual for quality improvement in the 1990s. The enemies, outdated bureaucratic management practices, are under attack. Our customers are not satisfied with the quality of service we provide and are demanding a change in how government works. Government can provide quality services. The change is up to you!

Don Ritter
Former Congressman, Pennsylvania

Acknowledgments

Quality Management for Government has been developed based on information from a wide variety of authorities who are specialists in their respective fields.

The following publications were used as the basic resources for this book. Portions of these publications may have been used in the book. The text, ideas, definitions, or artwork that have been used are reproduced with the permission of the respective publishers. Federal government publications are in the public domain.

Applegate, Carolyn, Susan Hocevar, and Kenneth W. Thomas. *Total Quality Management in Ten Exemplary Department of Defense Organizations: Lessons Learned, Innovative Practices, and Quality Measurements.* Monterey, Calif.: NPS-AS-92-003, Naval Postgraduate School, November 1991.

AT&T. *AT&T Quality Improvement Process Guidebook.* Baskin Ridge, N.J.: AT&T, 1988.

Carr, David K., and Ian D. Littman. *Excellence in Government: Total Quality Management in the 1990s.* Washington, D.C.: Coopers and Lybrand, 1990.

Crosby, Philip B. *Quality Is Free*. New York: McGraw-Hill, 1979.

————. *Quality Without Tears*. New York: McGraw-Hill, 1984.

Deming, W. Edwards. *Out of the Crisis*. Boston: MIT Center for Advanced Engineering Study, 1986.

Department of Defense. *Quality and Productivity Self-Assessment Guide for Defense Organizations*. Washington, D.C., 1990.

Dertouzos, Michael L., Richard K. Lester, and Robert M. Solow. *Made in America: Regaining the Productive Edge*. Cambridge, Mass.: MIT Press, 1989.

Federal Quality Institute. *Federal Total Quality Management Handbook*. Washington, D.C.: U.S. Government Printing Office, 1990.

————. "The Federal Quality Awards Program." First International Symposium on Productivity and Quality Improvement with a Focus on Government. Washington, D.C., February 10–12, 1992.

Hunt, V. Daniel. *Quality in America: How to Implement a Competitive Quality Program*. Homewood, Ill.: Business One Irwin, 1992.

————. *Managing for Quality*. Homewood, Ill.: Business One Irwin, 1993.

Juran, J. M. *Juran on Planning for Quality*. New York: Free Press, 1988.

Juran, J. M., and Frank M. Gryna, eds. *Juran's Quality Control Handbook*. 4th ed. New York: McGraw-Hill, 1988.

LMI (Mansir, Brian E., and Nicholas R. Schacht). *An Introduction of the Continuous Improvement Process, Principles and Practices*. Bethesda, Md.: Logistics Management Institute, August 1989.

LMI. *Total Quality Management—A Guide to Implementation*. Bethesda, Md.: Logistics Management Institute, August 1989.

National Technical Information Service. *A Guide to Benchmarking in Xerox*, NTIS Publication PB91-780106. Springfield, Va.: NTIS, 1990.

Office of the Deputy Assistant Secretary of Defense for Total Quality Management. *Total Quality Management Guide*. Vols. 1 and 2. DoD 5000.51-G, February 15, 1990.

Osborne, David, and Ted Gaebler. *Reinventing Government: How the Entrepreneurial Spirit Is Transforming the Public Sector.* Reading, Mass.: Addison-Wesley, 1992.

Peters, Thomas J., and Robert H. Waterman. *In Search of Excellence.* New York: Harper and Row, 1982.

Peters, Thomas J., and Nancy Austin. *A Passion for Excellence.* New York: Random House, 1985.

Reliability Analysis Center. *A Guide for Implementing Total Quality Management.* State-of-the-art report, Report SOAR-7. Rome, N.Y.: Rome AFB, 1990.

Rogers, Everett M. *Diffusion of Innovations.* New York: Free Press, 1983.

Scherkenbach, William W. *The Deming Route to Quality and Productivity.* Washington, D.C.: CEEPress, 1988.

U.S. Department of Transportation. *Lessons Learned: Getting Started/Revitalizing Your TQM Effort,* Vol. 1 no. 2. January 1992.

U.S. General Accounting Office. *Management Practices—U.S. Companies Improve Performance Through Quality Efforts.* GAO/NS1AD-91-190, May 1991.

U.S. General Accounting Office. *Quality Management—Survey of Federal Organizations.* GAO/GGD-93-9BR, October 1992.

Walton, Mary. *Deming Management at Work.* New York: G. P. Putnam, 1990.

Xerox. *USMG Partnership: The Way We Work.* Rochester, N.Y.: USMG Printing Office, 1988.

The continuous improvement concepts used in this book are from "An Introduction to the Continuous Improvement Process—Principles and Practices" developed by LMI under DoD contract MDA903-85-C-0139. We thank DoD and LMI for permission to use their material.

The preparation of a book of this type is dependent upon an excellent staff, and I have been fortunate in this regard. Special thanks to Donald Keehan and Ronald Fraser for their research assistance. I also appreciate the careful and conscientious editing by Susan Messer and the careful and accurate preparation of the manuscript by Valerie J. Western.

Many individuals provided material, interview comments, and insights regarding how to improve quality management in government. I appreciate their input and help in shaping this book. Special recognition is noted for **Jim Abbott,** IRS One Stop Accounting System; **Jack Adams,** Naval Aviation Depot (Cherry Point); **Peter Angiola,** Office of the Under Secretary of Defense for Acquisition, Total Quality Management; **James T. Benn,** Norfolk Naval Shipyard; **Ken Biddle,** Defense Industrial Supply Center; **Theresa A. Brelsford,** Assistant Commissioner for Public Service and Administration, U.S. Patent and Trademark Office, U.S. Department of Commerce; **Peter Brightbill,** California Department of Consumer Affairs; **Dr. Laurie A. Broedling,** former deputy undersecretary of defense for total quality management (now with NASA); **Jim Buckman,** president, Minnesota Council for Quality; **Carolyn Burstein,** Federal Quality Institute; **Pat Callahan,** IRS Federal Tax Deposit System; **Governor Anne H. Carlson,** state of Minnesota; **David K. Carr,** partner, Coopers & Lybrand; **Clifford Carroll,** 1926th Communications; **Marianne K. Clarke,** National Governors' Association; **Karen Cleaves,** Defense Contract Management District; **former Governor Bill Clinton,** state of Arkansas; **Governor Mario M. Cuomo,** New York State; **Martha Curry,** IRS Cincinnati Service Center; **General Jack Daily,** NASA TQM Program; **Jodi Davenport,** IRS Center at Fresno, California; **Eric N. Dobson,** National Governors' Association; **Linda M. Doherty,** Department of the Navy; **David Ellison,** assistant city manager, city of Lubbock, Texas; **Joanne Z. FitzGibbon,** New York State, Department of Economic Development; **Mary Hamilton,** director for quality management, U.S. General Accounting Office; **Jim Folz,** Sacramento Air Logistics; **Colonel Bill Friel,** Air Force Logistics Command, assistant to the commander for quality, HQ AFLC/QP Wright-Patterson AFB, Ohio; **Joan Griffey,** U.S. Patent & Trademark

Office; **James E. Hamilton,** Chief Quality Assurance Support Division, IRS; **Dr. Mary A. Hartz,** total quality management section leader, IIT Research Institute; **Don Hodgen,** VA Regional Office; **Colonel Jim Hintz,** Aeronautical Systems Division; **Julie Lambert,** American Productivity and Quality Center, Texas; **John Leitch,** assistant director, General Government Division, U.S. General Accounting Office; **Ian D. Littman,** director, total quality management, Coopers & Lybrand; **Ray Malatino,** director of quality, Naval Air Systems Command; **Shelby McCook,** quality administrator, state of Arkansas; **John McGinn,** director of the DCMD Northeast TQM Office, Defense Logistics Agency; **Ron Mertens,** Board of Commerce and Industry, Wichita Falls, Texas; **Kristine Mossinghoff,** coordinator, "Quality Texas,"; **Jane Newsome,** McLennan Community College, Waco, Texas; **Jan Partain,** Arkansas Quality Management Program, Arkansas Industrial Development Commission; **Donna Rosefield,** award administrator, North Carolina Quality Leadership Foundation; **Timothy Reardon,** San Francisco Region, Wage & Hour; **Dr. Curt W. Reimann,** director, Malcolm Baldrige National Quality Award, National Institute of Standard and Technology; **Joseph Sensenbrenner,** Sensenbrenner and Associates; **Barbara Shatto,** Veterans Administration Medical Center—Kansas City; **Mary Sibley,** U.S. Department of Transportation; **Tina Sung,** Federal Quality Institute; **Les Sullivan,** Greater Houston Quality Group, NASA Johnson Space Center; **Governor Pete Wilson,** state of California; **Patricia B. Wood,** Federal Quality Institute.

Permissions Acknowledgments

Grateful acknowledgment is made to the following for permission to reprint portions of previously published materials.

- Portions from David Osborne and Ted Gaebler, *Reinventing Government*, © 1992 by David Osborne and Ted Gaebler. Reprinted with permission of Addison-Wesley Publishing Company, Inc.

- Portions of "Quality Template" and related research material reprinted from *Quality in America: How to Implement a Competitive Quality Program* by V. Daniel Hunt. Published by Business One Irwin, 1992. Reprinted with permission of Technology Research Corporation.

- Portions of "Total Quality Management Initiatives in State Government," April 1, 1992; "Promoting Quality Businesses: A State Action Agenda," 1992; and "Designing and Implementing a State Quality Award," February 1993, by Eric Dobson, National Governors' Association, have been reprinted with permission. Portions of this material were previously published by ASQC in *Quality Progress* Vol. 26 no. 5, May 1993, entitled "The State of the States," and is reprinted with permission of ASQC.

1 Quality Management in Government Today

*The people who work in government are not the prob-
lem; the systems in which they work are the problem.*

David Osborne and Ted Gaebler
Reinventing Government

Reinventing Government

In their book entitled *Reinventing Government,* David Osborne and
Ted Gaebler reiterated the *Time* magazine cover question "Is Government Dead?" As the 1990s unfold, the answer—to many Americans—
appears to be yes.

Our public schools are the worst in the developed world. Our health
care costs are out of control. Our courts and prisons are so overcrowded
that convicted felons walk free. And many of our proudest cities and
states are virtually bankrupt.

Confidence in government has fallen to record lows. By the late
1980s, only 5 percent of Americans surveyed said they would choose
government service as their preferred career.

Only 13 percent of top federal employees said they would recommend a career in public service. Nearly three out of four Americans said
they believed Washington delivered less value for the dollar than it had
10 years earlier.

In 1990, the bottom really fell out. It was as if all our governments
had hit the wall, at the same time. Our states struggled with multi-
billion-dollar deficits. Our cities laid off thousands of employees. Our
federal deficit ballooned toward $400 billion.

1

Since the tax revolt first began to sweep the nation in 1978, the American people have demanded, in election after election and on issue after issue, more performance for less money. And yet, during the recession of 1990 to 1992, our leaders debated the same old options: fewer services or higher taxes.

Today, public fury alternates with apathy. We watch breathlessly as Eastern Europe and the Soviet republics overthrow the deadening hand of bureaucracy and oppression. But at home we feel impotent. Our cities succumb to mounting crime and poverty, our states are handcuffed by staggering deficits, and Washington drifts through it all like 30 square miles within the Beltway cut off from reality.

Yet there is hope. Slowly, quietly, far from the spotlight, new kinds of government institutions are emerging. They are lean, decentralized, and innovative. They are flexible, adaptable, and quick to learn new ways when conditions change. They use competition, customer satisfaction, and other nonbureaucratic mechanisms to get things done as creatively and effectively as possible. And they are our future."[1]

Osborne and Gaebler have stated that the fundamental problem today is

> *Not too much government or too little government. We had debated that issue endlessly since the tax revolt of 1978, and it has not solved our problems. Our fundamental problem is that we have* the wrong kind of government. *We do not need more government or less government, we need* better *government. To be more precise, we need better* governance.
>
> *Governance is the process by which we collectively solve our problems and meet our society's needs. Government is the instrument we use. The instrument is outdated, and the process of reinvention has begun.*[2]

Quality Is Good Government

One management approach that has been successfully demonstrated to help reinvent government is quality management. Quality management is much used but often vaguely defined. A recent report by the General

Accounting Office (GAO), *Management Practices: U.S. Companies Improve Performance Through Quality Efforts,* described quality management as "a new approach to the art of management that seeks to improve product quality and increase customer satisfaction by restructuring traditional management practices." The overriding objective of quality management is customer satisfaction. Quality management is not so much a specific set of activities as it is a management approach in which every employee is empowered with direct responsibilities related to the quality of the products or services provided by the organization.

Although quality management principles will be applied in unique ways to each organization, several attributes common to successful organizations can be identified.

- *Effective leadership.* Quality management cannot be achieved unless senior executive leaders are committed to achieving excellence. Each leader must relinquish some control and become a facilitator for change.

- *An emphasis on customer satisfaction.* The key to developing quality services lies in understanding, respecting, and responding to the customer. Successful organizations engage in open, continuous, two-way communication with their customers. Successful organizations use ongoing measures of customer satisfaction to alter services and processes.

- *A commitment to continuous improvement.* Successful organizations adopt management practices that encourage employees to continually identify and act upon opportunities to improve.

- *Strategic planning.* To become successful, organizations must develop a long-term strategy that addresses training, employee development, relationships with suppliers, technology application, and other factors bearing on quality.

- *Enlightened human resource management.* Changes in the way work is organized produce corresponding changes in demands for human resource development. Employees must develop the deeper and broader skills needed to participate in team decision making. An organization pursuing quality management must be committed to continuously upgrading and improving the skills of its work force. Employer-employee cooperation is essential. Such cooperation requires respect for employees' rights and for the organization's changing needs.

- *Quality assurance systems.* Organizations that practice quality management place a strong emphasis on preventing defects by continuously improving processes.

- *Effective information systems.* Quality management is predicated on decision making that uses reliable information and analysis to help make better decisions. The application of quality management principles goes well beyond establishing systems to ensure service or product quality. It addresses the structure and operation of the entire government organization.

Early interest and efforts in quality management in the United States occurred primarily in the private sector, where firms spurred by intense competition from Japan began to examine Japanese approaches to management. This intense competition stimulated U.S. attention to the role of quality management systems in improving quality. The increased interest in Japanese management methods was soon accompanied by research in the United States that documented that organizations can also reduce their costs by improving quality.

During the mid-1980s, the quality movement began to act as a catalyst to private sector industries; now, quality management practices are becoming a focal point in the public sector. Private sector businesses undertake fundamental change for reasons of efficiency and survival; likewise, today, the federal and state governments are faced with tremendous pressure to economize. The last few years of austere funding have provided an impetus to change and improve, by challenging government organizations to increase productivity and cope with shrinking budgets. To face this challenge, public managers have begun to embrace the quality movement as a path by which progressive management practices can impact cost, efficiency, and quality of government services.

Clearly, the taxpayer has not been satisfied with the services provided by either federal or state government but quality management can help provide better government. A quality management focus requires a human resources revolution that emphasizes people. Can the public sector offer its customers the same quality of services they have come to expect from the private sector? The answer is yes. As proof, many government agencies *are* achieving higher quality, productivity, and cost savings, as shown in the case studies provided in chapter 5.

State of the Practice

Quality management is being applied today in federal, state, and local governments. This book addresses the application of quality management to all three levels of government organizations. Today we may read about success in applying quality management in the private sector, or even in the Department of Defense; but great success is also being obtained in local education programs, state police organizations, and state governments such as Arkansas and Ohio, that are aggressively applying quality management to their state government agencies as well as supporting their business community.

As shown in Figure 1.1, the majority of government activity takes place at the state and local levels. There are more than 83,000 governmental units in the United States—one federal government, 50 state governments, and thousands of local governments for cities, counties, and towns.

Status of Quality Management in the Federal Government

Former Congressman Donald Ritter requested that the GAO examine quality management in the federal government. In response, in October 1992, the GAO released an excellent status report entitled "Total Quality Management—Survey of Federal Organizations," Report Number GAO/GGD-93-9BR. The GAO's objective was to obtain information on the status and scope of quality management implementation in the federal government. To accomplish its objective, the GAO sent questionnaires to the heads of more than 2800 civilian and Department of Defense installations. The GAO asked the installation heads to assess the results of their quality management activities. The GAO also made follow-up visits to a sample of 30 installations to determine the extent to which documentary support for quality management implementation efforts was available and to validate responses.

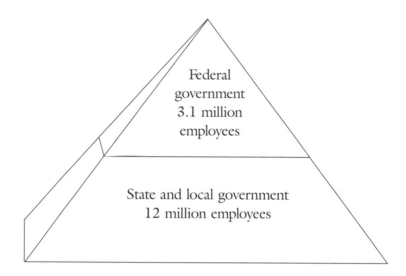

Figure 1.1.   Full-time U.S. public employees in government today.

In the GAO survey, federal installations reported a wide range of quality management activity. As shown in Figure 1.2, about 68 percent of all respondents said they were involved in some quality management efforts. The survey also found that most of these activities were no more than two years old. Furthermore, about half of the 32 percent of installations without quality management activities said they planned to implement such activities in the future.

To fully examine the status of quality management, the GAO defined quality management phases that indicate how far along, or *mature,* installations were in implementing their programs. The maturity phases are as follows:

Phase 1—Deciding whether to implement quality management

Phase 2—Getting started

Phase 3—Implementing

Phase 4—Achieving results

Phase 5—Institutionalizing

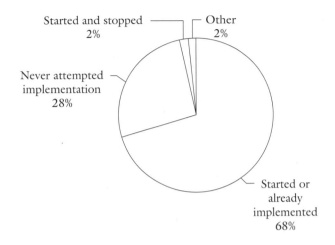

Started and stopped
2%

Other
2%

Never attempted
implementation
28%

Started or
already
implemented
68%

Source: General Accounting Office Report, GAO/GGD-93-9BR, October 1992, p. 10.

Figure 1.2.   Level of federal quality management activity.

Respondents were asked to place their organization in one of the maturity phases. Their analysis shows that about half the organizations reported being in the early stages—namely phases 1 and 2. In terms of those organizations achieving significant results, about 15 percent were in phases 4 and 5; only 4 percent judged themselves to be actually in phase 5.

Moving from the early start-up efforts through implementation takes time. The responses indicated that the first year is spent in the decision and start-up phases (phases 1 and 2). The average age for phase-3 organizations was about 2.5 years, and organizations took an average of three years to get to phase 4.

Institutionalizing quality management, however, appears to require fairly long-term efforts. Phase-5 organizations reported that they have been involved in quality management an average of slightly less than five years.

As noted earlier (Figure 1.2), 28 percent of the organizations reported that they had never attempted quality management. In response, they were asked to identify barriers to implementation. GAO categorized the answers into leadership, training, strategic planning, employee involvement, measurement and analysis, customer focus, and other issues. As shown in Figure 1.3, management leadership issues were the most frequently mentioned barrier.

Among those organizations that have quality management efforts, most have put a management and implementation structure in place. For example, according to the GAO, 82 percent of the organizations have established quality councils, and 76 percent have established quality improvement teams.

GAO asked respondents about the extent of their involvement in 43 activities commonly undertaken by organizations involved in quality management. GAO used the Malcolm Baldrige National Quality Award and the Federal Quality Institute Awards to categorize activities expected of organizations involved in quality management. The categories included leadership, employee training and recognition, strategic

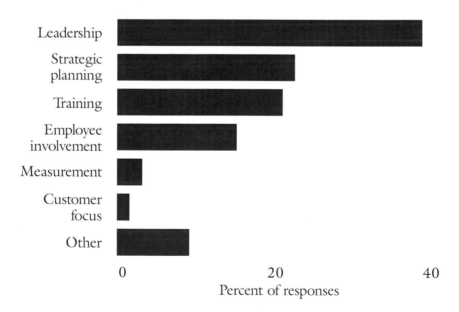

Source: General Accounting Office Report, GAO/GGD-93-9BR, October 1992, p. 14.

Figure 1.3.   Barriers to initiating quality management.

planning, empowerment and teamwork, measurement and analysis, customer focus, and quality assurance. Installations reported that these quality management activities increased in proportion to the maturity phase. In general, organizations identifying themselves as more mature in quality management also more frequently said they were doing these 43 activities.

GAO also asked about employee involvement. Respondents indicated that about 33 percent of the employees (20 percent of the managers and 33 percent of the nonmanagers) were actively involved in such quality management activities as teams, councils, and training. Phase-4 and phase-5 organizations reported an overall 25-percent employee involvement rate.

Incentives and training linked to participation appear to be used more frequently in more mature organizations. On average, 42 percent of the organizations surveyed reported providing teams with rewards and recognition. The average increases to 79 percent for phase-4 and phase-5 organizations. Further, 33 percent of all organizations reported having quality goals in employee performance plans, whereas 60 percent of the phase-4 and phase-5 organizations reported having such quality goals. Finally, 57 percent of all respondents reported training in group process and problem-solving skills, while 88 percent of phase-4 and phase-5 organizations reported such training.

The government clearly appears to have a very active interest in quality management (see Figure 1.4). About two-thirds (68 percent) of the federal installations GAO surveyed reported that they were involved in some way, and another 15 percent are planning quality management implementation. Moreover, although GAO found wide interest, quality management efforts are generally new—the average reported age being less than two years. This newness is reflected in employee participation levels, which are generally low compared to the potential levels reported by mature organizations. Further, the responses to the GAO study indicate that as the organizations mature in implementing quality management, and as they invest time and effort in the activities needed to carry on these quality management initiatives, they find that the barriers become less difficult, and they reap greater benefits.

> • Active interest in quality management in federal government.
> • Involvement very new to federal government organizations.
> • Organizations that have invested time and effort report greater benefits.

Source: General Accounting Office Report, GAO/GGD-93-9BR, October 1992.

Figure 1.4. GAO quality management adoption observations.

Status of Quality Management in State and Local Government

Many state and local governments over the past few years have begun to adopt quality management. In most cases, quality management awareness and implementation programs started in private sector business organizations within the state. By 1990, state and local governments recognized that they should "lead by example" and implement quality management within their government organizations. Today we have aggressive programs in Minnesota, Arkansas, Texas, Ohio, Iowa, North Carolina, New York, and others to expand awareness in the business community and, as is the case in Arkansas and Ohio, to implement quality management within the state government.

In their latest report, entitled "Promoting Quality Business," the National Governors' Association has presented several guidelines for promoting better government by implementing quality management principles. As state and local governments seek to provide increasing levels of service with fewer resources, they have increasingly recognized the need to operate efficiently and effectively. Thus, a 1992 survey by the National Governors' Association found that nearly three-fourths of the states have initiated quality management improvement efforts.

While state and local governments can learn from the experiences of successful companies, applying quality management principles in the public sector will require some modification. It is, for example, more difficult to identify customers of public agencies. It is also problematic to measure results precisely. Annual budget cycles and the need for politicians to show short-term results often make it difficult to adopt long-term perspective. Finally, implementing quality management practices often is time-consuming and, if poorly planned, can be expensive.

Despite these obstacles, a number of advantages can be realized from implementing quality management practices in government. Implementation can

- Show the business community that the government is committed to workplace excellence

- Help ensure that government is responsive to its citizens

- Give employees a larger voice in how their organization is run

- Help create a climate where creativity is encouraged

- Result in cost savings associated with improved efficiency

One way to approach quality management in state and local government is to start small, perhaps using one or two agencies as pilot sites. The government also can provide information on quality management practices and encourage agencies to voluntarily participate in quality improvement programs. To promote the application of quality management practices, the government could create a support network for those agencies that choose to undertake quality improvement programs.

As one example, the state of Texas is using a loaned executive from Xerox to help coordinate and lead the Texas quality management initiative. Moreover, along with the Texas Quality Award (see Appendix C, section 4) and the Quality Texas initiative, the governor's office is creating a training and resource center for quality development in state government. All agencies in state government are involved in the effort, which focuses first on top executives and then works its way through the agency.

Another way states can promote quality management practices in the operation of state government is by investing in appropriate just-in-time training for all levels of state employees. (States can conduct training in quality management principles, tools, and technique training for specific teams or work processes when quality changes are being implemented.) Iowa, for example, has embarked on a statewide program to achieve excellence in state administration based on quality management. An executive awareness training session and a governor's planning and policy conference were held to introduce state executive managers and policymakers to the basic concepts of quality management and to the experiences of other state governments that have implemented quality management practices. In addition, 25 individuals from various state departments participated in a nine-week series of workshops on quality management.

More intensive training for top managers also was held to help them understand what implementing quality management requires and to help them decide whether they want to undertake a quality improvement initiative. The program initially will involve a small number of state agencies on a pilot basis.

In Ohio, the governor and cabinet have participated in an executive training symposium on quality management, an initiative recently adopted by the state government to develop greater efficiency in state operations. Other training symposiums will also be set up for seven (phase-1) agencies, with employee unions being part of the efforts.[3]

Quality Management Benefits

The General Accounting Office report entitled "Quality Management—Survey of Federal Organizations" examined quality management benefits in two ways: (1) effect on external customers as reflected by overall organizational performance and (2) effect on internal customers as reflected by internal operating conditions. The GAO asked respondents to assess quality management's effect on organizational performance in terms of the following:

- Productivity
- Cost reduction
- Product and service quality
- Overall service to customers
- Customer satisfaction
- Timeliness

As shown in Figure 1.5, most organizations said quality management has enhanced organizational performance—about 60 percent reported a somewhat positive to very positive impact, although a third said it was too early to judge. Of particular note, few negative effects were reported.

One example of customer service improvement was noted during a survey visit to the Veterans Affairs Insurance Center in Philadelphia. This office has reduced from 11 percent to 6 percent the frequency with which veterans had to make follow-ups on their inquiries regarding insurance benefits. In another example, at the Ogden Air Logistics Center, the failure rate on a bomb release was reduced from over 80 percent to less than 5 percent after an employee simply called the customer to determine if there were any problems with the item.

Also, the reported impact of quality management on overall organizational performance increases as maturity increases. Figure 1.6 shows

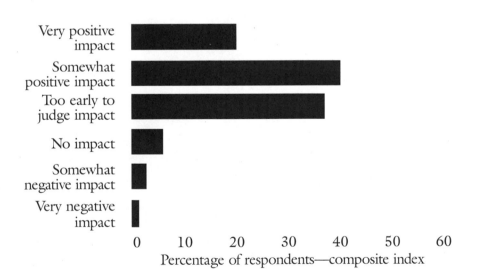

Source: General Accounting Office "Quality Management—Survey of Federal Organizations," GAO/GGD-93-9BR, October 1992, p. 32.

Figure 1.5.   Most federal installations report positive impact on performance.

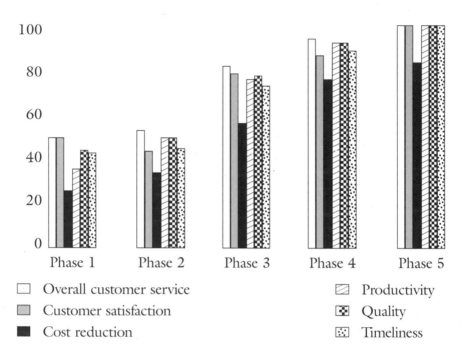

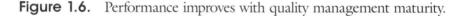

Source: General Services Administration Report GAO/GGD-93-9BR, October 1992, p. 33.

Figure 1.6. Performance improves with quality management maturity.

the six organizational performance measures and the way in which impact grows as organizations mature.

To assess internal operating conditions, GAO asked the installations to identify the impact of quality management on each of 13 internal operating conditions, such as communications and labor-management relations. Respondents said that quality management was affecting internal operating conditions in a positive manner, but not strongly. Also, about one-third of the respondents said it was too early to judge the impact.

One example of the benefits of improving internal operating conditions was provided during GAO's visit to the Internal Revenue Service's Ogden Service Center. According to Center officials, group process and problem-solving skills had been used for two years by a team that worked on taxpayer payment problems. During that period, the team had addressed a series of problems, such as the posting of taxpayer payments to the wrong accounts. This effort had helped reduce payment tracers by over one million and had also reduced erroneous payment-due notices to taxpayers.

In another example of quality improvement team activities, officials at the Defense Industrial Supply Center in Philadelphia described how a team had been given the task of identifying and reducing unnecessary reports and paperwork. The Center reported that the team's efforts have reduced paper consumption by millions of sheets.

The GAO also found that the top six indexes of internal conditions showed moderate or significant improvement due to quality management. The six indexes are

- Attention to customers' requirements
- Group process and problem-solving skills
- Internal communication
- Participatory management style
- Timeliness of internal processes
- Efficiency

Similar to the organizational performance area, benefits reported by mature organizations were double and triple the benefits reported by phase-1 and phase-2 organizations.

Quality Management Barriers

In its study, the GAO asked about the significance of 21 potential barriers to *implementing* quality management. Figure 1.7 shows the nine barriers said to be a moderate to very major problem by more than 39 percent of the respondents. Three key barriers were related to lack of employee training and support—for example, (1) employees didn't believe they were empowered to make changes, (2) employees lacked sufficient information on how to use quality management tools, and (3) employees lacked information and training on quality management concepts and theory.

The GAO analysis of the data also showed that respondents believed barriers would decrease as their involvement in quality management

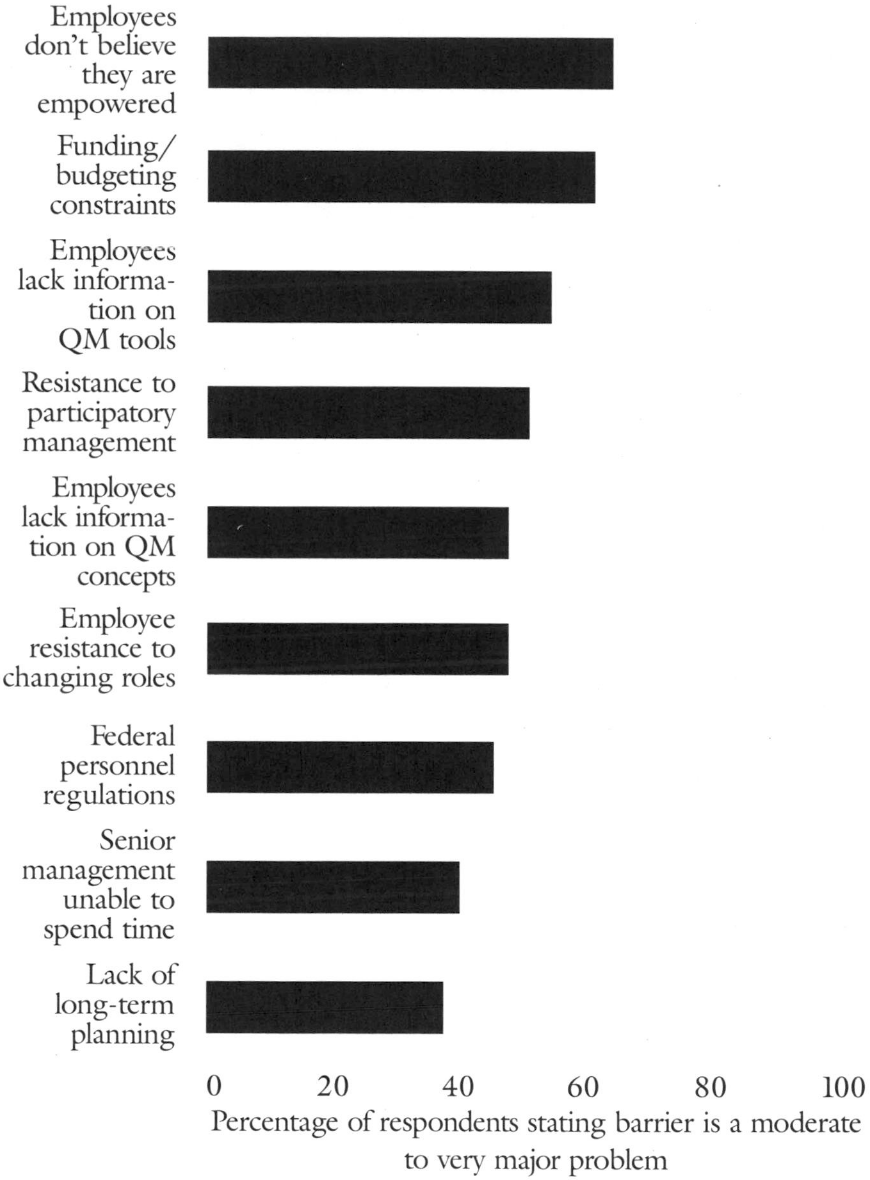

Percentage of respondents stating barrier is a moderate
to very major problem

Source: General Accounting Office Report GAO/GGD-93-9BR, October 1992, p. 40.

Figure 1.7.   Quality management barriers.

increases. For example, about 66 percent of the respondents in phases 1, 2, and 3 felt the first barrier—"employees don't believe they are empowered"—was a moderate to very great barrier. However, only 47 percent of the phase-4 installations saw this as a barrier, and only 23 percent of the phase-5 organizations reported it as a barrier.

Thus, the GAO study indicates that as the organizations mature in implementing quality management, and as they invest time and effort in the activities needed to carry on quality management initiatives, they find that the barriers become less difficult. Thus they reap greater benefits.

No Quick Fix

Perhaps the most daunting part of the challenge facing government is the nature of the change that the years ahead require. If the problem was just slow production, we could design faster machines. If the problem was simply one of poorly trained workers, we could attempt to redesign the education system to accommodate the needs of the modern worker. As we will see in the pages that follow, however, governments must prepare for massive changes in their basic culture that determines how they operate.

Unlike mechanical fixes, cultural change takes time and is hard work. When it comes to building quality into a government organization where it does not now exist, there is simply no quick fix. Interviews with quality leaders have repeatedly confirmed how difficult it is for an organization to shift from a culture that condones or accepts poor quality to one that insists on high-quality processes, services, and products. Many organizations simply don't have sufficient energy and leadership to make the change, and for them the future is bleak. Change may be difficult, but what's the alternative? In the 1990s, as we shall demonstrate repeatedly in this book, the "quick fix" mentality is the problem, not the cure.

When confronting a new crisis or problem, individuals and organizations characteristically react in a similar way: they deny that a problem exists. The denial period may last a brief moment, or it may never end. Nonetheless, until the individual or organization overcomes this initial stage in the problem-solving process and faces reality, the crisis will remain unsolved. Those government organizations entering the 1990s with a business-as-usual attitude and an unwillingness to acknowledge reality are stuck—for a moment or forever—in denial. Until they get over, or go around, this barrier, they are setting themselves up for continued failure.

The Rest of the Story!

Quality Management for Government has been created to provide you with a series of self-contained chapters to speed your awareness and understanding of the fundamentals of quality management. It is written in a clear, straightforward manner for federal and state government leaders, quality champions, and team members.

Chapter 2 provides an introduction for government leaders. It covers the background, context, and unique vocabulary of quality management. It also explains the differences between government and private-sector implementation, and the changes needed to create a quality management work culture and management system.

The approaches proposed by the leading quality gurus are described and demystified in chapter 3. There, we provide a balanced view of today's leading quality improvement methods based on the philosophy of Deming, the Juran approach to planning and implementation, and the modular methodology taught at the Crosby Quality College. The unique benefits of each approach are compared and assessed to help you choose the methods that best fit your own unique needs. This book does not suggest that there is only one "right" guru methodology to improve your management system.

Chapter 4 includes a description of the key criteria for both federal and state government quality awards. First, the form and structure of the federal quality awards are described in detail. Next, the chapter addresses the structure of the Malcolm Baldrige National Quality Award as it is used by state quality improvement leaders in Minnesota, New York, North Carolina, and so on. You will see that some states have adopted only the top-level Baldrige criteria to encourage their communities to begin the quality improvement journey. These limited criteria are sometimes referred to as *Baby Baldrige* awards.

As shown in chapter 5, success is contagious. By reading case studies of successful quality management adoption in organizations such as the IRS, the U.S. Air Force, the Departments of Commerce, Interior, and Labor, and Veterans Affairs, federal government leaders and employees can see that quality works in organizations like their own. Chapter 5 also introduces you to the role then-Governor Bill Clinton played in actively supporting quality management in both the Arkansas business community and his leadership in implementing quality management within the Arkansas state government. Moreover, several states with substantial quality award program experience have been selected as case studies. These cases illustrate quality initiatives directed toward the products and services of the states' business communities as well as their own internal operations in administration, education, and public safety via quality improvement.

Before you begin a quality management initiative, you'll encounter one fundamental question you must be able to answer for yourself and your co-workers: *Why* should we change? Today we hear often about the desire for change, but we must recognize the difficulty of changing the way we have done government business for so long. Chapter 6, then, provides 217 self-assessment questions that you can answer in about 20 minutes. These questions can help you focus on your application of quality management principles in your own office or organization. This self-assessment can illuminate the real need to change your organization by adopting quality management.

Chapter 7 describes how you can significantly improve your quality by developing a strategy based on your own unique needs and situation. Many quality strategies fail because an organization tries to improve by following a philosophy that does not show a clear path for implementation. Thus, chapter 8 describes the necessity for developing your own quality plan and the specific steps involved in doing so. Once the planning approach is defined in detail, the seven critical implementation steps for quality management can be adapted step-by-step, as shown in chapter 9.

Chapter 10 provides a basic introduction to the fundamental tools and techniques that you can use to better understand your processes and to provide a data source for decision making. The goal of this chapter is to familiarize you with the basics so that you can begin to base decision making on data rather than on seat-of-the-pants opinions. The Epilogue encourages you to be the quality champion within your organization and to act now to begin your implementation of quality management.

Notes

1. "As the 1990s unfold . . ." through ". . . And they are our future." is reprinted with slight adaptations from David Osborne and Ted Gaebler, *Reinventing Government: How the Entrepreneurial Spirit Is Transforming the Public Sector* (Reading, Mass.: Addison-Wesley, 1992), 1–2.

2. Ibid., 23–24.

3. The information in this section has been excerpted from Marianne K. Clarke and Eric N. Dobson, "Promoting Quality Business—A State Action Agenda" (Washington, D.C.: National Governors' Association, 1992), 10.

2   A Government Manager's Guide to Quality Management

Doing what's right isn't the problem. It's knowing what's right.

President Lyndon Johnson

What Is Quality Management?

Quality management is not a minor refinement of past managerial practices. What sets quality management apart from other approaches to management is a genuinely new perspective on how to best combine or reengineer the resources (people, budget, programs, processes) that make up a government organization. Quality management involves a unique set of principles, a new role for top management and co-workers alike, and an array of practices and techniques designed to implement these organizing principles. In other words, quality management is both a comprehensive managerial philosophy and a tool kit for its implementation.

Some government managers feel that quality management is a radical departure from traditional management practices due to its analytic focus on work-flow process redesign and statistical process control rather than function or product. Some question quality management's insistence that the customer is best equipped to define the quality of your work.

Some critics worry about the new roles assigned to the empowered co-worker in a quality management organization. Worker involvement and continuous process improvement are the basic sources from which quality flows. Every co-worker in a quality management organization has one central and common purpose—that is, to improve the quality of the organization's services and products in order to satisfy the customer.

21

In a quality management context, quality means meeting customer requirements and expectations the first time and every time. Customers have many potential requirements and expectations. But rather than the organization attempting to specify what it views as quality, a quality management organization determines what the customers want, and strives to meet, and even exceed, those requirements. Such an approach helps to identify the elements of quality that are of paramount importance to customers. It also recognizes that customers' expectations may change over time.

Quality management is a strategic, integrated management system for achieving customer satisfaction. It involves all managers and employees and uses quantitative methods to improve an organization's processes continuously. It is not simply an efficiency (cost-cutting) program, a morale-boosting scheme, a downsizing (right-sizing) program, or a project that can be delegated to operational managers and staff specialists. Furthermore, paying lip service to quality improvements, by merely using quality slogans to exhort workers, is inappropriate.

At the foundation of quality management (see Figure 2.1) are three principles: (1) focus on achieving customer satisfaction, (2) seek continuous improvement, and (3) give everyone responsibility.

The basic quality management message sent to government managers is this: If your organization is to remain responsive to changing customer demands, the organization must be ready and able to detect the need for change *and* to maintain the ability to make the needed changes.

In this context, we define quality management as the extent to which an organization's services satisfy its customer requirements. Moreover, *customers* can be internal as well as external to the organizational system. For example, services or products may flow to the person at the next desk or work area (an internal customer) rather than to a person outside the immediate organization (external customer).

Finally, the days of limiting the definition of quality to the soundness of the product—its hardness or durability, for example—are gone. The new kind of quality America rediscovered in the 1990s is far more cultural than physical. It's far more about the way processes are done than the nature of the processes.

Figure 2.1. Principles of quality management.

Historical Context

Modern industrial production techniques were perfected by the United States at the turn of the century. In the early 1900s, the United States had established the worldwide standard of management (see Figure 2.2), particularly in manufacturing. Influenced by the writings of Frederick W. Taylor, the father of scientific management, organizations sharply divided the functions of line workers from the processes of planning work. Organizations were established in a hierarchy of top managers, mid-level managers, specialists, and workers. Managers established the broad directions and policies for the organization to pursue, and they hired specialists to develop detailed instructions to govern how work was to be performed. Workers were told to follow instructions precisely without deviation.

Beginning about the same time, the United States benefited from an unprecedented influx of immigrants, giving American managers a

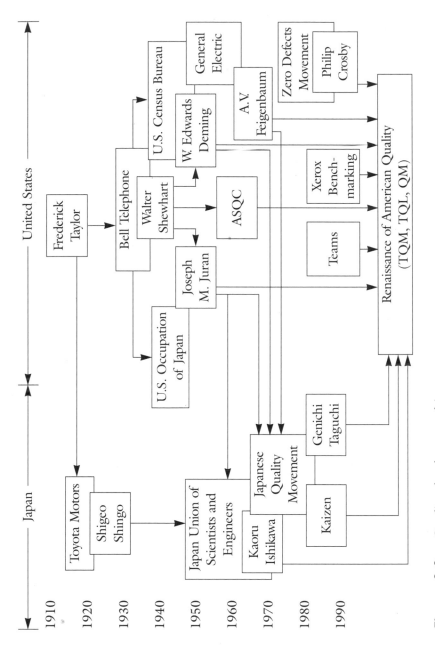

Figure 2.2.   Quality development history.

plentiful, inexpensive, and energetic work force. Because so many could not speak English, and most had little formal education, the management system of detailed direction with little input from the workers was generally effective.

This system worked reasonably well for the United States for decades. America had an unmatched combination of natural resources, advanced technology, inexpensive and productive labor, and a favorable political and economic structure. No one in the world could compete with American productivity. Americans produced goods and services efficiently, in volume, and at levels of quality unmatched in the world. At the end of World War II, America was at an even greater comparative advantage because Western Europe and Asia had been devastated by the war.

All that began to change in the 1950s. Japanese industrialists invited several Americans to instruct them on how to convert their war-focused industries to serve domestic consumption and to improve the image and quality of their products. Until then, Japanese products were generally recognized as inferior.

Dr. Joseph Juran was invited by the Japanese Union of Scientists and Engineers (JUSE) to advise Japanese executives. He emphasized the broad management aspects of quality and focused on planning, organizational issues, management's responsibility for quality, and the need to set goals and targets for improvement.

Dr. W. Edwards Deming was also one of the Americans to have a significant impact on Japanese industry. Through a series of lectures to members of JUSE, he taught them the importance of statistical process control and its impact on improving quality.

Other Americans, including Philip B. Crosby (zero defects) and Dr. Armand V. Feigenbaum (originator of total quality control) made important early contributions to the quest for quality. All stressed the important role that top management plays in establishing the climate and systems to give quality preeminence in an organization's mission, to ensure that everyone can contribute to this objective, and to empower the entire work force to improve quality.

The Japanese adapted the teachings of these Americans and others to their own culture. They developed the concept of *kaizen,* or continuous process improvement, and pioneered the use of quality circles—teams of workers who identify specific management problems and devise solutions.

In the mid-1980s, American industry began to recognize the need for customer satisfaction and, particularly in large corporations (Ford, Xerox, Motorola), began to adopt quality management principles. The federal government, however, began to focus on productivity rather than quality. President Reagan signed Executive Order 12552 on February 25, 1986, establishing a productivity improvement program for the federal government. Its goal was to improve the efficiency, quality, and timeliness of service to the public, with a 20-percent increase in selected areas by 1992. In late 1987, the leaders of the federal productivity effort consulted with officials of private corporations who had been among the leaders in the national quality and productivity movement. The private-sector representatives urged the government to change their focus and adopt quality improvement through quality management as the preferred approach to achieving both quality and productivity gains.

During the next two years, the shift to quality management began in earnest, with an emphasis on educating managers in all agencies about quality management practices and recognizing organizations that made significant progress. The Federal Quality Institute was established in 1988 to be a source of information, training, and consulting services to federal agencies on quality management. Its three major functions were (1) to provide quality-awareness seminars and follow-up consultation to senior federal managers, (2) to develop and maintain a roster of qualified private-sector consultants, and (3) to operate a resource center that would be a clearinghouse and referral source of information on quality management. Today, the role of the Federal Quality Institute is being reinvented to reflect the changes occurring because of the new administration.

The quality management initiative in the Department of Defense (DoD) began on March 30, 1988, when Secretary of Defense Frank Carlucci issued the "Department of Defense Posture on Quality" letter, which provided direction for implementing quality management concepts throughout the department. In this same time frame, federal civilian agencies such as the Internal Revenue Service, NASA Johnson Space Center, and the Kansas City Veterans Medical Center began to implement quality management. In some cases, state and local governments were ahead of the federal government both in fully realizing the potential of quality management in government and in terms of aggressively adopting its techniques in their state and local agencies.

Today, we see higher success rates in state and local government for quality management than we do in federal civilian agencies and the DoD. Of course, the government does have an opportunity to provide better government to its customers (the U.S. taxpayers)—by more aggressively adopting industry role model, state-of-the-art quality management practices.

The Language of Quality

Like any other field, quality management brings with it a new set of ideas and a new vocabulary to express these ideas. But be careful. While the quality management literature is full of familiar-sounding terms, many take on a somewhat different meaning when used in a quality management context. The language of quality vocabulary includes the following terms.

Process. The familiar definition of process is simply an agreed-upon set of steps. But, in the quality management context, *process* also refers to the logical way things are done in an organization. Quality management is based on a *continuous process improvement approach*, meaning that it involves a never-ending, cyclical search for ways to do things better.

Customer. In traditional management lore, attention is usually given only to the external customers. In quality management, however, there is a second, equally important customer. The end users of an organization's service or product located inside the organization are called the *internal customers*.

The seemingly simple supplier-customer relationship is complicated by the fact that the organization is *both* a customer of its suppliers (internal and external) and a supplier to its customers (both internal and external). A quality management approach brings the views of the suppliers and the views of the customers into harmony with each other. In graphic form, this relationship of the company to its many suppliers and customers is shown in Figure 2.3.

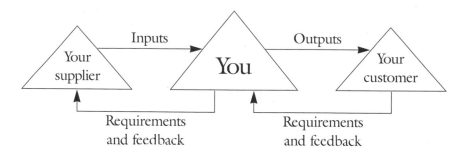

Source: AT&T, *AT&T Quality Improvement Process Guidebook* (Baskin Ridge, N.J.: AT&T, 1988), p. 69.

Figure 2.3.   Quality management customers—supplier model.

Customer requirements. The needs of the customers—both internal and external—constitute a company's customer requirements. The ultimate aim of the company is to satisfy these requirements, and thereby satisfy its customers.

Supplier specifications. Once an organization knows its customers' requirements, it can then determine supplier specifications. Quality management organizations reject the idea that their suppliers should be picked mainly on the basis of price. Far more emphasis is placed on whether a supplier can meet the organization's customer-driven specifications on a continuous basis, thus avoiding the introduction of defects into the organization's processes.

Benchmarking. A *benchmark* is a standard of excellence or achievement against which other similar products or services can be measured or judged. Simply speaking, benchmarking involves the following steps.

- Figuring out what to benchmark

- Finding out what the benchmark will be

- Determining how it's achieved

- Deciding to make changes or improvements in one's own practices to meet or exceed the benchmark

These four steps—while perhaps sounding fairly simple—require thinking and analysis. They require that you know your processes and practices down to the smallest detail. In a sense, benchmarking is a process of comparing—comparing results, outputs, methods, processes, or practices in a systematic way. One purpose of this book is to help you through the process of self-assessment, an aspect of benchmarking, as described in chapter 6.

Conformance. This term is closely linked to customer requirements. In the quality management context, *conformance* demands that products and services be measured against known and reliable customer requirements to ensure that they will, in fact, meet the customer's needs. Guesswork is not allowed. Dependence on historical data only is rejected. Conformance must be based on continuously updated data that reflect current, objective measures of customer needs.

Continuous process improvement (kaizen). The fundamental concepts for continuous process improvement are based on the Japanese management technique called *kaizen*. *Kaizen* means gradual, unending improvement—doing little things better every day. For government, *kaizen's* clear message is "do it better; make it better; improve it even if it ain't broke." *Kaizen* means making ongoing improvement involving everyone—top management, senior executives, mid-managers, and co-workers. *Kaizen* thinking is process oriented; it's also a management system that supports and recognizes your co-workers process-oriented efforts for improvement. If each of us did our job just a bit better every day, over the period of just one year we would see significant improvement in customer satisfaction, defect and error reduction, and worker productivity and attitude.

Data. Quality management is a data-driven approach to quality improvement. Information is presented in descriptive form using two basic kinds of data: measured *(variable data)* and counted *(attribute data).*

Statistical process control. Statistical process control (SPC) is a disciplined way of identifying and solving problems in order to improve performance. It involves use of fishbone diagrams to identify causes and effects of problems. Data are then collected and organized in various ways (graphs, Pareto charts, and/or histograms) to further examine problems. In addition, the data may be tracked over time (with control charts) to determine variation in the process. The process is then enhanced in some way, and new data are collected and analyzed to determine whether the process has been improved. Chapter 10 describes the tools and techniques of a data-driven quality management effort.

Variation. Dr. Walter Shewhart of the Bell Laboratories first made the distinction between controlled and uncontrolled variation due to what he called common and special causes while studying process data in the 1920s. He developed a simple but powerful tool called the control chart to dynamically separate the two variations. Since that time, control charts have been used successfully in a wide variety of process control situations, both in the United States and other countries, notably Japan. Experience has shown that control charts effectively direct attention toward special causes of variation when they appear and reflect the extent of common-cause variation that must be reduced by management action.

Several types of control charts have been developed to analyze both variables and attributes. However, all control charts have the same two basic uses. Using Shewhart's terms, they are

- As a judgment, to give evidence whether a process has been operating in a state of statistical control, and to signal the presence of special causes of variation so that corrective action can be taken

- As an operation, to maintain the state of statistical control, by extending the control limits as a basis for real-time decisions

Cross-functional teams. Knowledgeable, skilled employees are, of course, crucial to the quality management improvement process. However, each individual's unique skills can be substantially enhanced when co-workers come together from different disciplines within the organization to clarify and improve their processes. Teamwork is essential to the success of the quality management culture. One universal goal is to ultimately involve every member of the organization in relevant process-improvement team activity skills.

Teamwork does not necessarily imply that new organizational entities must be created. Rather, in most organizations it means that existing groups will begin working as teams, using the techniques that take advantage of interpersonal dynamics.

Most process-improvement teams mirror the natural work-group structures and thus overlay the existing organizational hierarchy. Additional teams are created to ensure cross-functional process improvement and attention to processes of special interest or broad application such as procurement-system improvement, technology advancement, information processing for specific problems, or process tool applications.

For the most part, creation of the team network flows from the top down. Training team members is an integral part of the deployment process. Training produces what H. James Harrington, author of *The Improvement Process,* calls a "waterfall effect" that systematically washes out the counterproductive ideas and signals as the culture is deployed down into the organization.

Each team, once created, engages in ongoing process-improvement activity that is appropriate to its level and area of responsibility. These activities include customer recognition, process definition, performance-requirements definition, performance measurement and assessment, and process-improvement activities. Multifunctional teams are particularly useful when work units depend upon one another for systems integration, materials, information, process simplification, and so on.

Employee empowerment. In many organizations, employees, by management design, are doers, not thinkers. They are expected to perform only to minimum standards. In quality management organizations, on the other hand, every single employee is expected to solve problems, participate in team-building efforts, and generally, expand the scope of his or her role in the organization. The goal of employee empowerment is to stop trying to motivate workers with extrinsic incentives, as is the case in traditional management practices, and build a work environment in which all employees take pride in their work accomplishments and begin motivating themselves from within.

This enhanced role of the worker draws on the thinking of Douglas McGregor during the 1950s and his familiar Theory X and Theory Y assumptions about the nature of the worker. He argues that the Theory X view is fundamentally flawed. His Theory Y assumptions, on the other hand, many of which underlie the quality management approach, invite a wider and more responsible role for the worker in an organization. A review of McGregor's two sets of assumptions, shown in

Figure 2.4, will facilitate a better understanding of the expanded role of the worker in quality management organizations in the 1990s.

Culture. In the quality context, *culture* does not mean going to the opera. *Culture* is the prevailing pattern of activities, interactions, norms, sentiments, beliefs, attitudes, values, and services in your organization. Many managers want to ignore culture. It is too nebulous, too difficult to fix. Some simply believe that all is well, or the old classic—if it's not broke, don't fix it.

Recently, a senior executive for a large government agency became a born-again quality advocate. He met late Friday with the Department Secretary to outline his plan to improve the organization's quality by changing its culture and adopting quality management concepts. All was well until the Department Secretary jumped up full of enthusiasm, and said he wanted the organization's culture changed by the close of business Monday!

One of the most difficult tasks for top management is to understand the impact of culture modification on its near-term and long-term strategic plans. Changing your organization's culture takes years, not days.

Quality Management Operating Practices

To define quality management is one thing. To implement it is another. As we shall see, quality management involves far more than tinkering with an organization's structure.

At the department or agency level, quality management is often compared to the adoption of a new work culture or philosophy. Shifting from a traditional, functional view of an organization to one based on work-flow process improvement is not an easy task.

The "essence of quality management is involving and empowering the work force to improve the quality of goods and services continuously in order to satisfy, and even delight, the customer."[1] To achieve this goal requires identifying customers and their needs, having a clear idea of how the organization plans to go about meeting expectations, and making sure that everyone in the organization understands the customers' needs and is empowered to act on their behalf.

There are few quick fixes for improving quality. Experience shows that it takes years to create a new environment, or culture, that places a

Theory X Assumptions of the Worker

1. The average human being has an inherent dislike of work and will avoid it if he [or she] can.

2. Because of this human characteristic of dislike of work, most people must be coerced, directed, [and/or] threatened with punishment to get them to put forth adequate effort toward the achievement of organizational objectives.

3. The average human being prefers to be directed, wishes to avoid responsibility, has relatively little ambition, [and] wants security above all.

Theory Y Assumptions of the Worker

1. The expenditure of physical and mental effort in work is as natural as play or rest.

2. External control and the threat of punishment are not the only means for bringing about effort toward organizational objectives. Man will exercise self-direction and self-control in the service of objectives to which he is committed.

3. Commitment to objectives is a function of the rewards associated with their achievement.

4. The average human being learns, under proper conditions, not only to accept but to seek responsibility.

5. The capacity to exercise a relatively high degree of imagination, ingenuity, and creativity in the solution of organizational problems is widely, not narrowly, distributed in the population.

6. Under the conditions of modern industrial life, the intellectual potentialities of the average human being are only partially utilized.

Source: Douglas McGregor, *The Human Side of Organizations* (New York: McGraw-Hill, 1960), pp. 33–34, 47–48.

Figure 2.4. McGregor's Theory X and Y.

premium on excellence; to build structures that will sustain and manage change; and to build an education system to support the expanded role for workers.

How then, does an organization achieve a commitment to quality management that meets this description? The quality management approach emphasizes several elements or practices, summarized in the following sections, that when integrated as a strategy of quality improvement result in the fundamental changes required (see Figure 2.5).

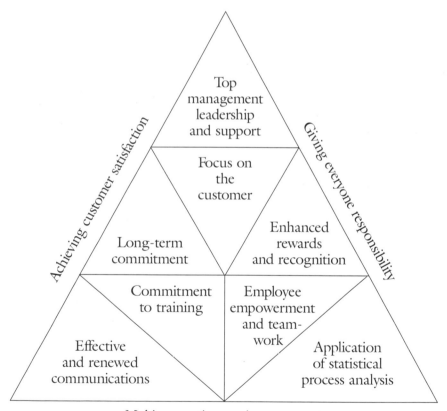

Source: Federal Quality Institute, *Introduction to Total Quality Management in Federal Government,* May 1991, p. 22.

Figure 2.5.   Synergy of elements of quality management.

Top Management Leadership

The primary, and perhaps the most critical, element in the quality management equation is the role of top management leadership and support. Top government leaders must be directly and actively involved in establishing a new environment that improves communications; accelerates the implementation of multifunctional teams; and encourages innovation, risk taking, pride in work, and continuous improvement on behalf of all customers. These top-level leaders set the tone, determine the theme, and provide impetus for action throughout the organization. They assert a clear vision of what the organization can achieve, and they communicate the quality policies and goals throughout the organization. This means providing an active, visible presence to all members of the work force as well as the resources, time, and training essential for the organization to improve its quality.

All employees, including union leaders, should be included in the early stages of the quality planning process in order to obtain an effective transition to quality management. The quality management leader empowers workers to make decisions. Gradually, leaders will shift their efforts from directing and controlling how the operations are carried out to identifying and removing barriers that prevent employees from meeting customer requirements and expectations. Leaders guide the fundamental cultural change in the organization from crisis management to continuous improvement.

In a quality management organization, co-worker empowerment means that the supervisory and control responsibilities that are traditionally reserved for senior managers are entrusted to cross-functional teams of workers who, on a day-to-day basis, transform inputs into outputs. Top leaders empower workers by giving each process team the freedom to set goals and the tools to achieve them. Ideally, the inspection function will no longer be needed in a quality management organization because each worker is committed to doing his or her job right the first time.

Strategic Planning

Strategic planning drives the government organization's improvement efforts. Planning for quality improvement is integrated into the overall strategic planning process, so that planning and achieving quality improvement become a part of the day-to-day management of the operation. Further, establishing a dynamic, participative planning *process* is as important as developing the plan itself.

A critical objective of quality management is to develop a climate or culture in the organization that encourages pursuit of excellence on behalf of customers and that nurtures risk taking and employee participation. A primary goal of the strategic plan is to map out the long-term strategy to bring about the cultural change. The plan establishes the goals for attaining superior levels of customer satisfaction and organizational performance. Thus, it both looks outward to the customer and focuses inward on the organization's processes. The plan is updated periodically and helps define how the organization intends to fulfill customer expectations over the next one, two, or five years.

All members of the organization contribute ideas to the plan and are aware of its implications for their own areas of responsibility. In organizations where employees are represented by unions, management should actively enlist the support and participation of union officials. Both management and organized labor benefit from the active involvement of labor in planning and carrying out the quality improvement processes.

Focus on the Customer

High-quality organizations seek not only to meet customer expectations, but also to go the extra mile and delight both their internal and external customers. Actively involving customers in the improvement process to find out exactly what they want is central to a quality management effort.

The concept of customer focus applies to both internal and external customers. Within an organization, work normally is organized so that the product of one worker is passed on to another before a final service or product is delivered. Under a quality management approach, any worker who delivers a service or product to someone else sees that person as a customer and attempts to respond to his or her needs and requirements in order to improve the quality of the final service.

If a government organization bases its strategy solely on its internal perception of its customers' needs, it is not likely to measure accurately what customers really want or what they think of current services. Only the customers know!

Tailored to its special needs, each organization should have a wide range of methods for obtaining and assessing customer feedback, including customer surveys, in-depth interviews of groups of customers, follow-up of customer complaints, collection of customer feedback at the time of service delivery, and third-party analysis of customer feedback. Customers should have easy access to the organization for obtaining information and resolution of their problems. Quality organizations adopt a service orientation as the primary means of achieving their mission.

Teamwork and Employee Empowerment

Once top management has made the long-term commitment to quality management, the most important and critical ingredient to achieving a quality commitment throughout an organization is employee involvement, empowerment, training, and teamwork. Work processes can only be improved when all people in the organization, top to bottom and horizontally across functions, are involved in making the changes. When the intelligence, imagination, and energies of the entire work force are engaged in the pursuit of the organization's goals, lasting results can be realized. People closest to the problems usually have the best information sources and solutions.

The idea of employee involvement, participative management, and empowerment is not unique to quality management. Indeed, many management practitioners claim to support the idea. Efforts often fall short however, not because of the absence of good intentions on the part of managers or workers, but because managers have not adopted specific systems and procedures to make employee involvement a routine part of providing better government.

The first step in achieving employee empowerment is to involve employees systematically in identifying and solving problems, through teams of employees working on specific process or operating issues, cross-functional problem-solving teams, and self-managing teams. The key is that employees be empowered to make real and lasting changes.

One of the most powerful employee-involvement techniques is to engage teams of co-workers (often called quality improvement teams or process action teams) in addressing immediate operational issues that the team itself helps identify and resolve. When co-workers participate in identifying and solving problems that are affecting the quality of the work they perform, they experience the satisfaction of making tangible contributions to the quality of their work and frequently are motivated to make continuing and lasting improvements to the work they do. Obviously, these results will not occur without the active support and responsiveness of management.

Employee involvement in quality improvement teams must be supported and reinforced by building into the organization's management system explicit recognition and support for the team concept. Management councils and other management bodies must be established and take responsibility for approving employee teams at the outset, assigning resources to let the teams perform their mission, and perhaps most importantly, authorizing changes in overall systems and policies necessary to implement the solutions.

The employee-involvement strategy should include organized labor at all stages in the process so that union leaders understand what is planned and can support the effort. Managers must be prepared to listen and, where possible, adopt recommendations of workers, delegating greater responsibility to lower levels in the organization. If managers do this, everyone will feel ownership of quality improvement and will exhibit personal pride in the work quality. Employees represent an almost unlimited source of knowledge and creativity that can be used, not only to solve problems, but also to continuously improve the quality of the services and products they produce.

Continuous Process Improvement

One of quality management's overall implementing methodologies is continuous process improvement. This means that each process team is constantly trying to improve the performance of its work process—from input from their supplier to output to their customers. The tools, described in chapter 10, that can be used in this never-ending quest for improvement are simple, yet effective.

In order to ensure that processes improve continuously, statistical data should be collected and analyzed on a continuing basis, with particular attention to variations in work processes. The causes behind these variations are important, since strategies differ depending on the type of variation detected, whether sporadic or chronic and, thus, a signal of deep-seated process problems. Statistical control methods are used to reduce rework, waste, and cycle time, and to measure the extent to which the government organization is satisfying its customers' demands.

Commitment to Training and Recognition

Often the missing element in efforts to improve work-flow processes is the training that will enable empowered teams of co-workers to do their job. This includes adequate training both in classrooms and on the job to ensure that employees are equipped with the skills to perform their work. It also includes training in the basic quality management concepts and skills such as teamwork, problem solving, team communication, and data collection and analysis using basic statistical tools.

Co-workers who make contributions to quality improvement should be recognized and rewarded in ways that are meaningful and timely. Reinforcing positive performance is a key ingredient for developing service excellence. An organization that claims to be focused on quality but, in fact, measures and rewards other things sends the wrong messages to its employees.

Nonmonetary awards and recognition can have a powerful and lasting impact on employee motivation and commitment. Many organizations facing stringent budget constraints and rigid compensation systems have found that creative (nonmonetary) recognition systems can go a long way toward achieving co-worker participation in service improvement.

Measurement and Analysis

Many managers depend on intuition and seat-of-the-pants judgments to solve problems. In a quality management organization, however, as many decisions as possible must be based on hard data.

Statistical process control systems are important, and they should be used to allow each work process improvement team in the organization to systematically measure the degree to which it is achieving its quality goals and the degree to which its output satisfies its customers' expectations. Seat-of-the-pants judgment is best replaced with objective data.

Data should be collected on a wide selection of customer-satisfaction indexes, such as supplier responsiveness, reliability, accuracy, and so forth. Measurement systems should also focus on internal processes, especially on key processes that generate variation in quality and cycle time.

Quality Assurance

In order to satisfy customer's quality requirements, the work processes used to produce services and products must be designed to prevent problems and errors from occurring in the first place. Quality assurance in a quality management environment focuses on improvement of each process rather than on the traditional controlling mode of inspecting and checking products at the end of operations, after the errors have already been made. Processes are designed both to prevent errors and to detect and correct them as they occur throughout the process.

As part of the emphasis on prevention and early detection, employees are trained to analyze incoming supplies. Suppliers are asked to assess and improve their processes to make sure that their incoming services or products are error free. Successful quality management organizations establish a partnership with both suppliers and customers to assure continuous improvement in the quality of their services and products. Employees should not accept defective or poor-quality work from their co-workers. Peer pressure is one of the great motivators for improved performance.

Quality Management Is Unique

Although adoption and integration of the basic quality management operating practices are important, leaders just beginning their quality improvement effort should realize that to obtain the full potential of quality management an organization will need fundamental change. When this transformation has occurred, everyone in the organization is continuously and systematically working to improve the quality of services, and the processes for delivering them, in order to maximize customer satisfaction. Quality management becomes a way of managing that is embedded in your organization, not simply a set of specific management techniques and tools.

It follows that successful quality improvement efforts require a long-term commitment and recognition that the effort is an unending journey. Although some early successes will be achieved, a cultural transformation to full use of the quality management approach will occur only gradually.

A quality management approach to management represents a unique blending of (1) *the objective, practical, and quantitative aspects* of management, for example, focusing on processes and using quantitative data and statistical analysis for decision making and (2) the *"soft" aspects of management,* for example, providing visionary leadership; promoting a spirit of cooperation, communication, and teamwork; and practicing participatory management. Many organizations, when deciding to undertake a quality management effort, focus on one or the other of these approaches. A fully successful effort requires attention to both.

Although many of the principles and operating practices summarized are familiar, and many managers believe they already practice them, many aspects of quality management are in fact unique.

- Many organizations claim to serve the customer first, but few systematically and rigorously identify the needs of customers, both internal and external, and monitor the extent to which those needs are being met.

- Many managers encourage employee involvement and empowerment, but few organizations adopt the specific practices that bring them about, such as reliance on teams of workers to identify and resolve specific operating problems. Where teams are used, few have been delegated sufficient authority to make changes or have been trained to use the full array of quality management tools.

- Although many organizations recognize the importance of measurement and analysis in decision making, many also measure the wrong things. Also, few organizations focus on internal processes across functions (such as purchasing requirements and supplier input to the product improvement effort) in order to assure that quality is built into the service system on a continuing basis.

- Many organizations have a system in place that they call quality control or assurance, but these systems are often designed to check for adherence to quality standards at the end of the process. In contrast, quality management creates procedures for assuring quality throughout every step of the process. Where every co-worker becomes a quality assurer.

Where quality management has been adopted by government organizations, the results have been startling. Co-workers at all levels focus on their customers' needs and are committed to and involved in the quest for quality. Management and co-workers form a team in seeking continuous improvement. Cumulatively, these changes frequently result in a significant change in the overall culture and atmosphere of the organization. Organization process becomes simpler, a larger percentage of co-workers are involved in operations, and a greater spirit of cooperation and working toward common goals emerges. Perhaps most significantly, a spirit of energy and excitement permeates the organization. Some characteristics that frequently result from traditional versus quality management approaches are summarized in Figure 2.6.

Is Government Different?

In *Reinventing Government,* Osborne and Gaebler state that "government and business are fundamentally different institutions. Business leaders are driven by the profit motive; government leaders are driven by the desire to get reelected. Businesses get most of their money from their customers; governments get most of their money from taxpayers. Businesses are usually driven by competition; governments usually use monopolies."[2]

Differences such as these create fundamentally different incentives in the public sector. For example, in government, the ultimate test for managers is not whether they produce a product or profit. They succeed if they please the elected politicians. Because politicians tend to be driven by special groups, public managers—unlike their private counterparts—unfortunately factor interest groups into every equation.

Traditional way of managing	Quality management
The organization structure is hierarchical and has rigid lines of authority and responsibility.	The organization structure becomes flatter, more flexible, and less hierarchical.
Focus is on maintaining the status quo (don't fix it if it ain't broke).	Focus shifts to continuous improvement in systems and processes (continue to improve it even if it ain't broke).
Workers perceive supervisors as bosses or cops.	Workers perceive supervisors as coaches and facilitators. The manager is seen as a leader.
Supervisor/subordinate relationships are characterized by dependency, fear, and control.	Supervisor/subordinate relationships shift to interdependency, trust, and mutual commitment.
The focus of employee efforts is on individual effort; workers view themselves as competitors.	The focus of employee efforts shifts to team effort; workers see themselves as co-workers.
Management perceives labor training as costs.	Management perceives labor as an asset and training as an investment.
Management determines what quality is and whether it is being provided.	The organization asks customers to define quality, and develops measures to determine if customers' requirements are met.
Primary basis for decisions is on "gut feeling" or instinct.	Primary basis for decisions shifts to facts and systems.

Source: Federal Quality Institute, *Introduction to Total Quality Management in Federal Government*, May 1991, p. 24.

Figure 2.6.   Traditional management versus quality management approach.

Osborne and Gaebler continue: "Governments also extract their income primarily through taxation, whereas businesses earn their income when customers buy products or services of their own free will. This is one reason why the public focuses so intensely on the high cost of government services, exercising a constant impulse to *control*—to dictate how much the bureaucrats spend on every item."

All these factors combine to produce environments in which public employees view risks and rewards very differently than do private employees. "In government, all the incentive is in the direction of not making mistakes," explains Lou Winnick of the Ford Foundation. "You can have 99 successes and nobody notices; one mistake, and you're dead."

There are many other differences between government and business. Government is democratic and open; hence, it moves more slowly than business, whose managers can make quick decisions behind closed doors. Government's fundamental mission is to "do good," not to make money; hence, the cost-benefit calculations of business turn into moral absolutes in the public sector. Government must often serve everyone equally, regardless of people's ability to pay or their demand for service; hence, it cannot achieve the same market efficiencies as business. One could write an entire book about the differences between business and government. Indeed, James Q. Wilson, the eminent political scientist, already has. It is called *Bureaucracy: What Government Agencies Do and Why They Do It.*

The government does not operate in a profit-driven competitive environment; it is constrained by congressional restrictions. It can be characterized largely as a service industry emphasizing administrative processes. But despite its unique character, significant gains in quality have, in fact, been realized by application of quality management principles to a wide range of government agencies involved in numerous functions, including health care, education, scientific research, defense systems, administration, intelligence, repair and maintenance, and logistics. Many segments of government have now embarked upon a long-term quality management effort, and a governmentwide effort to encourage adoption of quality management is underway.

In some respects, the incentive for government is similar to that which induced many private companies to embark upon a quality management effort: a crisis of survival. In light of severe budget cutbacks, government managers are pressed to carry out their current missions more effectively. But if anything, the demand for quality government service is increasing. When a customer of American Express finds he or she can receive a new credit card and cash within 24 hours anywhere around the world, the same person as a taxpayer wonders why it takes three months to receive an IRS refund. And, in fact, IRS can now deliver a refund in dramatically less time due to application of quality management principles.

Implementation of these principles of quality management in government is a significant task. Making far-reaching, lasting changes will be difficult. The government is a huge conglomerate of activities and functions generally operating under inflexible and outdated management practices and principles. Thus, the quality management effort in government should focus on breaking down the rigidity and excess structure of the government and should devise ways to enlist the energies and talents of the work force to meet the new challenges of America.

The Cost of Quality

One of the more compelling reasons why early quality leaders traded in traditional practices for quality management practices was the projected cost of poor quality if they did governance as usual. Once leaders realize how costly their old way is, mainly because it actually builds poor quality and unnecessary costs into the process, shifting to a new, defect-free process becomes very attractive. According to *A Guide for Implementing Total Quality Management,* from the Reliability Analysis Center, the "cost of poor quality has been quoted by various sources as being between 15 percent to 50 percent of the cost" of operations. One of the most effective actions government managers can take to improve productivity in any organization is to improve the quality of its processes, focusing on reduction of rework.

Specifically, in *Quality Is Free,* Crosby zeros in on the cost of quality: "Quality is free. It's not a gift, but it is free. What costs money are the unquality things—all the actions that involve not doing jobs right the first time." Crosby states that quality is not only free, it is an honest-to-everything money saver. Every penny you don't spend on doing things wrong, over again, or instead of becomes a budget-saving opportunity.

Although literary license allows phrases such as *Quality Is Free* to make a point, you must recognize that it takes substantial up-front leadership, training costs, and process-change costs to fully implement quality management. But once fully implemented, these implementation costs are absorbed; and the benefits in reduction of rework alone can justify the investment in quality management.

The key event, then, in an organization's journey toward quality management is an awareness among top management that its budgets already reflect the costs of not doing things right the first time around, that they must change their definition of quality, and that to obtain maximum benefit, the quality management program should be implemented organizationwide and involve everyone at all levels.

Simply stated, with quality management you can use your budget wisely and avoid wasting it. At Xerox, the cost of quality is measured by what a division, department, or team is spending for its overall quality. There are three kinds of measurements in cost of quality.

Cost of conformance—spending that results in products or services that conform with customer requirements. Conformance means that work outputs are being measured against known customer requirements and are meeting those requirements.

Cost of nonconformance—spending that results in products or services that do not conform with customer requirements. Such costs are measured in terms of the time needed to go back and do a job over. Nonconformance costs can also result from exceeding your customer requirements.

Cost of lost opportunities—costs that result from losing a customer due to lack of quality.

Figure 2.7 will help you visualize the cost shifts that can be expected before and after your organization adopts a quality management approach. Implicit in this cost-of-quality diagram is the notion that the organization will continuously set, and achieve, higher quality standards.

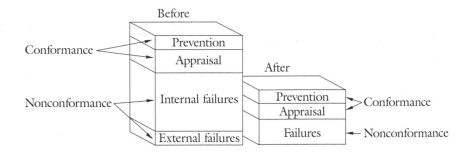

Source: U.S. Department of Defense.

Figure 2.7. The cost of quality: before and after quality management adoption.

Quality Management Dos and Don'ts

The following dos and don'ts are a compilation by the U.S. Department of Transportation of lessons learned in government agencies to guide you in your quality management improvement efforts.[3]

DOs

- **Do** capitalize on previous experiences/lessons learned.

- **Do** act in concert, not unilaterally.

- **Do** keep organizational mission, rather than turf, in the forefront.

- **Do** see yourself as a leader of change.

- **Do** invest "up front" to get results "down the road."
  —IRS Ogden Service Center

- **Do** keep the message simple and uncomplicated.
  —Social Security Administration

- **Do** make use of communication opportunities to reinforce quality.
  —Social Security Administration

- **Do** concentrate on attitude instead of tools and techniques in the beginning.
  —Social Security Administration

- **Do** it, don't study it to death.
  —*Department of Interior*

- **Do** generate champions using early project teams.
  —*Social Security Administration*

- **Do** build quality into the system; this is key to its continuity.
  —*Internal Revenue Service*

- **Do** involve middle managers early on.
  —*Department of Interior*

- **Do** interject quality improvements in government documents that may appear unrelated.
  —*Department of Commerce*

- **Do** tailor training to fit your organization's needs.
  —*Army Aviation Systems Command*

- **Do** include input from your customers in setting your course of direction and in prioritizing activities.
  —*Army Aviation Systems Command*

- **Do** involve unions early in the process.
  —*Department of Interior*

. . . and DON'Ts

- **Don't** call it quality management if you don't want to, but do quality management.
  —*Federal Lands Highway*

- **Don't** expect much and you won't be disappointed. Plan what you are going to do, but don't plan so carefully that you never get started.
  —*Federal Lands Highway*

- **Don't** force one approach on all subordinate level organizations.
  —*Department of Interior*

- **Don't** view quality management as a short-term fix.

- **Don't** require bureaucratic approvals for quality initiatives; it stifles the process.
  —*Department of Commerce*

- **Don't** have training that is long on philosophy and short on practical application of concepts, tools, and disciplined problem solving.
  —*Army Aviation Systems Command*

- **Don't** lose sight of your organization's mission. This is often the most obvious characteristic of a true bureaucracy.

- **Don't** concentrate on statistical process control in the beginning—work on attitudes.
  —*Social Security Administration*

The Transition to Quality Management

Earlier in this chapter we discussed the shift from traditional management to quality management practices. Once this shift takes place, quality management practices will displace existing practices—that is, they will become standard operating procedures—in most federal, state, and local government organizations. Until that paradigm shift takes place, however, the process of introducing and institutionalizing a set of new management ideas in an existing organization will continue to require your active leadership.

Each new procedure introduced into an organization is certain to upset the status quo. Workers who identify personally with the status quo will, in turn, feel vulnerable and insecure. They are likely to resist the new ideas and the changes in behavior required to implement them. For this reason, if a new idea is to evolve from a new concept into an actual practice in an organization, it needs continued support from your quality champions.

A full-time champion can help overcome the resistance the change process will generate and help settle the myriad of problems and barriers that will crop up from day to day. In the absence of a dedicated champion, a new idea will falter before it is routinized. A quality management champion, an individual who leads by his or her own active participation, is needed to inspire others to participate fully in the change process. Thus, a successful quality management champion will do the following:

- Visibly support the organization's quality management strategy

- Insist on the team approach

- Measure his or her success by customer satisfaction
- Build feedback loops within the firm and to suppliers and customers
- Meet goals

Figure 2.8 illustrates the four stages through which a new idea such as quality management must pass before it is institutionalized in your organization. These stages are as follows:

Stage 1:   The source of the new idea, such as the quality management concept, is located *outside* the target organization, but the quality management concept captures the interest of an organizational *insider.*

Stage 2:   An *insider* (or group of insiders) makes the decision to adopt the new idea.

Stage 3:   Once the decision to adopt the idea is made, an internal change process is set in motion to incorporate the new idea. Characteristically, a *champion,* a person with strong personal convictions concerning quality management, sufficient formal or informal authority, and expertise or some other mix of desired qualities, is given responsibility for the day-to-day implementation process.

Stage 4:   Only when the new idea is finally internalized and accepted as the way things are done in an organization is the champion's job complete.

In their book, *In Search of Excellence,* Thomas Peters and Robert Waterman, Jr., identified the "fired-up champion" as an indispensable ingredient present in all the best-run organizations. They define the champion's role like this: "The champion is not a blue-sky dreamer, or an intellectual giant. The champion might even be an idea thief. But, above all, he's the pragmatic one who grabs onto someone else's theoretical construct if necessary and bullheadedly pushes it to fruition . . . Champions are pioneers, and pioneers get shot at." The organizations that get the most from champions, therefore, are those that have "rich

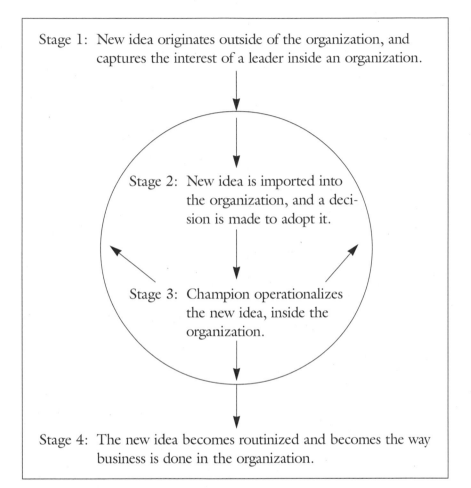

Stage 1: New idea originates outside of the organization, and captures the interest of a leader inside an organization.

Stage 2: New idea is imported into the organization, and a decision is made to adopt it.

Stage 3: Champion operationalizes the new idea, inside the organization.

Stage 4: The new idea becomes routinized and becomes the way business is done in the organization.

Figure 2.8.   The quality management idea-adoption-implementation process.

support networks so their pioneers will flourish. This point is so important it's hard to overstress. No support system, no champions. No champions, no innovation."

The question now is does your organization have a quality management champion? If not, why not you?

Notes

1. Federal Quality Institute, *Introduction to Total Quality Management in the Federal Government* (Washington, D.C.: U.S. Government Printing Office, May 1991), 9.

2. David Osborne and Ted Gaebler, *Reinventing Government: How the Entrepreneurial Spirit Is Transforming the Public Sector* (Reading, Mass.: Addison-Wesley, 1992), 20–21.

3. U.S. Department of Transportation, *Lessons Learned: Getting Started/Revitalizing Your TQM Effort,* vol. 2, no. 2 (January 1992), 6–7.

3　The Quality Gurus

There is nothing more difficult to plan, more doubt-
ful of success, nor more dangerous to manage than the
creation of a new order of things. . . . Whenever his
enemies have occasion to attack the innovator they do
so with the passion of partisans, while the others
defend him sluggishly so that the innovator and his
party alike are vulnerable.

Niccolo Machiavelli
The Prince, 1513

More Than One Way

The Innovators

At the turn of the century, most Americans believed that leaders were born, not made. The idea that anyone could develop leadership traits was only gradually accepted. Today, however, the study of leadership is a part of many business school curriculums. The diffusion of quality management practices throughout government has followed a similar path, as managers cautiously redefined how they view, and perform, their work during the past decade. In the past several years, we have seen both the federal and state governments become aware of and adopt quality management in their effort to provide better government.

Like innovators before them, Philip Crosby, Dr. W. Edwards Deming, and Dr. Joseph M. Juran are change agents, spreading the notion that government leaders can, and must, learn to build quality management performance into their organizations and that quality management is neither a matter of chance nor an act of magic. But since change involves risks for individuals and organizations alike, with each new idea also comes resistance to change. Only slowly are familiar habits and beliefs traded in for new ones. As you read in chapter 2, the diffusion of new ideas and successful change processes—whether occurring societywide or just within individual organizations—pass through predictable stages.

Figure 3.1 groups innovation adopters into five categories, from innovators to laggards. This classification scheme helps us better appreciate the process of quality management change in several ways. First, it places the quality management movement in government into a longer range, historical context and suggests that Crosby, Deming, and Juran—the innovators of new ideas—started a societywide change process. Second, we also see that the early adopters, (such as the winners of the Malcolm Baldrige National Quality Award, the Presidential Award for Quality, the Quality Improvement Prototype Award, the Senate Quality Award, the NASA Quality Award, and the State Quality Awards), who first embrace the new ideas, represent only a fraction of the potential adopters.

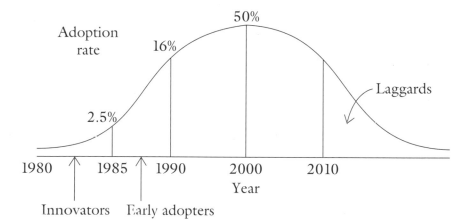

Figure 3.1. Distribution of adopters of quality management in government.

Finally, as quality management ideas spread into the government at large, dependence on the guru-dominated diffusion process used by the relatively few early adopting organizations will be modified. In its place, we will see adoption of customized, mix-and-match approaches that better accommodate the needs of thousands of adopting organizations in the years ahead. Thus, in the future, the reliance on a single guru will be dead.

Toward Customized Adoption

In Japan in the 1950s, quality management innovators achieved a charismatic appeal. Only in the early 1980s, as these innovators spread their ideas among American industrial clients who were feeling the impact of global competition did quality management begin to gain a similar appeal in the United States. Under the influence of a single innovator, organizations tended to adopt a more-or-less pure approach—à la Crosby, Deming, Juran, or some other guru. Not until the middle and late 1980s were the ideas of these innovators popularized in America, and industry began to implement their concepts.

Today, federal and state government organizations are on the verge of mass adoption of quality management practices. In this emerging era, the one-on-one, guru-dominated approach becomes less and less able to keep up with the demand as the number of adopters skyrockets. In the meantime, the experiences of the early adopters have combined with the methods promoted by the gurus and with other new concepts (for example, benchmarking and teamwork). With all these ideas percolating through the government community, it seems only natural that mix-and-match, customized approaches to quality management will replace the original, guru-dominated approach.

Is There One Best Approach?

The remainder of this chapter introduces the basic ideas and concepts of a few of the leading quality management experts. These experts, it should be stressed, represent just a sampling of a still larger community of quality and management thinkers, including Armand V. Feigenbaum, Kaoru Ishikawa (deceased), and Rosabeth Moss-Kanter. The three quality management experts highlighted here do, nonetheless, offer a wide range of approaches to better understand quality management today.

Deming's approach is selected because of his well-known role in the reconstruction of Japan's industrial base following World War II and his broad, philosophical approach to change with an emphasis on a statistically based implementation process and concern for people. Juran's contribution, on the other hand, contains a distinct product-development flavor and a systematic, three-step methodology to help managers zero in on quality management implementation.

Because Crosby stresses a well-structured, stage-by-stage development of an organization's culture, his model may have greater appeal for those executives interested in a more incremental, road map approach.

Caution: Don't assume that a single best method should, or does, exist. Only you can decide. If, after comparing the Crosby approach to those of Deming and Juran, for example, you conclude that Crosby's model fits exactly the needs of your organization, you might consider adopting it wholesale. On the other hand, after a careful comparison of the strengths and weaknesses of each approach, you may decide that a pick-and-choose approach is the way to go. For example, you might use a version of Crosby's maturity grid at the organizationwide level, and a version of Deming's control chart approach at the subunit level.

The challenge facing America's government leaders in the 1990s is not simply to decide whether to adopt any quality management program, but to adopt one that best fits their specific organization's needs.

The Crosby School

Like Chester Barnard, a 40-year veteran of American Telephone and Telegraph and author of the 1938 classic study of management, *The Functions of the Executive,* Philip Crosby developed his total quality management ideas during a long corporate career. Rising through managerial ranks, Crosby was a vice president of ITT for 14 years. Crosby's insider corporate perspective is reflected in a down-to-earth approach to quality management. He believes an organization can learn and that top management should adopt a quality management style, not because it is the right thing to do, but because it is good for the bottom line.

The Problem Organization

Crosby believes that the problem organization will benefit most from his quality management program. In his book, *Quality Without Tears,* Crosby identifies a problem organization by the presence of five symptoms.

- The outgoing product or service normally contains deviations from the published, announced, or agreed upon requirements.

- The organization has an extensive field service or dealer network skilled in rework and resourceful corrective action to keep the customers satisfied.

- Management does not provide a clear performance standard or definition of quality management, so the employees each develop their own.

- Management does not know the price of nonconformance. Service organizations spend 35 percent or more of their operating costs doing things wrong and doing them over.

- Management denies that it is the cause of the problem.

In other words, virtually every organization is, by Crosby's definition, a *problem organization.* Why? Because managers traditionally attack problems as they crop up in the organization and seek random improvements. Top management, according to Crosby, is too quick to "send everyone else to school, set up programs for the lowest levels of the organization, and make speeches with impressive-sounding words. It is not until all the problems are pulled together, particularly the financial ones, that the seriousness of the situation is exposed."

Crosby's View of Quality

The real meaning of quality, Crosby asserts in *Quality Is Free,* suffers from several erroneous assumptions.

Quality is not

- Goodness, or luxury, or shininess

- Intangible, therefore not measurable

- Unaffordable

- Originated by the workers
- Something that originates in the quality department

Quality is

- Conformance to requirements; nonquality is nonconformance

To put this definition into practice, Crosby assumes that quality either is or is not present in the whole organization, that quality is the responsibility of everyone in the organization, and that quality is measurable. In addition, he cautions the quality-bound manager, "the process of instilling quality improvement is a journey that never ends. Changing a culture so that it never slips back is not something that is accomplished quickly."

Crosby's Quality Management Maturity Grid

The first step for an organization moving toward a quality management profile is to determine its current level of *management maturity*. Table 3.1, Crosby's Quality Management Maturity Grid, is used for this purpose. Along the left-hand margin are six measures of the sophistication of an organization's management style, including the attitude of top management, how the organization handles problems, and the cost of quality to the organization. Across the top are five levels, or stages, of quality management maturity. These range from *uncertainty*, in which an organization is characterized by the statement, "We don't know why we have quality management problems," to *certainty*, reserved for organizations in which top management can proclaim, "We know why we don't have quality management problems."

Once an organization has located its current maturity stage on the grid, it then implements an improvement program based on Crosby's 14 steps of quality management improvement (see Figure 3.1). Each step is designed as a building block to move the organization's management style toward the right-hand side of the maturity grid, passing through progressively higher level maturity stages. Only in the final stage is conformance to the organization's stated quality management requirements assured. A zero-defects culture—one in which the organization, in effect, does it right the first time—is established, and the cost of quality management is reduced to its lowest possible level.

Table 3.1. Crosby's quality management maturity grid.

Measurement categories	Stage I: Uncertainty	Stage II: Awakening	Stage III: Enlightenment	Stage IV: Wisdom	Stage V: Certainty
Management understanding and attitude	Fails to see quality as a management tool.	Supports quality management in theory but is unwilling to provide the necessary money or time.	Learns about quality management and becomes supportive.	Participates personally in quality activities.	Regards quality management as essential to the company's success.
Quality organization status	Quality activities are limited to the manufacturing or engineering department and are largely appraisal and sorting.	A strong quality leader has been appointed, but quality activities remain focused on appraisal and sorting and are still limited to manufacturing and engineering.	Quality department reports to top management, and its leader is active in company management.	Quality manager is an officer of the company. Prevention activities have become important.	Quality manager is on the board of directors. Prevention is the main quality activity.
Problem handling	Problems are fought as they occur and are seldom fully resolved; "firefighting" dominates.	Teams are established to attack major problems, but the approach remains short term.	Problems are resolved in an orderly fashion, and corrective action is a regular event.	Problems are identified early in their development.	Except in the most unusual cases, problems are prevented.
Cost of quality as percentage of sales	Reported: unknown Actual: 20%	Reported: 5% Actual: 18%	Reported: 8% Actual: 12%	Reported: 6.5% Actual: 8%	Reported: 2.5% Actual: 2.5%
Quality improvement actions	No organized activities.	Activities are motivational and short term.	Implements the 14-step program with full understanding.	Continues the 14-step program and starts Make Certain.	Quality improvement is a regular and continuing activity.
Summation of company quality posture	"We don't know why we have quality problems."	"Must we always have quality problems?"	"Because of management commitment and quality improvement programs, we are identifying and resolving our quality problems."	"We routinely prevent defects from occurring."	"We know why we don't have quality problems."

Source: Adapted from Philip B. Crosby, *Quality Is Free* (New York: McGraw-Hill, 1979), pp. 38–39.

Step 1.   **Management commitment.** Top management must be convinced of the need for total quality improvement and must make its commitment clear to the entire organization. This show of commitment should be accompanied by a written quality management policy, stating that each person is expected to "perform exactly like the requirement, or cause the requirement to be officially changed to what we and the customers really need."

Step 2.   **Quality improvement team.** Management must form a team of department heads (or those who can speak for their departments) to oversee quality management improvement. The team's role is to see that needed actions take place in its departments and in the organization as a whole.

Step 3.   **Quality measurement.** Methods for measuring quality, appropriately tailored to every activity, must be established to identify areas needing improvement. In accounting, for example, one measure might be the percentage of late reports; in engineering, the accuracy of drawings; and in purchasing, rejections due to incomplete descriptions.

Step 4.   **Cost-of-quality evaluation.** The budget office should make an estimate of the costs of quality to identify areas where quality improvements would be productive.

Step 5.   **Quality awareness.** Employees must be made aware of quality issues. They must understand the importance of product conformance and the costs of nonconformance. These messages should be carried by supervisors (after they have been trained) and through such media as films, booklets, and posters.

Step 6.   **Corrective action.** Opportunities for correction are generated by steps 3 and 4, as well as by discussions among employees. Employees' ideas for corrective actions should be brought to the supervisory level and resolved there, if possible. Such ideas should be pushed up further if that is necessary to get action.

Source: Adapted from Philip B. Crosby, *Quality Without Tears* (New York: McGraw-Hill, 1984), pp. 99–119.

Figure 3.1.   Crosby's 14-step program.

Step 7.   **Zero-defects planning.** An ad hoc zero-defects committee should be formed from members of the quality management improvement team. This committee should start planning a zero-defects program appropriate to the organization and its culture.

Step 8.   **Supervisory training.** Early in the process, all levels of management must be trained to implement their part of the quality management improvement program.

Step 9.   **Zero-Defects Day.** A Zero-Defects Day should be scheduled to signal to employees that the organization has a new performance standard.

Step 10.   **Goal setting.** To turn commitments into action, individuals must establish improvement goals for themselves and their groups. Supervisors should meet with their people and ask them to set goals that are specific and measurable. Goal lines should be posted in each area, and meetings held to discuss progress.

Step 11.   **Error-cause removal.** Employees should be encouraged to inform management of any problems that prevent them from performing error-free work. Employees need not do anything about these problems themselves; they should simply report them. Reported problems must then be acknowledged by management within 24 hours.

Step 12.   **Recognition.** Public, nonfinancial appreciation must be given to those who meet their quality management goals or perform outstandingly.

Step 13.   **Quality councils.** Quality professionals and team chairpersons should meet regularly to share experiences, problems, and ideas.

Step 14.   **Do it all over again.** To emphasize the never-ending process of quality improvement, the program (steps 1–13) must be repeated. This repetition renews the commitment of old employees and brings new ones into the process.

Figure 3.1. (continued)

The Crosby Quality College

The labels Crosby has given to each stage of his management maturity grid—that is, awakening, enlightenment, and wisdom—establish a mood of intellectual progress and reinforces the role of organizational learning in his "do-it-right-the-first-time" approach to quality management. In other words, wishful thinking won't work. Only constant, top-level effort will move an organization toward the right-hand side of the grid. To make sure this happens, the Crosby Quality College in Winter Park, Florida, offers a no-nonsense environment that reinforces again and again one basic theme: zero-defect management is possible.

"The main problem of total quality management as a management concern," says Crosby in *Quality Without Tears*, "is that it is not taught in management schools. It is not considered to be a management function, but rather a technical one. . . . However, with the pressure on quality erupting worldwide and the difficulty in getting senior management to do something about it, it becomes apparent that a new measurement is needed for quality management. The best measurement for this subject is the same as for any other—money."

The Crosby Quality College does not educate individuals per se. According to Crosby, "The college deals with whole companies, not with individuals." While at this college, every student activity, from hotel registration upon arrival to ownership of problems in class, is designed to reinforce *the* central message: conformance to requirements—the definition of quality—is both beyond compromise and financially wise.

The Deming Philosophy

Born in 1900, and recipient of a Ph.D. in mathematics and physics from Yale, W. Edwards Deming was first introduced to the basic tenets of traditional management principles in the late 1920s, as a summer employee at Western Electric's famous Hawthorne plant in Chicago. At the Hawthorne plant the revolutionary human relations studies of Harvard Professor Elton Mayo began to raise a fundamental question: How can organizations best motivate workers? Deming found the traditional motivation system in use at that time to be degrading and economically unproductive. Under that system, worker incentives were linked to piecework to maximize worker output. During the inspection process that followed, defective items were subtracted from the worker's piece-work credits. The virtues of an equalitarian workplace—clearly absent from this traditional model—comprise an enduring theme found throughout Deming's philosophy.

During the 1930s, Deming's collaboration with Walter A. Shewhart, a statistician working at Bell Laboratories, led to Deming's conviction that traditional management methods should be replaced with statistical control techniques. Deming recognized that a statistically controlled management process gave the manager a systematic capacity to determine when to intervene and, equally important, when to leave an industrial process alone. During World War II, Deming got his first opportunity to demonstrate to government managers how Shewhart's statistical quality management control methods could be taught to engineers and workers and be put into practice in busy war production plants.

Following the war, Deming left government service and set up a private consulting practice. The State Department, one of his early clients, sent him to Japan in 1947 to help prepare a national census in that devastated country. U.S. managers soon forgot their wartime statistical control lessons and continued their prewar love affair with traditional management practices, which prized production over quality management. Deming's evolving statistical process control (SPC) methods received a warm reception in Japan.

In fact, the Japanese now credit part of their postwar industrial renaissance to Deming's SPC-based philosophy of quality management. Each year in his name, the Union of Japanese Scientists and Engineers awards the Deming Prize to companies that have demonstrated outstanding contributions to product quality management and dependability. In addition, in 1960 the Japanese emperor awarded Deming the Second Order Medal of the Sacred Treasure, a tribute rarely paid to a foreigner.

The Quality Crisis

In his book, *Out of the Crisis,* Deming holds American managers responsible for causing a societywide quality management crisis. "Western style of management must change to halt the decline of

Western industry, and to turn it upward. . . . There must be an awakening to the crisis, followed by action, management's job. . . . The transformation can only be accomplished by man, not by hardware (computers, gadgets, automation, or new machinery). An organization cannot buy its way into total quality management."

Deming's philosophy puts quality management in human terms. When an organization's work force is committed to doing a good job, and it has a solid managerial process within which to act, quality management will flow naturally. Thus, a practical, composite definition of quality management might read this way: quality management is a method for generating a predictable degree of uniformity and dependability at low cost, and suited to the market.

Because Japan adopted statistical-based control techniques in the early 1950s, it has a 30-year head start on the United States. Deming estimates it will take American managers another 30 years to achieve the advanced level of statistical control now in wide practice in Japan. While Western managers have focused on outcome and practiced retroactive management, such as management by objectives, the Japanese have perfected quality management. In 1985, as quoted in *The Deming Management Method* by Mary Walton, Deming summed up his indictment this way: "Failure to understand people is the devastation of Western management." The U.S. quality management crisis is being prolonged by what Deming calls the seven deadly diseases associated with traditional management practices (see Figure 3.2).

Deming's 14 Points
To eliminate these underlying managerial diseases, Deming prescribes his 14-point cure, shown in Figure 3.3. Both the philosophical foundation for Deming's managerial transformation, and the role assigned to statistical quality management control in the execution of that philosophy, are present in his 14-point program of quality management. These points are so essential to his approach, Deming will not accept a new company client until its president has promised to faithfully implement *all* 14 points. Halfway measures will not do. If an organization is unwilling to change its management philosophy 100 percent to the Deming way, Deming passes that client by. Why? Because Deming is

1. **Lack of constancy of purpose.** An organization that is without constancy of purpose has no long-range plans for staying in operation. Management is insecure, and so are employees.

2. **Emphasis on short-term profits.** Looking to increase the quarterly dividend undermines quality and productivity.

3. **Evaluation by performance, merit rating, or annual review of performance.** The effects of these are devastating—teamwork is destroyed, rivalry is nurtured. Performance ratings build fear and leave people bitter, despondent, beaten. They also encourage defections in the ranks of management.

4. **Mobility of management.** Job-hopping managers never understand the organizations they work for and are never there long enough to follow through on long-term changes that are necessary for quality and productivity.

5. **Running an organization on visible figures alone.** The most important figures are unknown and unknowable—the "multiplier" effect of a happy customer, for example.

6. **Excessive medical costs for employee health care, which increase the final costs of goods and services.**

7. **Excessive costs of warranty, fueled by lawyers who work on the basis of contingency fees.**

Source: Mary Walton, *Deming Management at Work* (New York: G.P. Putnam's Sons, 1990), p. 19.

Figure 3.2. The seven deadly diseases.

convinced that about 85 percent of all quality management problems are caused by harmful management practices. Consequently, a CEO intent on changing the way production workers perform—without changing the obsolete management system—will, at best, only address 15 percent of the problems.

1. **Create constancy of purpose for improvement of product and service.** Dr. Deming suggests a radical new definition of an organization's role: Rather than focusing only on making money, the organization seeks to stay in operation and provide jobs through innovation, research, constant improvement, and maintenance.

2. **Adopt the new philosophy.** Americans are too tolerant of poor workmanship and sullen service. We need a new religion in which mistakes and negativism are unacceptable.

3. **Cease dependence on mass inspection.** American organizations typically inspect a product as it comes off the assembly line or at major stages along the way; defective products are either thrown out or reworked. Both practices are unnecessarily expensive. In effect, an organization is paying workers to make defects and then to correct them. Quality comes not from inspection but from improvement of the process. With instruction, workers can be enlisted in this improvement.

4. **End the practice of awarding contracts on the price tag alone.** Purchasing departments customarily operate on orders to seek the lowest price vendor. Frequently, this approach leads to supplies of low quality. Instead, buyers should seek the best quality in a long-term relationship with a single supplier for any one item.

5. **Improve constantly and forever the system of production and service.** Improvement is not a one-time effort. Management is obligated to continually look for ways to reduce waste and improve quality.

6. **Institute training.** Too often, workers learn their job from other workers who were never trained properly. Moreover, they are forced to follow unintelligible instructions. Clearly, they can't do their jobs well because no one tells them how.

7. **Institute leadership.** The job of a supervisor is not to tell people what to do, nor to punish them, but to lead. Leading consists of helping people do a better job and of learning by objective methods who is in need of individual help.

Source: Mary Walton, *Deming Management at Work* (New York: G.P. Putnam's Sons, 1990), pp. 17–18.

Figure 3.3. Deming's 14 points.

8. **Drive out fear.** Many employees are afraid to ask questions or to take a position, even when they do not understand what their job is or what is right or wrong. They will continue to do things the wrong way, or not do them at all. The economic losses from fear are appalling. To ensure better quality and productivity, people must feel secure.

9. **Break down barriers between staff areas.** Often an organization's departments or units are competing with each other, or have goals that conflict. They do not work as a team so they cannot solve or foresee problems. Worse, one department's goals may cause trouble for another.

10. **Eliminate slogans, exhortations, and targets for the work force.** These never helped anybody do a good job. Let workers formulate their own slogans.

11. **Eliminate numerical quotas.** Quotas take into account only numbers, not quality or methods. In contrast, they usually guarantee inefficiency and high cost. To hold a job, a person meets a quota at any cost, without regard for the larger organization.

12. **Remove barriers to pride of workmanship.** People are eager to do a good job and distressed when they cannot. Too often, misguided supervisors, faulty equipment, and defective materials stand in the way of good performance. These barriers must be removed.

13. **Institute a vigorous program of education and retraining.** Both management and the work force will have to be educated in the new methods, including teamwork and statistical techniques.

14. **Take action to accomplish the transformation.** It will require a special top management team with a plan of action to carry out the quality mission. Workers cannot do it on their own, nor can managers. A critical mass of people in the organization must understand the 14 points [and] the seven deadly diseases.

Figure 3.3. (continued)

Statistical Process Control

Identifying the Problem

The methodological core of Deming's quality management approach is the use of simple statistical techniques to continuously improve an organization's management process. Only through statistical verification, according to Deming, can the manager (1) know that he or she has a problem and (2) find the cause of the problem. Deming uses control charts, like the one shown in Figure 3.4, to identify the absence or presence of a quality problem. Since all human activity will contain unavoidable variations—that is, every product or service will differ slightly from all the others—an acceptable range of random variations must be established for every product or service.

Once measurable upper and lower control limits have been set for a product or service, and a control chart prepared to reflect these limits, the workers performing the activity periodically plot actual

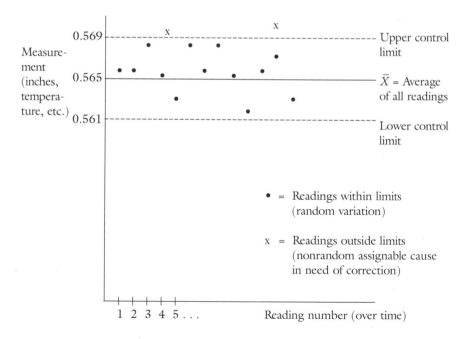

Figure 3.4. A typical Deming control chart.

measurements on the chart. When these measurements fall outside the acceptable random-variation range, the worker immediately knows that a nonrandom quality management problem exists.

Classifying the Problem's Cause

The next step is to identify the cause behind the problem. Two possibilities exist. The problem could result from a *common cause*, or one rooted in the basic management system and, therefore, potentially organizationwide. Fundamental design errors or imprecise machinery are examples of common causes. Alternatively, the problem could result from a *special cause*, or one stemming from a more isolated source, a few poorly trained workers in one department, for example.

Deming recommends using several additional charting methods to learn more about the factors causing the quality problems exposed in a control chart. Mary Walton, in *Deming Management at Work*, sums up the crucial role of statistics this way, "American managers pride themselves on hunches and intuition. When they succeed, they take credit. When they fail, they find someone to blame. But a quality management transformation rests on a different set of assumptions: decisions must be based on facts . . . [and] . . . it is helpful to display information graphically." Figure 3.5 summarizes the full array of Deming's charting techniques. More is said concerning the specific uses of these charting methods in chapter 10.

Correcting the Problem

The final step in the quality management cycle is for the manager and the workers to eliminate the cause of the quality problem by taking the necessary actions contained in the 14 points. These actions may range from redesign of a faulty manufacturing assembly line to a one-day training course in which workers learn how to operate a new office machine or better serve a new type of customer.

Boosting Performance

While finding and curing quality problems keeps an organization's activities within established quality limits, Deming uses control charts in another way to actually boost an organization's performance. By

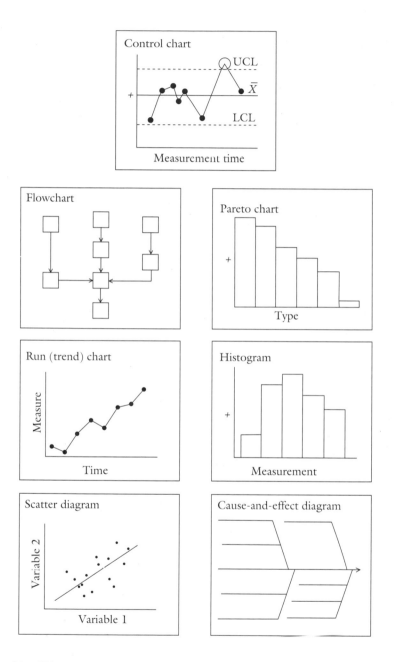

Source: Mary Walton, *Deming Management at Work* (New York: G.P. Putnam's Sons, 1990), p. 23.

Figure 3.5. Doing it with data—seven helpful charts.

narrowing the established range between the upper and lower random-variation limits for an activity, an organization will, in effect, deliberately create and then solve self-inflicted quality problems. The result is an increase in the organization's overall level of quality. In this way, managers can plan for and implement a long-range quality improvement program to provide better government.

Plan-Do-Study-Act Cycle

Deming envisions a never-ending, circular management process. The Plan-Do-Study-Act (PDSA) cycle is an adaptation of the work of Shewhart (PDCA cycle) that links the seven diseases, the 14 points, and the statistical techniques into a continuous process, without a starting or ending point. Only through the ongoing application of the four-stage cycle shown in Figure 3.6 can an organization attain and retain a superior quality management process. There are no shortcuts.

The Juran Philosophy

Joseph M. Juran was educated during the first quarter of this century in engineering and law. His outlook, in general, reflects a rational,

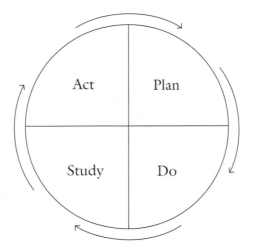

Figure 3.6.   The Deming PDSA cycle.

matter-of-fact approach to organization and one heavily dependent on sophisticated planning and quality management control processes. The focal point of Juran's quality management philosophy is the organization's individual service or product, not the organization per se. If the building blocks—each individual service or product—meet the customers' requirements, an organizationwide quality management program will emerge.

Like Deming, Juran also played a significant role in rebuilding Japan after World War II, and he also received the Second Class of the Order of the Sacred Treasure for "the development of quality control in Japan and the facilitation of U.S. and Japanese friendship." His search for underlying principles of the management process led to his focus on quality as the ultimate goal. Before becoming a quality management consultant and lecturer, Juran worked in both government and business organizations.

A National Quality Crisis

The basic societywide problem, according to Juran, is that U.S. government is caught up in a quality crisis and, while many government managers agree with him on the existence of the crisis, too few understand how to end it. Juran has identified two widely held but wrong assumptions that are preventing government managers from finding solutions to their problems.

The first error in thinking is this: many managers have not yet realized that they, not the workers, must shoulder the responsibility for the performance of their organization. Until top management begins to plan quality into its service and products, rather than actually planning a lack of quality into them (as is presently the case), the quality crisis will continue. Complementing the first erroneous assumption is the fact that managers also fail to realize the great productivity gains to be made once quality management becomes their top priority.

Juran's Quality Trilogy

The challenge facing managers, according to Juran, is to abandon the traditional approach to planning, which carelessly introduces quality flaws into the process. The traditional approach depends on an inspection and rejection process to find and correct quality problems without ever redesigning the planning process itself.

Adoption of Juran's quality trilogy requires that an organization, once and for all, redesign its service, product planning, and control systems and then, through an ongoing improvement program, ensure that the basic causes of quality flaws are permanently eliminated. This means an organization's planning system should contain a single, universal thought process that supersedes the particular processes used in the production of an individual product. It also stresses the adoption of Juran's definitions of quality presented in *Juran on Planning for Quality*. "*Quality* [is] (1) product performance that results in customer satisfaction; (2) freedom from product deficiencies, which avoids customer dissatisfaction. A shorthand expression that conveys both meanings is *fitness for use.*"

Trilogy Parts
Conceptually, Juran divides quality into three prime parts.

- Quality planning
- Quality control
- Quality improvements

While planning, controlling, and improving managerial processes have long been considered fundamental executive functions, Juran asserts that they are seldom combined in a structured way—as they are in the quality trilogy—for managing quality. Figure 3.7 describes the way in which Juran's three-part approach is designed to reduce the cost of quality over time.

Quality Planning
In Juran's approach to quality management, the central task is "developing the products and processes required to meet customers' needs." To accomplish this task, he recommends a road map as shown in Figure 3.8. During the quality management planning stage, an organization prepares to meet established quality management goals. The result of the planning stage is a dependable process that can be trusted to perform as planned under operating conditions.

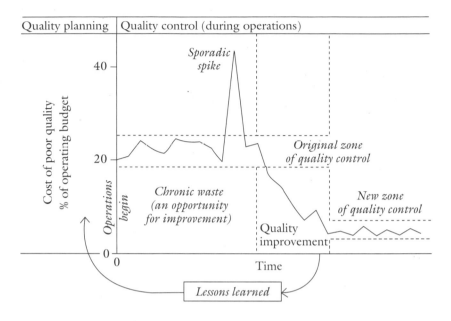

Source: J. M. Juran, *Juran on Planning for Quality* (New York: Free Press, 1988), p. 12.

Figure 3.7.   The Juran trilogy reduces the cost of quality.

Quality Control

Control processes are designed to ensure that the quality management goals set in the planning stage are, in fact, being met during the actual production or rendering of the organization's services and products. Figure 3.9 illustrates Juran's quality control process.

Quality Improvement

Unlike quality planning and quality control processes, which logically fit together to form a step-by-step, product-idea-to-quality-product continuum, quality management improvement is the means by which an organization selectively identifies and implements change on a subsystem level. Quality planning and quality control establish a stabilized quality culture, or foundation, throughout an organization. The third part of the trilogy, however, known both as quality improvement and Juran's *breakthrough sequence,* is the means for managers to find and remedy

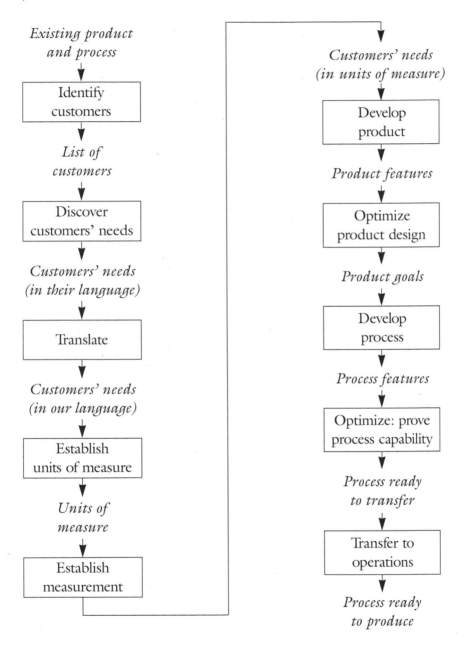

Source: J. M. Juran, *Planning for Quality* (New York: Free Press, 1988), p. 15.

Figure 3.8.   The quality management planning road map.

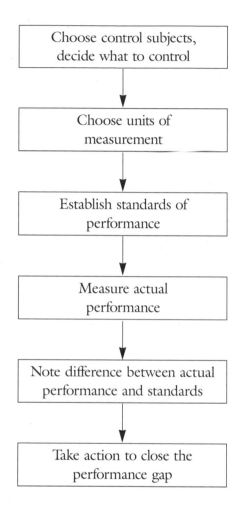

Source: Adapted from J. M. Juran, *Juran on Planning for Quality* (New York: Free Press, 1988), p. 14.

Figure 3.9. Based on Juran's quality approach.

the basic quality-limiting causes imbedded in the organization. Juran expressly warns that the improvement phase of his trilogy is not to be considered a quick-fix exercise. Instead, whenever a basic cause leading to a quality failure is identified, Juran insists that the planning-control processes be altered to permanently prevent that cause from occurring again.

The breakthrough process described in Figure 3.10 is used in conjunction with Juran's planning and control processes while the trilogy is first being installed in an organization. It is also used as a troubleshooting tool to keep the planning-control sequence running smoothly after it is established in the organization. Juran uses the term *breakthrough* to emphasize that this part of the trilogy is the means to achieve unprecedented levels of quality performance in an organization. Juran estimates that approximately 80 percent of the problems identified with

1. **Break through attitudes.** Managers must first prove that a breakthrough is needed and then create a climate conducive to change. To demonstrate need, data must be collected to show the extent of the problem; the data most convincing to top management are usually cost-of-quality figures. To get the resources required for improvement, expected benefits must be presented in terms of cost and return on investment.

2. **Identify the vital few projects.** Pareto chart analysis is used to distinguish the vital few projects from the trivial many and to set priorities based on problem frequency.

3. **Organize for breakthrough in knowledge.** Two organizational entities should be established: a steering group (executive steering group) and a diagnostic group (process action team). The steering group, composed of people from several departments, defines the program, suggests possible problem causes, gives the authority to experiment, helps overcome resistance to change, and implements the solution. The diagnostic group, composed of quality management professionals and sometimes line managers, is responsible for analyzing the problem.

Source: Adapted from "Quality Planning Road Map," in J. M. Juran, *Juran on Planning for Quality* (New York: Free Press, 1988), p. 14.

Figure 3.10. Quality improvement process.

4. **Conduct the analysis.** The diagnostic group studies symptoms, develops hypotheses, and experiments to find the problem's true causes. This group also tries to determine whether defects are primarily operator controllable or management controllable. (A defect is operator controllable only if it meets three criteria: operators know what they are supposed to do, have the data to understand what they are actually doing, and are able to regulate their own performance.) Theories can be tested by using past data and current production data and by conducting experiments. With this information, the diagnostic group then proposes solutions to the problem.

5. **Determine how to overcome resistance to change.** The need for change must be established in terms that are important to the key people involved. Logical arguments alone are insufficient. Participation is therefore required in both the technical and the social aspects of change.

6. **Institute the change.** Departments that must take corrective action must be convinced to cooperate. Presentations made to these departments should explain the size of the problem, alternative solutions, the cost of recommended changes, expected benefits, and efforts taken to anticipate the change's impact on employees. Time for reflection may be needed, and adequate training is essential.

7. **Institute controls.** Controls must be set up to monitor the solution, see that it works, and keep abreast of unforeseen developments. Formal follow-up is provided by the control sequence used to monitor and correct sporadic problems.

Figure 3.10. (continued)

breakthrough analysis, including defect rates, are correctable only by improving the management control system. The remaining 20 percent are attributable to the actions of the operating work force.

Cost-of-Quality Accounting System

To keep top management interested in, and supportive of, the department-level quality management planning process, Juran uses a cost-of-quality (COQ) accounting system. This system demonstrates how cost effective it really is to shift to a quality management process. Here is how it works.

By comparing the costs of implementing Juran's appraisal and prevention process to the costs of detecting internal and external product failures, an executive can determine an optimal level of effort. In the early stages of implementing a quality management process, every dollar invested in appraisal and prevention activities cuts the organization's external and internal failure costs by far more than one dollar. As the defect rate and failure costs drop in response to the widespread adoption of quality management processes, the organization's level of investment will be optimal whenever a dollar spent on appraisal and prevention equals a one-dollar reduction in detecting and fixing failures. Since the costs of finding and preventing the last few defects in a production system are extremely high—higher than the costs saved if these defects were eliminated—the optimal quality management level is somewhat less than a 100-percent, defect-free system.

Comparative Assessment

Before comparing the quality management approaches of Crosby, Deming, and Juran, let's place the ideas of these innovators into their larger, societal framework. As a group, they all advocate the need for a greater commitment to quality management in the government. But each holds his own view of what causes the quality vacuum. Table 3.2 attempts to identify the genesis, or the root causes, of the quality management challenge facing government. Crosby locates the roots of the problem within the organization itself. Juran and Deming, on the other hand, trace organization-based quality management problems back to the values found in post–World War II U.S. society.

Table 3.2.   Three theories of the quality management challenge for government.

	Nature of the crisis	Cause of the crisis	Solution	Definition of quality
Crosby	Communication failure within the organization	Lack of commitment to quality	Organizational culture committed to quality	Conformance to organization's own quality requirements
Deming	Loss of competitiveness	Societal and organizational acceptance of low quality	Society and organization committed to quality	Dependable, customer-satisfying product or service at a low cost
Juran	Loss of competitiveness	Organizational acceptance of low quality	Organization committed to quality	Product or service that is fit for use

The Early Adopters

A measure of the adoption of quality management principles and practices in the last 10 years is shown in Figure 3.11. The figure provides a partial listing of the growing number of organizations that have adopted the ideas of Crosby, Deming, and Juran.

Common Ground

The various quality management approaches explored here build on a solid base of commonly held expectations and assumptions. In many

- Aeronautical Systems Division, Wright Patterson Air Force Base
- Air Force Logistics Command
- Defense Contract Management District
- Defense Industrial Supply Center
- Equal Employment Opportunity Commission
- IRS Center at Fresno, California
- IRS Center at Ogden, Utah
- IRS Cincinnati Service Center
- IRS Federal Tax Deposit System
- IRS Ogden Service Center
- IRS One Stop Accounting System
- Kenmore–Town of Tonowanda Union Free School District, New York
- NASA Johnson Space Center, Houston, Texas
- NASA Lewis Research Center, Cleveland, Ohio
- Naval Air Systems Command, Washington, D.C.
- Naval Aviation Depot, Cherry Point, North Carolina
- Naval Publications and Forms
- New York State Police, Albany, New York
- Norfolk Naval Shipyard, Norfolk, Virginia
- Patent and Trademark Office
- Sacramento Air Logistics, Sacramento, California
- San Francisco Region, Wage and Hour, San Francisco, California
- State of Arkansas
- State of Ohio
- State of Minnesota
- State of New York
- Veterans Administration Medical Center, Kansas City
- Veterans Administration Regional Office and Insurance

Figure 3.11. The leading quality management adopters in government.

respects, the approaches are far more alike than they are different from one another. Each approach

- Requires a very strong top management commitment
- Shows that quality management practices will save, not cost, money
- Places the responsibility for achieving quality management primarily on the managers and the systems they control, not on the workers
- Stresses that quality management is a never-ending, continuous improvement process
- Is customer oriented
- Assumes a shift from an old to a new organizational culture
- Is founded on building a strong management/worker problem-solving team

But, the differences do matter and will influence a manager's decision to adopt portions of one approach over the other. So let's compare and contrast Crosby, Deming, and Juran on a number of key issues.

What Is the Nature of the Organization?

Crosby

More so than the others, Crosby's approach has an unmistakable, organizationwide, team-building flavor. The organization is treated almost as if it were a whole, living organism that evolves through time toward higher levels of self-awareness.

Deming

Resident in Deming's view of the organization is a deep current of social responsibility. The purpose of the organization is to stay in business. But why? Not to make a lot of money, but to lend stability to the community it serves and to treat all workers with the respect naturally due every human being. The Deming approach has a moral philosophical tone that is absent in the others.

Juran

Juran's outlook focuses more on the parts of the organization than on the whole. Of course, the whole does matter, but the path to a healthy organization is to make sure each part is fine-tuned. Juran seems to invite the use of his trilogy on an isolated, troubled division or department.

Is a Step-by-Step Implementation Process Readily Apparent?

Crosby and Juran

In both of these approaches, we have a feeling that a starting point and an end point are visible. Crosby's maturity grid and Juran's trilogy might be called user-friendly.

Deming

With Deming, a road map does not necessarily exist. Without a tutor's guiding hand, one might not readily know where to start the journey to implementation of Deming's philosophy.

Can the Approach Be Implemented Piecemeal?

Crosby and Deming

Both these approaches are holistic, and neither invites a piecemeal implementation strategy. That said, however, the Crosby model does more easily lend itself to prudent modifications to suit the host organization. Deming, on the other hand, calls for an almost instantaneous belief and total adoption of a new way of organizational life—one filled with significant culture and value shifts.

Juran

A danger, perhaps, in the Juran model is the apparent ease with which his methodology could be targeted only at parts of an organization *(islands of quality)*. For example, a manager attempting a piecemeal implementation of Juran's methods might forget that, in the end, the entire organization must share a deep commitment to quality management. While Juran selectively picks his subunits for application of the quality management improvement process, he still requires an organizationwide commitment.

How Well Does Each Approach Handle Resistance?

Crosby and Juran

Resistance to change is inevitable, but it need not be a barrier. Crosby's learning-based model is perhaps best suited to accommodating resistance. It allows the individual to acknowledge his or her doubts and then appease them through education and training. Juran also accommodates resistance by insisting that changes be justified through analysis and team-building processes.

Deming

On the surface, one can easily conclude that Deming's approach is dogmatic and uncompromising. In many respects, Deming himself cultivates this image. Yet, his statistical methods are, in effect, learning tools. They not only structure problems in objective ways that make them easily understood but also disarm critics of change by depending on facts, not gospel.

Where Do We Go from Here?

Adopting a quality management program is a big decision and one that should be made with care and only after consultation with others in your organization. Consider the advice given to Alice by the Cheshire Cat, when, during her adventures in Wonderland, she could not decide which of two paths to take.

> "Cheshire Puss," Alice began, rather timidly . . .
> "Would you tell me please, which way ought I go from here?"
>
> "That depends a good deal on where you want to get to," said the Cat.
>
> "I don't much care where—" said Alice.
>
> "Then it doesn't matter which way you go," said the Cat.

"—so long as I get somewhere," Alice added as an explanation.

"Oh, you're sure to do that," said the Cat, "if you only walk long enough."

From: Lewis Carroll, *Alice's Adventures in Wonderland* (1865)

If, like Alice, you really don't care where you and your organization are going, then it really doesn't matter what you do regarding quality management. But if you do care, then which way you go will make all the difference in the world.

Just Pick One

As Tom Peters notes in his book, *Thriving on Chaos,* "You should have a system. There's a lot of controversy here: Should you follow W. Edwards Deming, father of the Japanese total quality management revolution via statistical process control? Or Phil Crosby, author of *Quality Is Free,* and so prominent that GM bought a 10 percent stake in his organization? . . . Or Joseph Juran? Or invent a system of your own? Eventually you will develop your own scheme if you are successful."

During the mid-1980s, when quality management was first gaining some acceptance in government, it really didn't matter which approach—Crosby, Deming, or Juran—was adopted. Simply by following any one of the gurus, the early adopting organizations were well ahead of competitors still operating under traditional management practices. Those days are over. In the 1990s, as more organizations turn to quality management strategies out of necessity, just to maintain their performance positions, they will need to carefully compare approaches and adopt the quality management initiatives that best suit their organization.

The Situational Approach

Perhaps the single most crucial step for a manager preparing to adopt and implement a quality management program is an honest and frank appraisal of the current status of the organization. For starters, answer the following questions carefully.

- How will the organization react to change?
- Who are the potential champions of the change?
- What are realistic expectations for the organization?
- How much time is available to make changes?
- Will you make an organizationwide effort, or will you target a single subunit?
- How will you measure results?

During your assessment, keep good notes. You will benefit from constructing an "As-Is/To-Be" chart that summarizes and compares your organization's current quality management situation with your vision of it in the future.

Picking a Strategy

This chapter has been designed to first introduce you to, and then compare the ideas of, a few of the leading quality management gurus. Once you have a feel for your organization's current needs and the deep commitment required as you take your initial step toward quality management, you can begin to consider how the strategies of Crosby, Deming, and Juran apply specifically to your situation.

As discussed earlier, each approach has a number of common elements. The decision to adopt elements of one approach over another, therefore, will probably hinge on the unique nature of your organization. For example, a highly technical organization employing many engineers may find Juran's approach far more appealing than the idealistic approach favored by Deming. An organization with a history of strong organizational development may find Crosby's model culturally more comfortable.

Table 3.3 provides a comparison of Crosby's 14 steps, Deming's 14 points, and Juran's seven-point breakthrough sequence. In the table, each step and/or point is shown as it relates to one of eight generic quality management implementation tasks. Four of the task categories are people-oriented tasks, and four are technical in nature. The table will help you compare the relative weight each of quality management gurus gives to each of the eight quality management categories. With an idea

Table 3.3. Comparative assessment matrix: quality management tasks.

	Crosby's 14 Steps (Figure 3.1)*	Deming's 14 Points (Figure 3.3)*	Juran's 7 Points (Figure 3.10)*
People-oriented tasks			
Build top management commitment	1	1	1
Initiate teamwork	2, 10, 13	4, 9	3, 5, 6
Improve quality awareness	5, 7, 9, 12	2, 3, 8, 10 11, 12	5
Expand training	8	6, 7, 13	5
Technical tasks			
Measure quality	3	3, 4	4
Recognize cost of quality	4	3, 4	2
Take corrective action	6, 11	14	6, 7
Continuously improve process	14	5	7

*Note: Refer to figures noted for detailed description of each step or point delineated.

of the strengths and weaknesses of your current organization in mind, try to decide which of the eight categories will present the greatest challenge as you begin your quality management program. If, for example, you anticipate that building an awareness of quality management in your organization will be a particularly difficult challenge, you may want to take a closer look at Crosby and Deming, since their approaches have a strong awareness-building focus.

Quality Demystified

This chapter has been both a historical and an intellectual introduction to the central ideas behind the quality management movement. As with all innovations that challenge a long-held set of beliefs and practices, quality management has not been quickly accepted in the government community. While the ideas of Deming are as American as apple pie, they were first exported in the 1950s to Japan, where they ripened, and only recently have they been imported back into the United States.

Having surveyed a range of definitions of quality and a variety of well-known approaches to implanting quality management in an organization, you are ready to seriously consider the development of a specific quality management methodology for your organization. While you do take risks whenever you upset an organizational status quo, I hope you can see the enormous benefits the introduction of quality management can offer your organization.

Hopefully, this chapter has also helped demystify the aura that often surrounds the quality gurus. Crosby, Deming, and Juran do, indeed, offer new insights into a leader's role in the management process. But no magic is hidden behind their ideas. With determination, every government employee can learn to achieve a higher level of quality management. What the gurus cannot do, however, is supply that precious ingredient—the will to act. That comes from within and is developed bit by bit. By the time you have finished this book, you should have acquired both the tools and the desire to put quality management into practice.

The final message contained in this chapter is this: There is no one best way. A situational approach, in which government leaders carefully match their unique organizational environment to a customized quality management program, is the recommended route to achieving quality services.

4 American Government Quality Awards

To win the award, business, government organiza-
tions, and educational institutions must demonstrate
a commitment to quality products and services, a
quality work force, and cooperative labor-manage-
ment relations.

Governor Mario M. Cuomo

This chapter describes federal and state government efforts to improve quality and productivity in both the public and private sectors through quality award programs. This suite of quality self-assessment awards is shown in terms of their importance in Figure 4.1. As part of the reinventing of government activities, federal and state quality awards are changing to reflect the Baldrige National Quality Award criteria as the preferred quality management standard.

The Federal Quality Awards Program

Dick O'Brien and Victoria Elder, program administrators for the federal quality awards program at the Federal Quality Institute, describe the federal awards program this way: "Two awards are given annually to federal organizations that have successfully implemented quality management—the Presidential Award for Quality and the Quality Improvement Prototype (QIP) Award. Many people have heard of the Malcolm Baldrige National Quality Award. Many have seen the Cadillac commercials on TV. Few, however, know about the organizations receiving the Federal Quality Awards—the Federal sector's equivalent of the Baldrige Award."

Figure 4.1.   Quality award hierarchy.

Both the Quality Improvement Prototype Award and the Presidential Award for Quality were created with two purposes in mind: The first is to recognize federal organizations that have implemented quality management in an exemplary manner, resulting in high-quality products and services and the effective use of taxpayer dollars. Recognition is an integral part of quality management, and must play a central role in the advancement of the quality revolution in this country.

The second purpose is to use winners as models for other federal organizations, showing how a commitment to quality leads to better products and services and more satisfied customers. By publicizing the efforts of the award winners, the Federal Quality Institute encourages and facilitates the implementation of quality management throughout the federal government.

The Federal Quality Awards Program grew out of President Reagan's Quality and Productivity Improvement Program. This program required agencies to develop strategies for improving the quality, productivity, timeliness, and cost effectiveness of major federal programs. A group of private-sector executives advised those who administered the program at the Office of Management and Budget (OMB) to focus on quality improvement in order to achieve productivity improvement and cost savings. With this advice in mind, the Quality Improvement Prototype Award and Presidential Award for Quality were created in 1988.

The Federal Quality Awards Program has changed dramatically in the past several years. In 1988, quality management was a very new concept in federal government—not many organizations had embarked upon the quality journey. To stimulate the federal adoption of quality management, in that first year, the staff at the Office of Management and Budget sought out examples of quality improvement in federal agencies, and designated four of them quality improvement prototypes. There was no competition, no formalized process. In addition, the Executive Office of the President requested agencies to submit applications for the Presidential Award for Quality, but no award was presented.

In 1989, the Quality Improvement Prototype Award application consisted of 10 questions. The questions were rather general, and they elicited 58 applications that depicted widely divergent quality improvement efforts. The Office of Management and Budget staff read them all, culled out examples that actually reflected the principles and practices of quality management, visited several sites, and selected six prototype winners.

In 1989, the name and focus of the Presidential Award for Quality changed—from productivity to quality. The first set of criteria was patterned after the Malcolm Baldrige criteria, and applicants were asked to describe their quality improvement efforts. For the first time, outside judges were used to assess the applications and conduct site visits. The first Presidential Award was presented by the vice president of the United States to the Naval Air Systems Command.

The process currently used to evaluate applicants for both the Quality Improvement Prototype Award and the Presidential Award for Quality began in 1990. A structured evaluation process, patterned after those used for the George Westinghouse Total Quality Management Awards and the Baldrige Award, was created. Examiners and judges who had experience with quality improvement were selected from public- and private-sector organizations. A set of criteria was developed for the Quality Improvement Prototype Award, based on the Baldrige Award criteria. And finally, a set of scoring guidelines was created that described various levels of quality management implementation for each of the criteria. These guidelines have become an invaluable tool in the evaluation process—benchmarks against which to measure the scope and approach of an organization's quality efforts.

Twenty-seven organizations submitted applications based on the new Quality Improvement Prototype Award criteria, but many more of them than the previous year actually described the practice of quality management. The judges selected three 1990 Quality Improvement Prototype Award winners based on the examiners' evaluations. However, in 1990, none of the eligible agencies felt they had made enough progress to successfully meet the standards outlined in the Presidential Award for Quality application package.

In 1990, the functional responsibility for quality management implementation in the federal government was transferred from Office of Management and Budget to the Federal Quality Institute. The Federal Quality Institute sees the awards program as one of the primary and most successful means of providing guidance and leadership to federal organizations that want to improve the quality of their products and services.

In 1991, there were 34 applications for the Prototype Award. Thus, it was time to refine the awards criteria, scoring guidelines, and evaluation process. Once again the caliber of applications indicated that significant strides had been made in federal quality management implementation. Moreover, the scores of the winners and finalists demonstrated that new levels of improvement had been achieved. The Federal Quality Institute had so many substantive and worthy applicants that it decided to formally recognize the eight finalists as well as the two Quality Improvement Prototype winners.

In 1991, also, the Federal Quality Institute used the structured Quality Improvement Prototype Award process to evaluate Presidential Award applicants. Although it was difficult to orchestrate the evaluation of its two large applicants (both had approximately 100,000 employees), the process proved successful. The judges and examiners selected a 1991 winner—the Air Force Logistics Command. And as O'Brien and Elder describe it, the process is still evolving.

A significant change has been made in the eligibility criteria for the 1992 President's Award for Quality. Previously, only high-level organizations (for example, bureaus, major commands) that had at least one sub-component designated as a prototype could apply for the President's Award for Quality. Both of these qualifiers were eliminated for the 1992 Award. Applicants for the 1992 Award must be autonomous, have their own defined mission, and provide products and services to the American public. This allows "subsidiaries" of large organizations to apply for the award, just as may be done for the Baldrige Award.[1]

Presidential Award for Quality

According to 1992 application criteria, the annual Presidential Award for Quality, administered by the Federal Quality Institute, was created with the following purposes in mind.

- To recognize federal government organizations that have implemented quality management in an exemplary manner, resulting in high-quality products and services and the effective use of taxpayer dollars

- To help promote quality management awareness and implementation throughout the federal government

To apply for the Presidential Quality Award, an applicant organization must

- Be a part of the federal government, staffed by federal employees.

- Have no fewer than 500 full-time employees.

- Be autonomous, with its own defined mission.

- Provide products or services to the American public (with the exception of Department of Defense organizations, whose primary customers are frequently other military organizations). An administrative or support organization is not eligible.

Each cabinet department and executive agency may submit a maximum number of applications for the Presidential Quality Award according to its size.

- Up to 50,000 employees—two applications.

- Up to 95,000 employees—three applications.

- Over 95,000 employees—four applications.

- Department of Defense may submit a maximum of three applications for *each* service (Army, Navy, and Air Force), and a *total* of three additional applications for the other Defense agencies.

These limits are set to encourage agencies to conduct internal reviews and select the best nominations. The award process should not be used as a substitute for agency organizational assessments.

Winners of the Presidential Award, including organizational subcomponents, may not reapply for four subsequent years. For example, the winner of the 1989 Presidential Quality Award—the Naval Air Systems Command (NAVAIR)—cannot reapply until 1994. NAVAIR's depots and other subcomponents are similarly ineligible. An application that does not satisfy these requirements will not be evaluated.

The timetable for award processing is as follows:

Applications available	May
Notification of intent to apply due	June 24
Applications due	September 25
Application review	October 14–15
Site visits	October 26—December 18
Final judging	January 13–14
Award presented	May

Application

To apply for the Presidential Quality Award, complete a nomination form and prepare the written application. The application must be able to stand on its own. It is particularly important to describe the mission, products, and services of your organization so that individuals unfamiliar with the organization can fully understand its business. Descriptions should assume no prior knowledge of the organization. Responses should be concise and quantitative where possible. Statements should be supported by facts and information. Agencies should designate a centralized coordinator responsible for submitting applications.

To apply, mail or deliver 10 copies of the complete application package (including nomination form) to the following address.

Presidential Award for Quality
Federal Quality Institute
National Building Museum, Room 333
401 F Street, NW
Washington, DC 20001

Evaluation and Recognition

Evaluation Process
A panel of examiners from public- and private-sector organizations will evaluate the applications. Points will be assigned to the written descriptions of each element based on the scoring guidelines. No examiner will review applications from organizations within his or her own agency or from organizations with which he or she has a relationship.

Site Visits
A maximum of five finalists will be selected based on the application scores. Examiners will conduct site visits of the finalists to supplement and validate information contained in the applications. Finalist organizations may be asked to bear site-visit costs for up to three examiners.

Final Selection
A panel of judges, also comprised of public- and private-sector representatives, will select a maximum of two winners from the finalists based on the evaluations of the written applications and the results of the site visits.

Feedback
A feedback package based on the examiners' review and containing comments on strengths and areas for improvement will be prepared for each eligible applicant and sent to the head of the applicant organization.

Award Presentation

Presidential Quality Award winners will receive a custom-designed cut-crystal trophy. The awards will be presented at the National Conference on Federal Quality held annually in Washington, D.C. The Federal Quality Institute will showcase award winners throughout the year.

Winners' Responsibilities

The Presidential Quality Award was created to recognize quality organizations and to promote quality management education throughout the federal government. Accordingly, each award winner will be asked to

- Prepare a case study describing its quality management approach and accomplishments
- Produce a videotape that showcases its quality management efforts
- Participate in the national and regional conferences on Federal quality management
- Host on-site visits for interested groups

Award winners will bear the costs of case-study publication, video production, and travel to the conferences.

Award Criteria

The criteria are the basis for applying for the award and providing feedback to applicants. The criteria define a quality system. They represent the key elements of a quality improvement effort and demonstrate the relative importance and interrelationship of these elements. The criteria embody certain fundamental concepts of quality management.

- Quality is defined by the customer.
- The organization is driven by continuous improvement.
- The focus is on prevention of errors rather than detection.
- Everyone participates in quality improvement.
- Senior management creates quality values and builds the values into the way the organization operates.
- Employees are valued and recognized for their involvement and accomplishments.

The eight elements and their point values are as follows:

- Top management leadership and support (20 points)
- Strategic quality planning (15 points)
- Customer focus (35 points)
- Training (10 points) and recognition (5 points)
- Employee empowerment and teamwork (20 points)
- Measurement and analysis (15 points)
- Quality assurance (30 points)
- Quality and productivity improvement results (50 points)

The point distribution indicates the relative importance of each element in an integrated quality management system. The following passages further delineate the eight elements and call for specific information from the applicant.

Element 1. Top management leadership and support   20 points
This category examines how all levels of senior management create and sustain a clear and visible quality value system along with a supporting management system to guide all activities of the organization.

a. Describe the roles of key executives (head of applicant organization and senior managers) in quality management activities. Include specific examples of sustained, visible, and personal involvement in the development of an effective quality culture. Highlight any unique or innovative leadership approaches used.

b. Summarize the organization's policy on quality and describe how ownership of the policy by senior management was accomplished and how it is reinforced. Include key strategies used to involve all levels of management and supervision in quality.

c. Describe how senior management communicates its quality vision to all levels, functional units, and employees. Include recent actions that demonstrate the importance of quality values to the organization.

d. Describe how management has established a value system and environment in which individual and group actions reflect a continuous improvement attitude. Include actions taken to evaluate the extent to which quality values have been adopted throughout the organization.

e. Show trends in allocations to quality management efforts (for example, funds, staff, time, facilities, equipment) since the beginning of quality management implementation, expressed as a percentage of total budget. Describe plans for future allocations, showing the long-term perspective of the organization.

f. Describe specific steps senior management takes to create close cooperation across functional and divisional lines and in different locations to ensure consistent quality improvement throughout the organization.

g. Describe how managers are actively involved in removing barriers to excellence (for example, deregulating work, encouraging risk taking and innovation, delegating authority, and discouraging shortcut, quick-fix solutions).

h. Describe how senior management seeks and obtains the support, cooperation, and participation of the organization's union (if applicable).

i. Describe how the organization's quality policies and improvement efforts reflect its commitment to public health and safety, environmental protection, and ethical conduct.

Element 2. Strategic quality planning   15 points

This category examines the organization's quality planning process, quality plans, and how all key quality requirements are integrated into overall planning.

a. Indicate whether operational (one-to-two year) goals and strategic (three to five year) goals and objectives for quality improvement exist across the organization. Explain how they relate to the organization's mission and to the vision and values described in element 1. Give examples of the most important goals.

b. Give specific plans for quality improvement relating to the most important goals and objectives described in subelement a.

c. Describe the process used to establish operational and strategic quality improvement goals, and how goals and objectives are integrated into organizationwide planning and budgeting processes. Describe how these plans are implemented and managed on a routine basis.

d. Describe how employees, customers, and suppliers participate in the planning process.

e. Describe how the planning process is evaluated and improved.

f. Describe the principal types of data, information, and analysis used in planning, such as customer requirements, process capabilities, supplier data, and benchmark data.

Element 3.   Customer focus   **35 points**

This category examines the organization's overall customer service systems, knowledge of internal and external customers, and responsiveness and ability to meet requirements and expectations.

a. Describe how a knowledge of external customer requirements and expectations is obtained, how this information is shared with relevant employees, and how the employees use it.

b. Describe the methods used to identify internal customers, determine their requirements, and share this information with employees. Also describe how the employees use it.

c. Describe internal and external customer-feedback systems, including procedures for handling customer complaints, and how feedback information is used to improve products and services.

d. Describe the organization's service standards derived from internal and external customer requirements and expectations. Indicate how performance relative to these standards is tracked and used to ensure that customer needs are met.

e. Describe the organization's external customer-interface practices (that is, how customer-contact employees are empowered to resolve problems). Describe any special training for customer-contact employees.

    f. Describe how the organization evaluates and improves its process for (1) determining customer requirements and expectations, (2) receiving customer feedback, (3) handling customer complaints, and (4) interfacing with customers.

Element 4. Training   **10 points**
             and recognition   **5 points**

This category examines the organization's efforts to develop the full potential of the work force for quality improvement as well as the organization's efforts to use rewards and incentives to recognize individuals.

    a. Describe the organization's education and training strategy for quality improvement and how this strategy is integrated with the goals and objectives described in element 2. Describe approaches used to provide education and training (for example, just-in-time training and train-the-trainer).

    b. Describe how the education and training strategy described in subelement a is based on a systematic needs analysis.

    c. Describe the types of training provided for all levels of management in support of quality goals. Provide the number of managers who have received this training since the beginning of quality management implementation and the total number who are eligible.

    d. Describe the types of training provided for employees in support of quality goals. Provide the number of employees who have received each type of training since the beginning of quality management implementation and the total number eligible for each.

    e. Describe how the fiscal investment in education and training reflects the policy and priority on quality described in element 1 and quality plans described in element 2.

    f. Describe the organization's indicators of effectiveness of education and training activities and how the indicators are used to improve these activities.

g. Describe how contributions to goals and objectives described in element 2 are recognized and rewarded. Indicate whether and how team and peer recognition are used.

h. Describe methods used to develop a reward and recognition system that has value to the work force. Describe how members of the work force participate in the development of the system.

i. Provide trend data for the past three to six years in employee recognition (that is, percentage of both employees and managers recognized for both individual and team achievements).

Element 5.   Employee empowerment and teamwork   20 points
This category examines the effectiveness and extent of work force involvement in quality management, and the approaches used to enhance employee empowerment.

a. Describe the organizational strategy for involving and empowering the entire work force (including union members) to achieve quality goals and objectives described in element 2. In addition, discuss specific approaches for involving customers and suppliers.

b. Describe the specific approaches used to enhance employee empowerment (authority to act). Describe extent of empowerment in the organization, and give specific examples that illustrate the degree to which authority, rewards, information, and knowledge have moved to lower organizational levels.

c. Describe specific means available for members of the work force (both employees and managers) to become involved in quality management activities, both as individuals and on teams.

d. Provide trend data for the past three to six years related to work force involvement for *each type* of activity described in sub-element c. Express individual involvement as a percentage of the total work force. Provide number of teams operating in each year.

Element 6.   Measurement and analysis   15 points
This category examines the scope, validity, use, and management of data and information that underlie the organization's quality management

system; how the data are used to support improvement; and the process for developing measures.

   a. Describe the process for developing measures. Describe how measures relate to goals and objectives in the strategic plan as described in element 2.

   b. State whether measures relating to goals and objectives in the strategic plan exist; provide the most significant measures.

   c. Describe the organization's base of data and information used to measure progress toward goals and objectives. Indicate the scope of the data it contains (for example, relating to customers, suppliers, internal processes, program, or administrative areas).

   d. Describe the processes and/or technologies the organization uses to ensure that key data are accurate, consistent, valid, timely, and available to those who need them.

   e. Describe how and by whom data and information are analyzed to support quality improvement (for example, to identify problems, determine trends, or evaluate performance of key processes). Give specific examples.

   f. Describe the organization's approach to selecting areas to benchmark and organizations to benchmark against; the types of data collected; the ways that comparative data are used for improvement; and how the organization evaluates and improves the scope, sources, and uses of benchmark data.

Element 7. Quality assurance   **30 points**
This category examines the systematic approaches used by the organization to design, assess, control, and improve processes and inputs to produce quality products and services. Emphasis is on prevention rather than detection.

   a. Describe how new or improved products and/or services are designed and introduced to meet or exceed customer requirements (as described in element 3) and how processes are designed to produce and/or deliver these products and/or services.

b. Describe the principal means used by the organization to (1) ensure that processes are adequately controlled to meet design plans and customer requirements, (2) identify and solve root causes of specific problems that disrupt processes, (3) continuously improve processes, (4) verify that improvements will produce desired results, and (5) communicate changes to all relevant work units.

c. Describe the principal approaches used to assess quality, quality systems, and quality practices (for example, systems audits, product or service audits). Indicate the frequency of such assessments and how the findings are translated into prevention and improvements.

d. Describe how the quality of materials, components, information, and services furnished by external suppliers is assured, assessed, and improved. Indicate whether quality is considered when selecting suppliers.

**Element 8.   Quality and productivity   50 points
                improvement results**

This category examines the measurable results of the organization's quality improvement efforts. Data tables and graphs summarizing trends and achievement should be utilized as much as possible.

a. List at least five of the most significant indicators of the organization's mission performance as described in element 6; provide trend data for the past three to six years. Explain any adverse trends. Indicate how these data compare to industry standards, where applicable.

b. Provide trend data for the past three to six years indicating the level of external customer satisfaction with the quality of major products and services.

c. Provide trend data for the past three to six years for key organizational measures of quality, timeliness, or productivity (other than those listed in subelement a). In addition, provide trend data for the past three to six years for in-process (for example, rework rate) and end-item (for example, defect-rate) measures. For *each* measure listed, describe actions taken to produce those results.

d. Provide trend data for the past three to six years for performance of major external suppliers.

Scoring Guidelines

The panel of examiners use scoring guidelines to determine the appropriate number of points that should be assigned to each element. Figure 4.2 depicts the theoretical construct of the scoring guidelines. Two dimensions are measured: the *integrity of the approach,* and the *extent*

	Approach	Implementation
100%	• World-class; sound, systematic, effective; QM-based; continuously evaluated, refined, improved • Complete integration • Innovation	• Fully in all areas, functions • Ingrained in organizational culture
80%	• Well-developed, tested; QM-based • Excellent integration across functions	• In most areas, functions • Evident in culture of most groups
60%	• Well-planned, documented; sound, systematic, QM-based; all aspects addressed • Good integration across functions	• In many areas, functions • Evident in culture of many groups
40%	• Beginning of sound, systematic, QM-based effort; not all aspects addressed	• Begun in some areas, functions • Evident in culture of some groups
20%	• Beginning of QM awareness • No integration across functions	• Beginning in some areas, functions • Not part of culture
0%		

Source: Presidential Award for Quality application.

Figure 4.2. Presidential award scoring guidelines.

of the implementation of that approach. For example, the 80-to-100 percent range describes a world-class organization with a sound, systematic, effective, and quality management-based approach that is fully integrated and implemented across the organization. The 40-to-60 percent range describes an organization with a well-planned, sound, and systematic approach that is well integrated and implemented in many parts of the organization.

Based on a thorough review of the application and comparison to the scoring guidelines, the examiners will reach consensus on a specific percentage score for each element. The percentage will be multiplied by the total number of points possible for that element. For example, the examiners decide that Applicant A fits at the 65-percent mark for element 1. They would then multiply 0.65 by 20—the total number of points available for element 1—and arrive at a score of 13 for Applicant A's top management leadership and support. The examiners repeat this procedure for each of the other seven elements. The total score for the applicant organization is the sum of each of the eight element scores.

You can obtain a copy of the latest nomination form for the Presidential Quality Award at the following address.

> Federal Quality Institute
> Presidential Award for Quality
> National Building Museum, Room 333
> 401 F Street, NW
> Washington, DC 20001

Quality Improvement Prototype Award

The Quality Improvement Prototype Award, administered by the Federal Quality Institute, was created for the following reasons.

- To recognize organizations that have successfully adopted quality management principles and thereby improved the quality, timeliness, and efficiency of their services or products

- To use the Quality Improvement Prototypes (QIPs) as models for the rest of government, showing other agencies how a commitment to quality leads to better services and products and more satisfied customers.[2]

Applicant organizations must meet the following eligibility conditions.

- Have no fewer than 100 employees

- Provide services or products to customers outside the organization's agency (except for DoD, whose primary customer is the military)

- Provide mission-related services or products

In addition, each agency may submit one application for an administrative or support organization. The organization must cover an entire function, not just a branch or division of a function. For example, an application could be submitted for an entire finance department, but not for a payroll office that might be part of the department.

Each cabinet department and executive agency may submit a maximum number of applications for the Quality Improvement Prototype Award according to its size.

- Up to 20,000 employees—two applications.

- Up to 50,000 employees—three applications.

- Up to 95,000 employees—four applications.

- Over 95,000 employees—five applications.

- Department of Defense may submit a maximum of five applications for each service (Army, Navy, and Air Force) and a total of four applications for the other Defense agencies.

These limits are set to encourage agencies to conduct internal reviews and select the best nominations. The award process should not be used as a means to conduct organizational assessments.

Quality Improvement Prototype Award winners are ineligible to compete for four succeeding years. For example, winners of the 1988 Quality Improvement Prototype Award were eligible to apply for the 1993 Award.

Each applicant must complete a nomination form and prepare a written report that addresses each item listed under the attached criteria. The report must not exceed 30 pages. Five pages of illustrative attachments (charts, graphs, quality vision statements, and so on) may be added to the 30 pages. Pages in excess of these limits will not be examined.

Include a one- to three page summary that states the mission of the applicant organization and describes the products and/or services it provides, the customer of its products/services, and a brief history of when and why quality management was initiated. This summary is not counted as part of the 30-page limit for the written report. It is particularly important to describe the mission, products, and services so that individuals unfamiliar with the organization can fully understand its business.

The application must be able to stand on its own. Answers should assume no prior knowledge of the organization. Responses should be concise, factual, and quantitative where possible. Responses should also address what was done, why it was done, how it was done, and the outcomes of the actions taken. Care should be taken to fully define acronyms and terminology specific to the business of the applicant organization.

To apply, send five copies of the complete application package to the following address.

> Quality Improvement Prototype Award
> c/o Federal Quality Institute
> P.O. Box 99
> Washington, DC 20044-0099

Agencies should designate a centralized coordinator responsible for submitting applications. The coordinator must ensure that the quota for submissions outlined is observed and that all applicants meet the eligibility requirements. Agency submissions should be sent to the Federal Quality Institute as a package.

Application Criteria

Eight criteria will be used to evaluate applications.

Quality leadership (20 points)

Quality measurement and analysis (15 points)

Quality improvement planning (15 points)

Employee involvement (15 points)

Employee training and recognition (15 points)

Quality assurance (30 points)

Customer focus (40 points)

Results of quality improvement efforts (50 points)

Evaluation Process

Competition is based on a written application describing performance
in relation to the eight criteria listed. A panel of examiners from
public- and private-sector organizations evaluate the written applications relative to the criteria elements. No examiner will review applications from organizations within his or her own agency or from
organizations with which he or she is directly conducting business.
The scoring guidelines will be used by the panel of examiners to
assign points for each criterion. The panel of examiners will then select
a maximum of 10 finalists based on the application scores. Site visits
will be conducted for the finalists to supplement information contained in the applications.

A panel of judges, also composed of public- and private-sector representatives, will select a maximum of six prototypes from the finalists
based on the evaluations of the written applications and results of the
site visits. A feedback package containing the examiners' and judges'
comments on strengths and areas for improvement will be prepared for
all applicants and sent to the head of the applicant organization.

Recognition

Both finalists and Quality Improvement Prototype Award-winning
organizations will receive plaques from the director of the Office of
Personnel Management at the National Quality Conference held annually in Washington, D.C. Finalists will be recognized for their quality
efforts, and Quality Improvement Prototype winners will receive further
distinction in recognition of their achievements. The Federal Quality
Institute will showcase the finalists and Quality Improvement Prototype
winners throughout the year.

Work Products

Each finalist organization will be asked to

- Write a paper highlighting selected elements of its quality management effort
- Make presentations at regional quality conferences
- Host on-site visits for other interested organizations

Each prototype organization will be asked to

- Write a case study describing its quality management processes and achievements
- Host two workshops, one in Washington and one in the field, to share experiences with other agencies concerning improvement techniques and implementation approaches
- Participate in the National Quality Conference
- Participate in the production of a videotape
- Host on-site visits for other interested organizations

Costs

Finalists will bear the cost of travel to the site for one person from the panel of examiners and the cost of travel to the conferences. Prototypes will bear those same costs as well as costs of publishing the case study, producing the video, and traveling to the conferences and workshops. Estimated pro-rata costs for each Quality Improvement Prototype winner is approximately $15,000.

Schedule

Applications due	Aug. 30
Application review, site visits	Sept. 18–Nov. 22
Final judging	Dec. 9–13
Finalists, prototypes announced	Dec. 20
Finalists, prototypes meeting	Jan. 13–17

Award Criteria

The award criteria for the Quality Improvement Prototype Award are similar to those for the Presidential Quality Award. Refer to Quality Improvement Prototype Award application for additional information.

You can obtain a copy of the latest nomination form for the Quality Improvement Prototype Award by writing to the following:

> Federal Quality Institute
> Quality Improvement Prototype Award
> National Building Museum, Room 333
> 401 F Street, NW
> Washington, DC 20001

NASA's Quality and Excellence Award

The George M. Low Trophy is awarded to current NASA contractors, subcontractors, and suppliers in the aerospace industry who have demonstrated sustained excellence and outstanding achievements in quality and productivity for three or more years. The objectives of this award are to

- Increase public awareness of the importance of quality and productivity to the nation's aerospace program and industry in general

- Encourage domestic business to continue efforts to enhance quality, increase productivity, and thereby strengthen competitiveness

- Provide the means for sharing the successful methods and techniques used by the applicants with other American enterprises

The award may be given to as many applicants as demonstrate the level of excellence required over the period of time specified.

The award program is managed by the NASA Quality and Productivity Improvement Programs Division. The NASA Quality and Excellence Award is being revised to reflect the Baldrige National Quality Award criteria.

The award has an application for both large and small businesses. The purpose of having separate criteria for small business is to acknowledge the difference in documentation and availability of resources between large and small business. However, the best organizations, regardless of size, will already have processes that address all the major criteria. The degree of complexity and sophistication of these processes will vary with the size and requirements of the organization.

Prospective and active participants are encouraged to contact NASA at the following address and phone number for more information or for a copy of the current application guidelines.

Dr. Laurie Broedling
Office of Continued Improvement
NASA Headquarters
Washington, DC 20546
202-358-2100

The George M. Low Award evaluation criteria are summarized in the following sections.

1.0 Performance Achievements

1.1 Customer satisfaction. Emphasis in this element is on measurable and verifiable satisfaction of NASA and/or prime contractor requirements for overall organizational performance.

1.2 Quality. Emphasis in this element is on qualitative, quantitative, and substantiated accomplishments in both the design and delivery of quality products and services with an emphasis on continual improvement.

1.3 Productivity. The focus in this section is on demonstrated, quantifiable increases in output per unit of invested resource.

2.0 Process Achievements

2.1 Commitment and communication. The emphasis in this section is on demonstrated leadership in establishing a quality culture. The process changes necessary to empower employees at all levels and eliminate organizational barriers to continuous improvement must be documented.

2.2 Human resources activities. The focus here is on the quantitative evaluation of the programs and activities that are necessary to recognize the value of people to an organization.

State Quality Awards

The National Governors' Association, in its report entitled "Promoting Quality Business," notes that a number of states have established local-level awards that can be instrumental in promoting quality within the state government as well as the private sector. The state quality awards recognize organizations that meet a very discriminating definition of quality.

To help states develop their award approach, the State Quality Award Network (SQAN) was organized in 1992. "SQAN provides a network and a forum for state and community quality award administrators to communicate with each other and to share information and experiences so they can move their award programs forward," said John Politi, SQAN chairman.

SQAN conducts two meetings annually. One meeting is held in May in conjunction with the American Society for Quality Control's (ASQC's) Annual Quality Congress; the other is held in the fall. About 45 states are currently represented in SQAN. Representatives from the National Governors' Association, the U.S. Commerce Department's National Institute of Standards and Technology, the ASQC, and the Association for Quality and Participation are also members of SQAN.

Organizations competing for the state quality awards can use the process to identify the strengths and weaknesses of their quality programs. In addition, organizations that are in the early stages of adopting quality programs can utilize the award criteria as a framework for developing their own unique quality initiative.

Use of the Baldrige Award Criteria as Model

Since its establishment in 1987, the Malcolm Baldrige National Quality Award has become the accepted "gold standard" of quality practices. In *Management Practices,* GAO reported that increasingly organizations "view the criteria outlined in the Baldrige award application as useful diagnostic tools for evaluating the effectiveness of their management practices."

In turn, the trend is for state quality management strategies to adopt and promote consistency by adopting the Baldrige award criteria. Eight states have fully established Baldrige-based quality award programs, while another 19 states are in the planning stage, as shown in Figure 4.3. In addition, seven states administer U.S. Senate Productivity Awards. Under this program, which was established in 1982, each U.S. senator can present an award in his or her state to promote and recognize productivity improvements. The trend, however, is for states to move away from the U.S. Senate Productivity Awards and adopt the Baldrige award criteria.

Some states adopt all levels of the Baldrige award criteria, while others begin their quality initiatives by starting with the basic top-level criteria. The key to an effective state or local government quality program is to begin with the Baldrige criteria. Creating minor awards that don't conform with those criteria is a disservice to your community in the long term. The full Baldrige criteria prompt the "stretch goals" needed to improve quality in America.

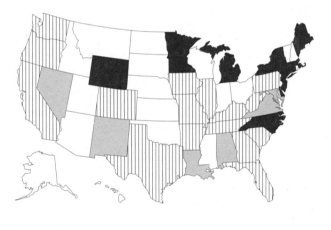

■ Quality award in place   ▨ Senate productivity award in place

▥ Quality award effort underway   ☐ No activity

Source: National Governors' Association, *Promoting Quality Businesses: A State Action Agenda* (Washington, D.C.: National Governors' Association, 1992), p. 10.

Figure 4.3. Status of quality award activity by state.

Beginning in this way, organizations can use the state award process to improve their knowledge of quality principles and practices before applying the Baldrige award criteria to their efforts. States can also draw on the expertise of those trained to be examiners and judges for the Baldrige award and use educational information developed in support of the Baldrige award. Perhaps even more important, the Baldrige award has credibility with the business community, and its use can promote consistency between state and national quality initiatives.

The following sections of this chapter introduce some state quality programs as models for your consideration. The top-level criteria used in state quality award programs such as the Minnesota Council for Quality Award are also summarized.

Minnesota Quality Award

According to *Business Week* (November 30, 1992) Minnesota has one of the top three quality programs offered at the state level. The Minnesota Quality Award is sponsored and administered by the Minnesota Council for Quality. The council's mission is to make the phrase "Produced in Minnesota" mean quality second to none.

The purpose of the award is to

- Encourage all Minnesota organizations to examine their current state of quality and to become more involved in the movement toward continuous quality improvement

- Recognize outstanding quality achievements throughout Minnesota

The award process promotes

- Awareness of quality as an increasingly important element of competitiveness

- Understanding of the requirements for quality excellence

- Sharing of information on successful quality strategies and the benefits derived from implementation of these strategies

The award process is patterned after the top-level requirements of the Malcolm Baldrige National Quality Award. Jim Buckman, president of the

Minnesota Council for Quality, believes that the Minnesota Quality Award approach encourages small- and medium-size organizations to participate and makes the award process less intimidating. Minnesota focuses on the 28 major Baldrige criteria while requiring less documentation than is needed for the federal-level award. This approach provides a logical "stretch goal" for local organizations, paving the way for their eventual participation in the actual Baldrige award.

An organization participates in the award process by submitting a Minnesota Quality Award Application Report. Applications are expected to provide information and supporting data on the organization's quality processes. Information and data submitted must be adequate to demonstrate that the applicant's approaches could be replicated or adapted by other organizations.

The award application is designed to serve not only as a reliable basis for making awards but also to permit a diagnosis of the applicant's overall quality system. All eligible award applicants receive feedback reports prepared by teams of quality professionals. In addition, award recipients are to serve as appropriate models of quality achievement for other Minnesota organizations.

The Minnesota Quality Award recognizes organizations in the state that have attained a high level of quality excellence and, thereby, a competitive advantage in the domestic and world marketplaces. Eligibility for the award is intended to be as open as possible to all Minnesota organizations. Any for-profit business or appropriate subsidiary located in the state of Minnesota may apply for an award. Minor eligibility restrictions and conditions ensure the award's fairness and consistency.

The award categories include the following:

1. Manufacturing
   Companies or subsidiaries (business units, divisions, or like organizations) that produce and sell manufactured products or manufacturing processes and those companies that produce agricultural, mining, or construction products.

2. Service
   Companies or subsidiaries (business units, divisions, or like organizations) that sell services.

3. Small business

   Complete businesses (not business subsidiaries) with fewer than 200 full-time employees. Business activities may include manufacturing and/or service.

In 1994, an additional award category for education will be established. Moreover, the state intends to establish categories for government and other nonprofit organizations at a later date.

Up to two "Highest Achievement" Minnesota Quality Awards may be given each year in each of the three award categories. Fewer than two awards may be given in a category if the high standards of the award are not met. Judges will make the final determination for all awards.

Each application will proceed through a two-stage review process. Stage one involves the application review by individual examiners. Stage two involves the consensus review by a team of examiners. Site visits will be conducted at higher-scoring organizations to verify and clarify the information in the application.

For additional information on the award, write to or call the following:

The Minnesota Quality Award
2850 Metro Drive, Suite 300
Bloomington, MN 55425
Attn: Mr. Jim Buckman, President
612-851-3181

Minnesota Quality Service Award

In 1989, the Minnesota Council for Quality initiated an award and recognition program called the Minnesota Quality Service Award. The purpose was to recognize those "unsung heroes" who have been "caught in the act" of giving superior service.

Hundreds of trained volunteers traveled across the state of Minnesota searching for individuals who give quality service. The recipients received a commemorative lapel pin, a letter of congratulations from the Minnesota Council for Quality, a certificate of commendation from the governor, and an invitation, along with their employer or supervisor, to a luncheon to honor them.

In 1991, more than 100 individuals received "Quality Service" awards at the Governor's Award Luncheon. In brief, the results were outstanding. Recipients, employers, and volunteers all agreed that this was a wonderful way of focusing customers on quality performance and recognizing individual quality service.

For additional information on the Quality Service Award, write to or call the following:

The Minnesota Quality Award
2850 Metro Drive, Suite 300
Bloomington, MN 55425
Attn: Mr. Jim Buckman, President
612-851-3181

New York Governor's Excelsior Award

Announced by Governor Mario Cuomo in 1991, the Governor's Excelsior Award recognizes and promotes a common standard of excellence in three major sectors of the state's economy—business, government, and education. The Governor's Excelsior Award program emphasizes the dynamic interplay of these sectors and their impact on the economy.

Modeled after the Malcolm Baldrige National Quality Award, the Governor's Excelsior Award offers a thorough and objective review process by which an organization can be evaluated on its excellence in quality products, programs, and services, and on its development of a quality work force.

The Governor's Excelsior Award is unique in two ways.

- New York is the first state to offer this high-caliber award not only to private-sector companies but also to public-sector agencies and educational institutions.

- The award application places heavy emphasis on the importance of a quality work force and labor-management cooperation.

Organizations throughout New York can use the Governor's Excelsior Award examination criteria not only to compete for the Award but also to measure themselves against standards of product, program, service, and work force quality that are benchmarked to the highest in the world. In addition, the Governor's Excelsior Award

- Promotes quality awareness and practices in New York State's businesses, educational institutions, and government agencies

- Recognizes quality achievements
- Publicizes quality strategies and programs
- Acknowledges the interrelationship of the public, private, and education sectors

The applicant pool includes manufacturing companies, state government, local government, and public and private educational institutions. Awards are available to both large and small organizations. Up to two awards are given in each of three sectors.

- Private sector, including manufacturing and service companies
- Public sector, including state and local government
- Education sector, including public and private schools, colleges, and universities

"The mission of the Excelsior Award is to raise the overall level of quality in the public, private, and educational sectors throughout the state," said Lt. Gov. Stan Lundine. "If New York is to remain the ninth largest economic power in the world, our companies must be globally competitive and poised for expansion and job creation. Of equal importance, government agencies and our educational institutions must also be 'world-class' in order to provide the best public services and to prepare our people to meet the challenges of the future."

All Excelsior Award applicants receive evaluation reports providing valuable guidance on improvement opportunities. In addition, the award has been designed to serve as a self-assessment mechanism for organizations committed to continuous quality improvement. The award examination process serves as a comprehensive road map for diagnosis and action. Excelsior Award recipients are quality role models, and are expected to assist other organizations through communication and educational activities. Privately or publicly owned manufacturing and service businesses, state or local government entities, and educational institutions located in the state of New York are eligible to apply for the Excelsior Award (see Table 4.1).

Subsidiaries of eligible organizations may apply if they primarily serve either the public or businesses outside the parent organization, and if they meet certain size and business activity-level requirements.

Table 4.1. New York State Excelsior Award categories.

Sector	Size (number of employees)		Number of awards
	Small	Large	
Private	1–100	101+	2
Public	1–500	501+	2
Education	1–500	501+	2

Applicants are required to obtain a determination of eligibility for the year in which an application is to be made.

Each of the three sectors will have specific application requirements. However, the award examination will be based upon the following common criteria, designed to set a quality-excellence standard for organizations seeking the highest levels of overall performance.

- **Leadership.** The senior executives' success in creating and sustaining a quality culture

- **Information and analysis.** The effectiveness of the organization's collection and analysis of information for quality improvement and planning

- **Strategic quality planning.** The effectiveness with which quality requirements are integrated into the organization's business plans

- **Human resource excellence.** The success of the organization's efforts to realize the full potential of the work force

- **Quality assurance.** The effectiveness of the organization's systems for assuring quality control of all operations

- **Quality results.** The organization's results in quality achievement and quality improvement

- **Customer/client satisfaction.** The effectiveness of the organization's systems to determine customer/client requirements and demonstrated success in meeting them

This application provides information on eligibility, examination criteria, review processes, timetables, and fees. As a set of standards, it provides a self-assessment tool for evaluating present and future operations. All award applications are reviewed by highly qualified examiners and judges who represent all three sectors and all areas of New York State. All applications remain anonymous throughout the award process. Only names of winners are announced.

For additional information concerning the award, write to or call the following:

> The Governor's Excelsior Award
> New York State Department of Labor
> Averill Harriman State Office Campus
> Building 12, Room 540A
> Albany, NY 12240
> 518-457-6743

or

> The Governor's Excelsior Award
> New York State Department of Economic Development
> Industrial Effectiveness Program
> One Commerce Plaza
> Albany, NY 12245
> 518-474-1131

The North Carolina Quality Leadership Award

Donna Rosefield, award administrator for the North Carolina Quality Leadership Award, noted that the North Carolina Quality Leadership Foundation has adopted the Malcolm Baldrige Award categories as the criteria for organizations to use in assessing themselves and defining an agenda for education and training. The criteria are used for award examination and are also the basis for internal organizational quality benchmarking and supplier assistance. The quality leadership criteria emphasize the following:

- Approach

    —Prevention-based systems, processes

—Continuous process improvement

—Benchmarks: internal, competitor, industry, world-class

- Deployment

—Integration of functions, including business support

—Customer-supplier relations—internal, external

- Results

—Elimination of waste, mistakes, defects

—Utilization and development of human resources

—Documentation of facts and trends

—Relation of process time and cost

In 1989, the governor's science advisor and the secretary of economic and community development hosted a meeting of representatives from North Carolina industry, government, and education. Following that meeting, task teams were formed with 51 volunteers to define the mission and to plan an organization and procedures to facilitate understanding and application of quality principles in North Carolina. In October of 1989, the planning teams met jointly at the North Carolina Quality Conference and decided to move forward with the formation of an educational foundation and to define a Quality Leadership Award for North Carolina. These goals were formally announced at the conference banquet. In early 1990, an advisory panel of state leaders met at the governor's mansion to review plans and progress.

In April of 1990, the North Carolina Quality Leadership Foundation was incorporated with the following mission.

- Encourage the pursuit of excellence and quality in the private and public sectors of the North Carolina economy.

- Promote quality awareness throughout North Carolina.

- Promote cooperative efforts between governmental, educational, and private organizations to expand training opportunities in manufacturing, service, and public sectors.

- Recognize quality achievements in manufacturing, service, and public sectors through an annual quality leadership award.

- Publicize successful quality strategies and initiatives of private and public organizations in North Carolina.

- Support and promote research programs or other activities that will encourage and enhance quality achievement in North Carolina.

- Promote training and education programs in the community colleges, public and private colleges and universities, and industry to enhance management and work force.

The incorporators were Dr. W. A. Smith, Jr., of North Carolina State University; Dr. Leigh H. Hammond of the North Carolina Community College System; and Dr. Earl R. MacCormac of the governor's office. The foundation provides support for educational, research, technology transfer, recognition, promotion, training, and evaluation activities.

The North Carolina Quality Leadership Awards Council was established in June of 1990 by Governor's Executive Order Number 119. The purposes of the council are to

- Enhance education and training of management and work force, both current and future

- Improve competitiveness of North Carolina business and industry, especially supplier relationships

- Encourage exchange of information toward quality improvement, especially through regional councils and industry associations

- Promote application of total quality management in North Carolina organizations

The council is responsible for approving and announcing award and honor roll recipients; adopting guidelines to examine applicants; approving appointments of judges and examiners; formulating changes in form or coverage of awards; and reviewing education, training, technology transfer, and research initiatives proposed by the North Carolina Quality Leadership Foundation.

The foundation provides the secretariat for the council, as well as operational support, including administration and training of the board of examiners. The North Carolina Department of Economic and Community Development, the University of North Carolina System, and the North Carolina Community College System may provide additional staff and administrative support on a voluntary basis.

Organizations are encourage to become involved in North Carolina Quality Leadership Foundation activities in the following ways.

- Entering the pursuit of excellence
  - —Self-assessment and benchmarking to identify strengths and opportunities for improvement
  - —Education and training enhancement
  - —Systems and operations improvement
  - —Customer-supplier partnerships
  - —Performance measurement
  - —Results documentation
- Targeting award candidacy
- Nominating examiners
- Encouraging suppliers and small businesses to participate
- Increasing educational, research, and knowledge transfer activities
  - —Management and work force development
  - —Regional networking, including industry associations and supplier relations
  - —Public-sector exchanges
  - —North Carolina Quality Conference and workshops
  - —Awareness briefings and seminars
  - —Knowledge-based course offerings
  - —Public service as quality ambassadors
  - —Financial support for educational and award evaluation activities

The basic educational functions of the foundation are as follows:

- Awareness
  - —Recognizing needs

—Learning what others are doing

—Adopting an external view

—Focusing on the customer

- Knowledge

—Existing principles, tools and techniques, systems and processes, change and organization-development approaches

—New concepts of cross-functional roles, strategic manage- ment, knowledge-based leadership, learning styles and processes

- Skills training

The foundation is not directly involved in developing employ- ees' skills for job entry or advancement, but it is concerned that educational institutions recognize the following skills and build them into their curricula.

—Basic literacy

—Technical, such as statistics

—Social/communication, such as problem solving and teamwork

—Management, such as quality management culture change

In order to measure quality improvement, an organization must establish its current baseline of performance. Self-assessment using qual- ity leadership criteria is a primary means of determining current status. The study is initiated by training key employees on the criteria and self- assessment procedures. Cross-functional teams must be formed, and a schedule must be set for the study. An outside facilitator may speed this process by sharing experience and providing objective progress reviews. Management and the selected team members should visit successful firms, participate in seminars and workshops, and exchange information in forums and focus groups.

To conduct the self-assessment, the team must collect and analyze data, write an assessment report based on quality leadership criteria, and identify strengths or opportunities for improvement. Scoring may be done by managers or by an objective outside source trained in the examination process, but this is not a requirement. All functions and employees should discuss the results.

The self-assessment is not an audit. An audit normally extends the concept—to report gaps in performance compared with standards, to prescribe corrective action, and to recommend responsibilities for follow-up assignments.

Key performance factors need to be identified, and a baseline established on current levels. Benchmarks of performance in external organizations are then used to identify targets for improvement. The assessment is based on objective facts and data, not anecdotes or pre-conceived ideas about accomplishment.

Organizations that successfully pursue excellence exhibit many of the following strengths.

- Management commitment and a public service role
- Aggressive quality goals in business plans
- Self-assessment conducted by cross-functional teams
- Benchmarks and standards used for outward focus
- Quantitative orientation for key measures
- Management and work force training and networking
- Proactive customer systems and partnerships
- Major investments in human resources and teams
- Experienced award examiners on staff
- Continuous improvement, prevention-based management system approach
- Approaches applied to all functions and internal/external customer/public interactions
- Results showing sustained trends over three to five years toward high-achievement objectives

Assessment reports should be precise, factual, and comprehensive in addressing quality leadership criteria. Experience in dealing with standards (ISO 9000 series or MIL-Q-9858A), industry acceptance (Bellcomm), and supplier certification or qualification (for example, Ford Q1) programs should be documented.

Gaining the competitive edge to assure survival is the primary goal of organizations that commit to the pursuit of excellence. Such organizations will achieve the following:

- Increased employee involvement and teamwork
- Reduced cost of poor quality
- Reduced development and delivery time
- Improved procurement, production, and support process performance
- Conservation of corporate resources and assets

The public will realize the following economic and social advantages.

- Job retention and/or expansion
- Quality of life enhancement
- Economic and industrial development
- Supplier base enlargement
- Resource conservation
- Tax base strengthening
- Public service improvement
- Work force preparedness
- Educational institutions' focus on excellence
- Government agencies performance improvement
- Reputation of state for economic and social well-being

Moreover, individuals gain the following personal and employment advantages.

- Job security
- Enhanced quality of work life
- Increased motivation and job satisfaction
- Skills that reflect the changing job market including
  —Cross-training for flexible assignment
  —Statistics for process control and improvement

—Problem solving

—Self-managed teams

—Coaching for participative management

• Consumer expectation

The North Carolina Quality Leadership Award has six award categories.

1. Large manufacturing

2. Large service

3. Medium manufacturing

4. Medium service

5. Small manufacturing

6. Small service

In addition, the North Carolina Quality Leadership Foundation annually announces an honor roll. The honor roll recognizes applicant firms that have demonstrated continuous quality improvement. They must have adopted prevention-based management approaches and quality systems, with a prognosis of greater deployment and/or sustained positive trends for key performance measures. Site visits are required for honor roll qualification. Public identification of honor roll designation will be at the discretion of the applicant.

The following list compares the criteria for the North Carolina Quality Leadership Award with the criteria for the Malcolm Baldrige National Quality Award.

The North Carolina Quality Leadership Award *does*

• Recognize the importance of education to management, and work force preparedness and human resources to the improvement process

• Stress the value of preparation, feedback, and involvement in the pursuit of excellence rather than the quest for a trophy

• Emphasize self-assessment and benchmarking, using Baldrige criteria

- Include an honor roll to recognize continuous quality improvement

- Define small organizations in terms of employees, assets, and sales

- Identify separate small-firm award categories for service and manufacturing to encourage subsidiaries, suppliers, and service firms to apply

- Simplify preparation by requiring a single quality system

- Encourage honor roll recipients to apply annually

The North Carolina Quality Leadership Award does *not*

- Limit the proportion of goods and services provided by an applicant-subsidiary to its parent firm

- Restrict the number of subsidiaries of an organization that may apply, including multiple or chain operations

- Require the majority of business activity, employment, or assets to be within North Carolina

- Allow complex applications that require supplemental sections

- Declare units related to a winner ineligible for five years

Texas Quality Award

The Texas Quality Award recognizes Texas organizations that demonstrate outstanding achievement in interpreting and applying quality improvement concepts. Volunteers from Texas companies, state agencies, and education institutions have donated their time and effort in creating this award.

Awards for the following types of organizations have been developed and were scheduled for implementation in 1993.

- Industrial organizations

- Service organizations

- Governmental agencies and nonprofit organizations

- Educational organizations

The criteria and processes are patterned closely after the Malcolm Baldrige National Quality Award criteria and processes. The criteria are designed to identify organizations that seek the highest levels of overall quality performance. The examination addresses all key requirements for achieving quality excellence as well as the important interrelationships among these key requirements.

This award will be part of a quality management initiative for the state of Texas endorsed by Governor Ann W. Richards. Her goal of providing "legendary customer service" in state government will be linked with quality management goals in the private sector.

The Texas Quality Award is designed to do the following:

- Promote quality awareness and practices in Texas businesses, government/nonprofit, and educational organizations

- Educate by documenting and communicating successful quality strategies and programs

- Foster teamwork among all organizations

- Stimulate the continuous improvement process by supporting innovation and benchmarking, information sharing, and supplier relationships

- Recognize quality achievements of organizations in Texas

These efforts raise the overall level of quality, thus enhancing economic development, job retention and creation, and the standard of living throughout the state.

For additional information, write to or call the following:

Texas Quality Award
c/o American Productivity & Quality Center
(Temporary Administrator)
123 North Post Oak Lane
3rd Floor
Houston, TX 77024-7797
Attn: Julie Lambert
713-681-4020

California Governor's Golden State Quality Award

Peter Brightbill of California's Department of Consumer Affairs is an advocate for the establishment of the state quality awards. California is developing its own unique award—the Governor's Golden State Quality Award—which focuses on "best business practices." The Governor's Golden State Quality Award will promote outstanding business practices by

- Identifying them
- Disseminating information about them
- Recognizing companies that practice them

The award will be presented in five categories.

- Quality in management
- Quality in the marketplace
- Quality in the workplace
- Quality in the community
- The Governor's Golden State "Quality Award"

The goal of the California quality award program is to enhance an organization's productivity by enhancing the quality of its products and services, and to accomplish that by enhancing the quality of the process by which they are conceived, designed, manufactured, distributed, and serviced, with particular attention to customer satisfaction. When speaking of quality, most people who are unfamiliar with quality principles think first of an organization's products or services. Yet the quality of a organization's products usually depends on the quality of the process that has conceived, designed, manufactured, distributed, and serviced them. Improving product and service quality, therefore, usually means improving the quality of the process of design, manufacture, distribution, and service on an organizationwide basis—a task that requires the active participation and cooperation of the organization's entire management and work force.

The Malcolm Baldrige National Quality Award

The Malcolm Baldrige award has become the benchmark for quality self-assessment in America. Many states have adopted the private-sector criteria delineated in the Baldrige award. Some states such as North Carolina and New York have adopted both the top-level and specific-item areas as criteria for their state awards. Others, such as Minnesota, have started their program by focusing only on the seven top-level categories. Minnesota has taken this "Baby Baldrige" approach to encourage broader participation by small- and medium-size organizations. The key is to use the fundamental Baldrige award criteria as standards and gradually add the stretch goal of applying for the Baldrige National Quality Award itself.

Each year, the Baldrige National Quality Award office issues the current application and submittal requirements. A copy of the complete, current Malcolm Baldrige Award criteria can be obtained free of charge from the following:

> Malcolm Baldrige National Quality Award
> National Institute of Standards and Technology
> Route 270 and Quince Orchard Road
> Administration Building, Room A537
> Gaithersburg, MD 20899
> Telephone: 301-975-2036
> Telefax: 301-948-3716

To provide a basic familiarization, we have condensed the top-level Baldrige award criteria here, retaining the Baldrige reference numbers for cross-reference purposes.

1.0 Leadership   (95 points)

The leadership category examines senior executives' personal leadership style and their involvement in creating and sustaining a customer focus and clear, visible quality values. Also examined is the way in which the quality values are integrated into the organization's management system and reflected in its expression of public responsibilities and corporate citizenship.

1.1 Senior executive leadership   (45 points)

Describe the senior executives' leadership, personal involvement, and visibility in developing and maintaining an environment for quality excellence.

1.2 Management for quality   (25 points)
Describe how the organization's customer focus and quality values are integrated into day-to-day leadership, management, and supervision of all organizational units.

1.3 Public responsibility and corporate citizenship (25 points)
Describe how the organization includes its responsibilities to the public in its quality policies and improvement practices. Describe also how the organization leads as a corporate citizen in its key communities.

2.0 Information and analysis   (75 points)
The information and analysis category examines the scope, validity, analysis, management, and use of data and information to drive quality excellence and to improve operational and competitive performance. Also examined is the adequacy of the organization's data, information, and analysis system to support improvement of the organization's customer focus, products, services, and internal operations.

2.1 Scope and management of quality and   (15 points)
performance data and information
Describe the organization's data and information used for planning, day-to-day management, and evaluation of quality and operational performance. Describe also how data and information are managed to ensure reliability, timeliness, and rapid access.

2.2 Competitive comparisons and benchmarking (20 points)
Describe the organization's processes, sources, scope, and uses of competitive comparisons, benchmarking information, and data to support improvement of quality and the organization's overall operational performance.

2.3 Analysis and uses of organization-level data   (40 points)
Describe how data related to quality, customers, and operational performance, together with relevant financial data, are analyzed to support organization-level review, action, and planning.

3.0 Strategic quality planning   (60 points)
The strategic quality planning category examines the organization's planning process and how all key quality requirements are integrated into overall business planning. Also examined are the organization's short- and longer-term plans and how quality and operational performance requirements are deployed to all work units.

**3.1 Strategic quality and organization   (35 points)
      performance planning process**
Describe the organization's strategic planning process for the short term (one to two years) and longer term (three years or more) for customer-satisfaction leadership and overall operational performance improvement. Describe also how this process integrates quality with the organization's operational performance requirements and how plans are deployed.

3.2 Quality and performance plans   (25 points)
Summarize the organization's quality and operational performance goals and plans for the short term (one to two years) and the longer term (three years or more).

4.0 Human resource development and management (150 points)
The human resource development and management category examines how the organization enables the work force to develop its full potential and pursue the organization's quality and operational performance objectives. Also examined are the organization's efforts to build and maintain an environment for quality excellence conducive to full participation and personal and organizational growth.

4.1 Human resource planning and management   (20 points)
Describe how the organization's overall human resource plans and practices are integrated with its overall quality and operational performance goals and plans, and address fully the needs and development of the entire work force.

4.2 Employee involvement   **(40 points)**

Describe the means available for all employees to contribute effectively to meeting the organization's quality and operational performance goals and plans; summarize trends in effectiveness and extent of involvement.

4.3 Employee education and training   **(40 points)**

Describe how the organization determines quality and related education and training needs for all employees. Show how this determination addresses the organization's plans and needs as well as supports employees' growth. Outline how such education and training are evaluated, and summarize key trends demonstrating improvement in both the effectiveness and extent of education and training.

4.4 Employee performance and recognition   **(25 points)**

Describe how the organization's employee performance, recognition, promotion, compensation, reward, and feedback approaches support the attainment of the organization's quality and performance plans and goals.

4.5 Employee well-being and satisfaction   **(25 points)**

Describe how the organization maintains a work environment conducive to the well-being and growth of all employees; summarize trends in key indicators of well-being and satisfaction.

5.0 Management of process quality   **(140 points)**

The management of process quality category examines the systematic processes the organization uses to pursue ever-higher quality and operational performance. Examined are the key elements of process management, including research and development, design, management of process quality for all work units and suppliers, systematic quality improvement, and quality assessment.

5.1 Design and introduction of quality   **(40 points)**
products and services

Describe how new and/or improved products and services are designed and introduced and how processes are designed to meet key product and service quality requirements and operational performance requirements.

5.2 Process management: product and   (35 points)
service production and delivery processes

Describe how the organization's key product and service production and delivery processes are managed to ensure that design requirements are met and that both quality and operational performance are continuously improved.

5.3 Process management: Business processes   (30 points)
and support services

Describe how the organization's key business processes and support services are managed so that current requirements are met and that quality and operational performance are continuously improved.

5.4 Supplier quality   (20 points)

Describe how the organization assures the quality of materials, components, and services furnished by other businesses. Describe also the organization's plans and actions to improve supplier quality.

5.5 Quality assessment   (15 points)

Describe how the organization assesses the quality and performance of its systems, processes, and practices and the quality of its products and services.

6.0 Quality and operational results   (180 points)

The quality and operational results category examines the organization's levels and improvement trends in internal quality, operational performance, and supplier quality. Also examined are current quality and operational performance levels relative to those of competitors.

6.1 Product and service quality results   (70 points)

Summarize trends in quality and current quality levels for key product and service features; compare the organization's current quality levels with those of competitors and/or appropriate benchmarks.

6.2 Organization's operational results   (50 points)
Summarize trends and levels in the organization's overall operational performance, and compare this operational performance with that of competitors and/or appropriate benchmarks.

6.3 Business process and support service results   (25 points)
Summarize trends and current levels in quality and operational performance improvement for business processes and support services; compare results with those of competitors and/or appropriate benchmarks.

6.4 Supplier quality results   (35 points)
Summarize trends in current quality levels of suppliers; compare the organization's suppliers' quality with that of competitors and/or with appropriate benchmarks.

7.0   Customer focus and satisfaction   (300 points)
The customer focus and satisfaction category examines the organization's relationships with customers and its knowledge of customer requirements and of the key quality factors that drive marketplace competitiveness. Also examined are the organization's methods to determine customer satisfaction, current trends and levels of customer satisfaction and retention, and these results relative to competitors.

7.1 Customer expectations: Current and future   (35 points)
Describe how the organization determines near-term and long-term requirements and expectations of customers.

7.2 Customer relationship management   (65 points)
Describe how the organization provides effective management of its relationship with its customers and uses information gained from customers to improve customer relationship management strategies and practices.

7.3 Commitment to customers   (15 points)
Describe the organization's commitments to customers regarding its products/services and how these commitments are evaluated and improved.

7.4 Customer-satisfaction determination   (30 points)
Describe the organization's methods for determining customer satisfaction, customer repurchase intentions, and customer satisfaction relative to competitors; describe how these methods are evaluated and improved.

7.5 Customer-satisfaction results   (85 points)
Summarize trends in the organization's customer satisfaction and trends in key indicators of customer dissatisfaction.

7.6 Customer-satisfaction comparison   (70 points)
Compare the organization's customer-satisfaction results with those of competitors.

The Baldrige system for self-assessment scoring is based upon three evaluation dimensions: (1) approach, (2) deployment, and (3) results. All self-assessment items require organizations to examine information in relation to one or more of these dimensions. Criteria associated with the evaluation dimensions are described here.

Approach

Approach refers to the methods the organization uses to achieve the purposes addressed in the self-assessment items. Criteria used to evaluate approach include one or more of the following:

- Degree to which the approach is prevention based
- Appropriateness to the requirements of the tools, techniques, and methods
- Effectiveness of the use of the tools, techniques, and methods
- Degree to which the approach is systematic, integrated, and consistently applied
- Degree to which the approach embodies effective self-evaluation, feedback, and adaptation cycles to sustain continuous improvement
- Degree to which the approach is based upon quantitative information that is objective and reliable

- Indicators of unique and innovative approaches, including significant and effective new adaptations of tools and techniques used in other applications or types of organizations

Deployment

Deployment refers to the extent to which the approaches are applied to all relevant areas and activities addressed and implied in the self-assessment. Criteria used to evaluate deployment include one or more of the following:

- Appropriate and effective application to all product and service characteristics
- Appropriate and effective application to all transactions and interactions with customers, suppliers of goods and services, and the public
- Appropriate and effective application to all internal processes, activities, facilities, and employees
- Evidence of improvement due to adaptation cycles

Results

Results refer to outcomes and effects in achieving the purposes addressed and implied in the self-assessment. Criteria used to evaluate results include one or more of the following:

- Quality levels demonstrated
- Scope of quality improvement
- Demonstration of sustained improvement
- Significance of improvements to the organization's business
- Organization's ability to show that improvements derive from its quality practices and actions
- Contributions of the outcomes and effects to quality improvement
- Rate of quality improvement
- Comparison with industry leaders

Figure 4.4 sets out the Malcolm Baldrige scoring guideline; it explains how evaluation scores are determined.

Score	Approach/deployment
0%	• Anecdotal information; no system evident in information presented
10% to 30%	• Beginning of a systematic approach to addressing the primary purposes of the item • Significant gaps still exist in deployment that would inhibit progress in achieving the major purposes of the item • Early stages of a transition from reacting to problems to preventing problems
40% to 60%	• A sound, systematic approach responsive to the primary purposes of the item • A fact-based improvement process in place in key areas addressed by the item • No major gaps in deployment, though some areas may be in the early stages of deployment • Approach places more emphasis on problem prevention than on reaction to problems
70% to 90%	• A sound, systematic approach responsive to the overall purposes of the item • A fact-based improvement process is a key management tool; clear evidence of refinement and improved integration as a result of improvement cycles and analysis • Approach is well deployed with no significant gaps, although refinement, deployment, and integration may vary among work units or system activities
100%	• A sound, systematic approach, fully responsive to all the requirements of the item • Approach is fully deployed without weakness or gaps in any areas • Very strong refinement and integration—backed by excellent analysis

Source: Malcolm Baldrige National Quality Award criteria.

Figure 4.4. Malcolm Baldrige scoring guidelines.

Score	Results
0%	• No data reported, or anecdotal data only • Data not responsive to major requirements of the item
10% to 30%	• Early stages of developing trend data • Some improvement trend data or early good performance reported • Data not reported for many to most areas of importance to the item requirements and to the company's key performance-related business factors
40% to 60%	• Improvement or good performance trends reported in key areas of importance to the item requirements and to the company's key performance-related business factors • Some trends and/or current performance can be evaluated against relevant comparisons, benchmarks, or levels • No significant adverse trends, or poor current performance in key areas of importance to the item requirements and to the company's key performance-related business factors
70% to 90%	• Good to excellent improvement trends in most key areas of importance to the item requirements and to the company's key performance-related business factors or sustained good to excellent performance in those areas • Many to most trends and current performance can be evaluated against relevant comparisons, benchmarks, or levels • Current performance is good to excellent in most areas of importance to the item requirements and to the company's key performance-related business factors
100%	• Excellent improvement trends in most to all key areas of importance to the item requirements and to the company's key performance-related business factors or sustained excellent performance in those areas • Most to all trends and current performance can be evaluated against relevant comparisons, benchmarks, or levels • Current performance is excellent in most areas of importance to the item requirements and to the company's key performance-related business factors • Strong evidence of industry and benchmark leadership demonstrated

Figure 4.4. (continued)

Notes

1. Dick O'Brien and Victoria Elder, "The Federal Quality Awards Program," International Symposium on Productivity and Quality Improvement with a Focus on Government, 1–6.

2. U.S. Office of Personnel Management, "1992 Quality Improvement Prototype Award Application" (Memorandum dated May 1991).

5 Quality Leaders in Government

The desire and necessity to improve government sys-
tems and the identification of total quality manage-
ment as a means of improvement are only two parts to
a three-part problem. The third part is committed
and determined leadership to make those improve-
ments comprehensive and continuous.

President Bill Clinton

This chapter provides success-story highlights from federal and state award-winning organizations that have demonstrated their ability to improve their customer satisfaction, performance, and productivity by effectively adopting quality management principles in their organizations. First we'll look at the federal quality leaders, then at the state and local quality leaders.

Federal Quality Leaders

This section describes some recent winners of the Presidential Award for Quality and the Quality Improvement Prototype Award, as well as some recognized leaders in quality management in the federal government. Refer to chapter 4 for award-submittal criteria.

Ogden Internal Revenue Service Center

The Ogden Internal Revenue Service Center operation is the winner of the 1992 Presidential Award for Quality. During the spring of 1985, newspapers around the country contained headlines such as these: "IRS Mistake-Rate High," "IRS Admits Refund Error," "Tax Filers Get Unhappy Surprise." Clearly the Internal Revenue Service (IRS) was caught in the middle of a customer satisfaction crisis.

The forerunner of this crisis was the government's drive for production at any cost. Like the rest of the nation, the IRS's problems in 1985 were symptomatic of our misplaced focus on production at the expense of quality. This focus on quantity led us to the quick-fix approach, addressing symptoms rather than root causes. Problems were not really solved, and thus, they often resurfaced. Major delays in tax processing resulted!

In turn, these delays triggered other problems throughout the IRS: volumes of erroneous notices, unlocatable tax returns, and a tremendous increase in taxpayer correspondence. Unfavorable public opinion regarding the agency's competence was painfully visible and could not be ignored. The IRS was in the middle of a crisis that was beginning to erode the very foundation of its operations.

As a processing center for the IRS, Ogden Service Center (OSC) was also caught up in the crisis. However, initiatives put in place in 1984 to restore quality to the operation helped the Center through this crisis. The Ogden IRS was able to regain control more quickly than would have been possible otherwise.

After the 1985 crisis, Ogden recognized that the quality initiatives already in place were just the beginning phase of quality improvement. In order to avoid another crisis, Ogden needed to refocus its priorities and channel the energy of its people in a new direction—toward a total quality organization (TQO). Over time, they identified a series of interlocking, driving principles designed to generate continuous improvement. As each principle was implemented, the momentum toward quality increased. These principles included the following:

- Structure
- Commitment
- Education
- Customer focus
- Involvement
- Recognition

Implementing these principles in an organization as large and complex as an IRS service center is a monumental task; however, it is a task that is vital in order to meet its customers' needs. To give you an appreciation of the challenge this task presented, the environment and the diversity of its day-to-day operations are summarized below.

The mission of the IRS is to "collect the proper amount of tax revenue at the least cost; serve the public by continually improving the quality of our products and services; and perform in a manner warranting the highest degree of public confidence in our integrity, efficiency, and fairness."

This mission is accomplished by the national IRS office, regional offices, district offices, and service centers working together. Service centers are the data-processing arm of IRS, and they work under the guidance of the national office.

Ogden is the largest of the 10 service centers in terms of its geographic area, serving taxpayers from 14 states. Located in Utah, the operation includes a main building and nine other locations comprising 21 acres of enclosed building space.

In 1991, Ogden processed 26 million tax returns, collected over $100 billion, and processed refunds for taxpayers totalling $9 billion. At its peak, Ogden employed 6300 employees—3400 permanent and 2900 who work as processing needs increase.

The Center is organized along two lines; one line directly processes tax returns (pipeline), and the other attends to other functions (nonpipeline).

The Ogden IRS process pipeline starts when operators place incoming mail into a computerized machine that sorts envelopes by type of return. Clerks extract mail from envelopes and perform a finer sort. All returns are assigned a unique serial number so they can be easily located. Payments are deposited into the Federal Reserve Bank within 24 hours.

Tax examiners review returns to ensure the necessary schedules and attachments are included, and then they code returns for computer entry. Data transcribers enter the information from the documents into the computer. Built-in computer checks identify math and other types of errors. Tax examiners correct returns rejected by the computer through the on-line error-resolution system. If additional information is needed at any point in the process, tax examiners contact the taxpayer. Finally, they transmit correct return information to the Martinsburg Computing Center in West Virginia, where permanent records are established. Taxpayers then receive refunds or notices of additional taxes due.

The following profile illustrates the intensity of Ogden's commitment to quality. Specific examples of initiatives, activities, and accomplishments are provided as well as the lessons they have learned.

Ogden's cultural and organizational changes began in 1984, when top-level managers attended a five-day training called Toward Excellence. This training was then given to 65 mid-level managers, who, in turn, shared these principles with the rest of their employees. Toward Excellence is based on Tom Peters and Zenger-Miller's philosophy, which emphasizes

- Innovating action
- Getting back in touch with employees
- Existing for the customer
- Fostering individual commitment

This program triggered a communication breakthrough that led to the development of an organizational structure within Ogden Service Center that would steer all quality improvement endeavors. This structure would provide a firm base for the Center's interlocking principles and include quality councils, a value system, quality improvement teams, task teams, and measurements of progress.

In January 1986, their senior executives established the Service Center Quality Council to lay the foundation for quality improvement. The council met weekly, and it only discussed quality issues. The local president of the National Treasury Employees Union (NTEU), Chapter 67, served on the coordinating committee for the council. The council developed the following goals.

- Provide quality awareness and training
- Formulate quality policies and goals
- Establish and support project systems
- Establish measures for progress on quality improvement

Knowing that a value system was essential, the council established the following core values.

- Respect for the individual
- Service to the customer
- Quality as a way of life

The next step in developing the value system was to define quality. The council soon learned through roundtable discussions that quality had different meanings to different people, even among its own members. To eliminate confusion, the council established the Ogden Service Center's definition of quality as meeting valid requirements and performing up to expectations.

Its core values, definition of quality, organizational goal, and mission statement combine to form the value system of their total quality organization (TQO) (see Figure 5.1). One method communicates its

---

A total quality organization

- Trusts and empowers employees to deliver a quality product
- Has a common vision shared by everyone
- Upholds the highest standards of ethics and integrity
- Advocates, recognizes, and rewards risk taking and creative thinking
- Focuses on long-term improvement
- Improves work processes to prevent mistakes from occurring
- Bases decisions on customer-focused quality standards
- Inspires all employees to take ownership of the quality process
- Openly discusses problems and sees defects as opportunities for improvements

---

Figure 5.1.   Ogden IRS quality-focused mission statement.

value system throughout the organization by displaying framed copies of the value on managers' desks. The Center also exhibits its organizational goal, "Excellence in Everything We Do," in main entrances to all buildings, in conferences rooms, and so on.

An important turning point in the development of Ogden Service Center's quality improvement process came in 1986, during a period of self-assessment. Mid-level managers throughout the Center felt left out of the quality improvement effort and voiced their concerns to council members. (In essence—"All this talk about quality improvement, but they haven't asked for my input.")

In response, their director decided that mid-level manager teams, or subcouncils, were needed to bring these mid-level managers into the quality improvement process and gain their support and commitment. Thus, in August 1986, the council established subcouncils for each division. Subcouncils included division chiefs, branch chiefs, and in some divisions, section chiefs. After the signing of a joint agreement, two NTEU representatives were added to each subcouncil. The subcouncils were named after each of the six divisions; the Tax Accounts Division Joint Quality Subcouncil, for example.

A night quality council was formed to enhance the quality initiatives on night shift. The night manager serves as a member of both the joint quality council (JQC) and the night quality council, providing a link between day and night shifts. Other members of the night council include first-line managers, a section chief, and NTEU representatives.

Soon, union officials wanted to form an NTEU quality council. The NTEU quality council supports the joint quality subcouncils by networking and improving communications. Meetings include discussions on quality initiatives and training in group dynamics skills. The NTEU quality council is composed of NTEU representatives from each subcouncil. These representatives are bargaining employees who are members of NTEU.

Another technique used to involve working-level employees is the establishment of grass-roots quality councils. The JQC recommended that such councils be formed under the umbrella of subcouncils. These councils are composed of first-line managers, employees, and union representatives. They meet on a regular basis. Their mission is to promote the quality process among nonmanagerial employees. With the addition of these councils, all levels of the organization have a voice in the quality process.

• Lesson learned:

All people need a voice in the quality process.

Ogden leaders recognized that the structure had to include a process to solve chronic problems. Quality improvement process (QIP) teams were established to solve such problems. These teams are cross functional and composed of both management and employees from areas where chronic problems are identified. Team members volunteer to be part of the quality process. They use a project-by-project approach modeled after Juran's planning methodology. This approach, shown in Figure 5.2, is a very structured eight-step process for team problem solving.

Subcouncils nurture and support QIP teams. As teams are formed, subcouncils prepare charters defining team missions, which become signed contracts between councils and teams. Here is an excerpt from

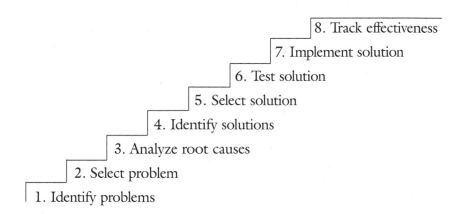

Source: *Introduction to Total Quality Management in the Federal Government,* May 1991, p. 16.

Figure 5.2.   Eight-step problem-solving process.

the charter of the Taxpayer-Caused Notices Teams: "IRS wants to mail quality, correct notices to taxpayer, even when the taxpayers have caused the problem. The team's purpose is to identify the primary causes for taxpayers' errors that result in erroneous notices." Charters also identify the responsibilities of councils and team members. Teams come to councils for direction and to update councils on their progress.

To further support QIP teams, OSC established a quality improvement staff with program analysts. These quality improvement analysts combine the duties of teacher, promoter, facilitator for councils, and consultant for the quality process. When OSC first formed QIP teams, members were trained individually rather than as a group. This inhibited the team-building process. Analysts now train entire teams together "just in time" in the eight-step process and in decision-making techniques. By training together from the beginning, team members become unified.

When teams are formed, members sign contracts with their part-time facilitators. Contracts set boundaries and expectations to define roles. For example, a contract might specify that the facilitator should intervene if the team process is not being followed. Part-time facilitators assist teams in building group dynamics and encourage them to follow the eight-step process. Team members and their facilitator meet regularly as they move through the problem-solving process. Diagnostic analysis or sampling is done outside of meetings. All team members and part-time facilitators serve on teams in addition to performing their regular responsibilities.

Employees from all levels of the organization nominate and submit team projects. At first, some proposed projects were too large and not suited to the process. Thus, the problem of reorganizing and establishing a set of specific criteria for selecting QIP team projects was addressed. The resulting criteria ask the following questions.

- Is the problem chronic or systemic?
- Is it do-able?
- What will be our return on the investment?
- What impact does this problem have on the customer?

> • Lesson learned:
>
> Quality improvement process team projects must be manageable in scope.

By the end of 1991, employees formed 56 teams, completed 41 of the projects, and involved over 500 people. An additional 106 people currently serve on councils and sustain teams. Not only does the organization benefit from improved systems, but team members increase their overall knowledge of service center processing and networking capabilities. One former team member says, "When we have a problem in our area, we now have contacts in other areas to help solve the problem." Team members use their new team-building and analytical skills in their day-to-day responsibilities. Their enthusiasm for the process encourages other employees to become involved.

Their teams have

- Improved customer service
- Realized cost benefits of $3,730,959 through 1991
- Achieved intangible benefits

Commitment from all levels—top management, the union, and front-line workers—accelerates the progress of the quality movement.

From their training, Toward Excellence, supervisors adopted the technique of managing by wandering around the workplace. This practice allows daily interaction between employees and serves as a tool for asking and answering questions.

> • Lesson learned:
>
> Management must listen to employees.

Today, top management continually demonstrates its commitment to quality by teaching quality training classes, employing new management skills, and opening meetings with quality-related comments. As the principles of the total quality organization reach all levels, they create an environment of cooperation. In this atmosphere, the union has become a vital partner in spreading the quality message as well. An excellent example of such a partnership is the teaching of quality leadership classes by union officials in cooperation with management. Additionally, union representatives from OSC councils united with management to teach quality concepts to all employees in a three-hour orientation. The union also shares in teaching QIT training.

The union is always looking for ways to assist employees in achieving quality goals. For example, the local union president chairs the Career Development and Training Action Team. Although only in the planning stages, the core curriculum will include courses in basic skills such as English, math, quality, and the rights and responsibilities of employees. Advanced classes will be designed for specific work areas and include customer service training and management courses. Participation in these after-hours, self-taught courses will earn employees extra points for their evaluations. The program hopes to assist employees in career advancement and develop a work force capable of producing quality products and services.

When other agencies visit Ogden Service Center to learn about its quality initiatives, the union president participates with the director and other management officials. Together, they introduce their quality improvement process and explain their accomplishments. A union official states, "I've been involved in the quality process since the beginning, and I can see it working through an improved work atmosphere, better overall communication, and better rapport between management, union, and employees."

- Lesson learned:
  Union partnership is essential.

Employees are the vital energy of any organization. One of their managers states, "Our efforts for improvements will be directed to our customers' needs through every employee, because every employee has the power to make a difference."

Ogden Service Center's quality process can only succeed if everyone in the organization is informed, involved, and committed. As one employee comments, "Start with quality as part of our new-hire orientation, and it becomes a daily part of processing our work." The Center introduces all new hires to quality concepts and their obligations to their internal and external customers. This is accomplished through a video presentation featuring the director. This introduction instills the quality vision at the very beginning of the employee's career.

The commitment of their employees is demonstrated through their performance and willingness to accomplish any task. For example, the mail area achieves excellent productivity results. Staffed with only 82 employees, this area handles enormous quantities of mail. Productivity in this area has direct impact on the taxpayer and all areas of the organization. Mail sent to the taxpayer must be released on a timely basis; at the same time, the volumes of incoming mail must be sorted and opened.

- Lesson learned:

  Employee commitment is the key to quality.

Education provides the tools employees use to integrate quality in their daily working environment and opens a forum for presenting quality goals. The Center uses many avenues of education to communicate its quality vision, including both formal and informal training and awareness activities. As one employee so aptly put it, "Employees will give quality service and job performance when given adequate instructions, support, materials, and motivation."

The Center's management discovered that when it included quality in its training, the quality vision was effectively communicated to employees. For instance, in the technical skills training classes, the commitment to quality and customer service is reinforced. The following goals are introduced to each new hire and reemphasized in all the training classes.

- Establish a quality climate where quality is first among equals with schedule and cost.
- Emphasize product and service quality by eliminating systemic flaws up front.
- Improve responsiveness to the customer inside and outside Ogden Service Center.
- Focus on improving work systems and processes through the use of project teams.
- Integrate quality standards and measurements.

In short, employees are taught that quality is greater than any one system or process. It becomes a way of thinking, approaching, and accomplishing their work. As one employee said, "I have known these quality definitions since the day I entered the Ogden Service Center work force."

- Lesson learned:

  Introducing quality management creates quality-minded employees.

At Ogden Service Center, employees have reexamined the word *customer.* They recognized that every tax return represents a taxpayer, who is their external customer. To improve customer service, they literally started from the inside out by identifying their internal and external customers' needs.

They defined their internal customers as anyone within the IRS—co-workers in all areas of the Ogden Center, other centers, district and regional offices, and the national office. A top-level manager said, "Before this definition, they didn't recognize in-house people as customers. They did not consider that some actions taken in one area may be detrimental to another down the line."

As a result of this analysis, management realized it needed to embed this new concept of customer service throughout the Center. It began educating employees with a training program called "Close Encounters of the Customer Kind." This training emphasizes who the customers are and what employees' responsibilities are to them. Now employees recognize in-house people as customers and have established open communication lines among all functional areas.

The staff solicits feedback from in-house customers through its outreach programs. For example, the communications and customer service operation in the computer room annually sends a quality questionnaire to all branches in the Center. The questionnaire asks other branches to rate the service they receive from the computer room. After compiling the data, communications and customer service employees perform an outreach program. They meet with all OSC branches one-on-one to discuss any corrective actions required.

- Lessons learned:
  —We are our own customers.
  —Happy employees are better employees.
  —Working as partners has increased quality.

The staff makes quality happen through its day-to-day continuous process improvement accomplishments. As one top executive expressed it, "Our real momentum comes from all persons making hundreds and thousands of small changes that continually raise the overall quality of the entire organization." Moreover, managers have introduced several means for formally acknowledging these efforts: designating quality champion and a quality week, posting quality boards, writing thank-you letters, and instituting instant-recognition and community-recognition programs.

As one specific example, in 1987, Ogden Service Center established a bimonthly recognition ceremony for quality champions. Senior management and union officials attend these recognition ceremonies along with mid-level managers, champions, their managers, and guests. The director, division chiefs, and union officials personally recognize each champion during the ceremony. Opening remarks during the recognition ceremony include a definition of champions. This definition was written by one employee and adopted.

C ustomer oriented
H ard working
A mbitious
M ake sure the job's done right
P roud of their work
I nnovative
O pen to new ideas
N ever shirk assignments
S old on quality

Managers, union representatives, and others can nominate people whose work performance and attitude reflect true quality characteristics. Members of the joint quality subcouncils bring narratives describing branch quality champions to council meetings. From these narratives, members select a division champion. This same procedure takes place at the JQC level. The JQC selects a Service Center Quality Champion from division champions. They have recognized 1026 branch quality champions, 342 division champions, and 87 Service Center champions from 1987 through 1991.

> • Lesson learned:
>
> Champions serve as role models because of the qualities they exhibit.

Ogden Service Center's success with quality principles enables it to face the challenges of change. OSC realizes that the quality process is not an easy one but that it has many rewards. As long as the organization remains focused on its quest for excellence, however, it can provide quality services to its customers.

U.S. Air Force Aeronautical Systems Division

Since the earliest days of aviation, Aeronautical Systems Division (ASD), located at Wright-Patterson Air Force Base in Dayton, Ohio, has led the world in developing air power for combat capability. From the early 1900s, when Orville and Wilbur Wright contracted to deliver the first miliary aircraft, to the stunning performance of the F-117 stealth fighter jet in Operation Desert Storm, ASD has been synonymous with aeronautical advances and aviation technology and has been recognized for its excellence in military research and development.

The largest product division of Air Force Systems Command (AFSC), ASD is responsible for the research, development, and acquisition of aeronautical systems to support the Air Force's operational commands, the U.S. Navy and U.S. Marine Corps, and selected foreign customers. The AFSC's five largest customers are Tactical Air Command, Strategic Air Command, Military Airlift Command, Air Force Special Operations Command, and Air Training Command.

With a work force of almost 14,000 people, and managing approximately one-fifth of the Air Force budget each year, ASD is responsible for 300 essential Air Force, tri-service, and foreign ally development and acquisition programs, totaling over $24 billion annually. If ASD were a private company, it would rank 16th in the annual Fortune 500 business listing.

Millions of people watched Operation Desert Storm on television and saw "smart" bombs that could literally be aimed right down the airshaft of a hardened shelter and stealth fighter planes that flew missions in downtown Baghdad without receiving so much as a scratch. These weapon systems performed in what appeared to be a well-choreographed exercise. But the audience only saw the final result. It did not see the years of research and development that went into designing and building the aircraft, engines, electronic warfare systems, bombs, and missiles. The audience did not see the painstaking hours of research and development, or the years spent in the acquisition process required to get major weapon systems from the drawing board to the operational unit. This is the mission of ASD. A special moment in ASD's journey toward quality management occurred in 1992. The Federal Quality Institute named ASD one of the Presidential Quality Award winners.

The impetus for the division's involvement in a quality improvement process dates from the Air Force's emphasis on improving productivity and reliability of its systems in the early 1980s. Top management commitment was first documented in August 1984 when the ASD Command drafted a quality improvement strategy for ASD describing an eight-step improvement process to be used as the basis for pursuing improvement with contractors. The eight steps were listed as follows:

1. Top management commitment
2. Multifunction teamwork
3. Measurement
4. Failure-cost evaluation
5. Corrective action
6. Awareness
7. Recognition
8. Refinement and expansion

This strategy laid the groundwork for ASD's present-day approach. Today, ASD has 31 total quality (TQ) teams, each representing a cross section of employees from throughout the division, and each operating four basic systems: the education system, which makes all employees aware of the benefits of the TQ process and how to operate it; the search-for-opportunity (SFO) system, which capitalizes on ideas for improving the organization; the corrective action system, which uses corrective action teams (CAT) to solve problems identified by the employees and their steering committee; and a measurement system, which gauges progress.

Critical process teams are chartered by the steering committee to analyze and revise those processes that cause the organization difficulty or are targeted for further improvement. Corrective action teams are often formed to work out tangential problems that are identified by the critical process teams. This structure permits all employees to participate in improving the organization—turning ideas into actions.

Over the years, the ASD leadership planted the seeds of change with the ASD and organizational visions. Leaders nurtured those seeds with their personal involvement, and now they are witnessing the growth of a quality culture. For example, the "FACTS" office was founded purely on the principles of TQ. That is, ASD established an office to focus on meeting the customers' needs by extracting the maximum individual contribution to the team. Accordingly, this encourages risk taking and allows mistakes. In the "FACTS" office, mistakes are acceptable as long as something is learned, and people continue to seek improvements. The key is for people to realize that they are empowered to act on their own and are fully supported by management.

Leadership with vision is essential, but the quest for continuous improvement is perpetuated by teamwork. ASD recognizes this and requires that team-building sessions be conducted at the three critical phases of a program's inception: at program initiation, at the start of source selection, and after contract award. The third phase includes the winning contractor in the team-building session—a concept unheard of several years ago, and a clear indication of ASD's improving customer-supplier partnerships.

Faced with reduced budget authority and a 25 percent reduction in personnel, ASD now recognizes teamwork and empowerment as critical to its continuing success. Every one of ASD's internal organizations has established a formal quality management structure involving executive steering committees, total quality management teams, corrective action teams, and critical process teams. Nearly every one of ASD's 14,000 employees is involved in improving the quality of ASD products and services. But, as essential as these teams are to working out "high pain" issues, ASD has carried the idea of employee involvement in quality improvement beyond the formal quality management structure and strives to make it the way the entire organization does business.

Teams formed with military personnel, civilians, and support contractors work together with no distinctions made between members because of job title or rank. These teams promote participatory management at all levels and serve as conduits through which leaders can encourage personnel to achieve goals.

Teamwork has become a way of life at ASD. Quality-of-life "Proud Look" (self-help) teams have stimulated ASD employees to improve the appearance of their work environment, which is essential to employee morale. Across ASD, personnel have voluntarily stayed after duty hours or come in on weekends to do everything from painting walls to planting flowers, designing and installing recognition lobbies, redecorating conference rooms, and holding an Earth Day to do general cleanup around one of the buildings.

ASD is committed to the continuation of quality management throughout the entire organization. Involvement in teams and process improvement groups has mainstreamed quality fundamentals into the organization's day-to-day operations. All units now provide a higher quality product. Employee-developed initiatives have enabled ASD to turn products around quicker, provide new and better products, improve service response time, and lower costs.

Today, ASD is shifting its emphasis from skills training to skills application. Meanwhile, it continues to emphasize the strengths that propelled it this far—newcomer orientations, newsletters, training, leadership by example, and empowerment—so that people get the job done right.

Following Operation Desert Storm, AFSC organizations started or accelerated 152 action items that represent the short-term payoff of being responsive to the customer. ASD's General Yates said, "When we have a crisis, our people can respond in high gear." Of course, 152 items are too many to mention here, but the following sample represents the can-do attitude of ASD organizations.

- Developed and built a Y duct to improve cooling air to the avionics during ground maintenance; fabricated by the 4950th modification shop at ASD; 15 units were shipped in 40 days after go-ahead.

- Weapon-arming lanyards or cords were damaging the aircraft conformal fuel tanks; over 8000 improved lanyards shipped within 30 days after go-ahead.

- In response to an urgent call from the secretary of the air force for a new weapon that would defeat hardened command and control bunkers, a team was assembled with members from the armament directorate of Wright Laboratory at Eglin AFB, the Tactical Air Warfare Center, the Tactical Air Command, the Air-to-Surface Weapons SPO, the U.S. Army, and several contractors. The team developed a laser-guided bomb (known as the GBU-28) made from old gun barrels, tested the concept, and successfully delivered the weapons on target in less than six weeks of effort from initial design to operational use over Iraq.

U.S. Department of Commerce—Patent and Trademark Office

In 1989, the Department of Commerce Public Services and Administration (PSA) took its first steps toward quality improvement. PSA is one of six primary organizations of the Patent and Trademark Office (PTO), is located in Arlington, Virginia, and is made up of eight offices. It is supported by 750 employees and a budget of $70 million. The mission of the PTO is to administer laws related to patents and trademarks by

- Examining patent and trademark applications, issuing patents, and registering trademarks

- Disseminating patent and trademark information to the public

- Encouraging a domestic and international climate in which intellectual property can flourish

In addition to handling PTO's administrative functions, PSA also carries out significant line programs directly related to the mission of the PTO. PSA is responsible for three major kinds of activities.

- Preexamining national and international patent applications and processing those applications for printing and publication as issued patents

- Providing public services related to patent and trademark copy sales, recording assignments (ownership) of patents and trademarks, certifying records, performing patent and trademark search services, and supplying general PTO information

- Managing typical administrative services related to procurement, mail processing, space, telecommunications, copier management, and other support services

Senior managers assessed PSA's strengths and identified several problems that were facing the organization. At the time these included

- Increased workloads. From 1981 to 1989, the filing of patent applications increased 42 percent and the filing of trademark applications increased 51 percent.

- Emphasis on production over quality.

- Costly rework and numerous customer complaints.

- High turnover rates. In fiscal year 1989, the turnover rate was 24 percent.

- Increasing adverse actions and employee grievances.

- Archaic work processes.

To supplement these known facts, the managers developed and conducted an employee attitude survey to obtain information and perceptions from employees and supervisors about their jobs, work units, and supervisors. They researched several surveys administered in other government agencies and designed their own, based on the best one they reviewed and their own particular concerns. They surveyed all PSA employees and took extreme care to protect the anonymity of those responding.

After the survey was conducted, the results were summarized and analyzed by an expert outside the agency. While the results were generally positive, the summary analysis provided information about the climate of the organization and pointed out areas for improvement. Concerning the job itself, three problem areas surfaced: unchallenging work, lack of information and supplies, and the need for involvement in decisions. While almost all supervisors reported that they sought out their employees' ideas on better ways of doing the job, less than half the employees said their supervisors were actually doing it.

With regard to the work unit, the survey findings called for improved cooperation among employees and work units, more equitable distribution of work among work unit members, and better furniture and equipment. Of special concern was the projected turnover rate. The survey results indicated that 42 percent of the employees who had been in their job for less than four years planned to leave the organization within the next year.

Of particular importance, the survey pointed out a direct relationship between how the employees perceive the quality of the work their unit produces and the pride they have in their work unit. Those employees who felt their work unit produced high-quality services and products were proud of their work unit. Management distributed a summary of the survey results to all PSA employees, as well as to the union officials, and discussed the findings.

Many of PSA's prior efforts to make organizational improvements had resulted in ongoing Patent Trademark Office programs and in the installation of good management practices. However, after evaluating its own organization, PSA management knew it had to change its organizational culture if it wanted to improve. Moreover, this change needed to start with a vision of where management wanted to go. It needed an underlying philosophy that would endure as the core value or focus for all employees' efforts.

Rather than following a particular philosophy or a methodology of a specific quality expert, senior management looked at various approaches and developed what seemed best for the organization. The assistant commissioner—the top management official—led senior managers in a three-day workshop to focus on what made private-sector companies successful; why the Japanese have been so successful in the quality of their products; what was working well based on their own experiences and those of other areas in the federal government; and what was not working well. At that workshop, senior managers articulated the vision statement or overall goal for PSA, identified key principles for success, and launched TEAMWORK (Together—Employees And Managers WORK) to adopt quality management. The workshop culminated several months of discussing the need to change and to create the vision for that change.

Next, assistant Commissioner Theresa Brelsford led a workshop session with all 100 managers and supervisors to describe the existing situation, to identify where the agency was headed, and to introduce a draft of the recently drafted vision. As she told the group, "We can do a hundred times better if we involve every manager and supervisor in PSA as a team to help us plan for PSA's future."

Included in this session was a presentation about the results of the employee attitude survey, given by the outside expert who had completed the analysis. The group openly acknowledged that the organization had problems, and it expressed a real interest in doing something about them. Assistant Commissioner Brelsford challenged the group to change its organizational culture: "If we think we're as good as we can be, we're as good as we're going to be." Senior management encouraged managers and supervisors to provide their comments and ideas for their organizational visions. Everyone actively participated in brainstorming sessions, priority setting, and the development of action plans. Senior management then held similar sessions with the remaining PSA employees to review the existing conditions and seek their ideas. After input from managers, supervisors, and other employees, senior management crafted a final philosophy statement that identifies the goal and key principles of their organization.

The quality vision, their goal, is to "consistently achieve customer satisfaction in carrying out their mission."

TEAMWORK represents the collective abilities, efforts, and commitment toward this vision. The key principles articulated are as follows:

- Commitment to quality
- Respect for individuals
- Involvement of everyone
- Creativity and innovation for continuous improvement

These principles guide the agency's selection of actions as it sets priorities and makes choices.

The goal and key principles for success that the employees and managers developed are not unique, but they are theirs. Employees bought into these goals and principles as they heard convincing reasons to change and as managers fostered their ownership in the process. Every person in the organization had the opportunity to participate in the development of its vision. The success of the Patent and Trademark Office quality improvement activities stems from a combination of special attention to customers and review of processes.

PSA has dramatically changed the ways in which employees receive and respond to customer feedback. Their emphasis is now on a strong, proactive outreach program to seek and collect customer input and feedback. Instead of assuming they know their customers' requirements, they are asking and listening. Moreover, the manner in which employees handle and respond to customer feedback has become more participatory and customer focused. They no longer believe that response to customers is the sole responsibility of management and specialized customer service groups. Everyone, each employee at every level, plays an active part in customer service. Focusing on their customers, both external and internal, is at the forefront of all that they now do.

PSA has used customer feedback to determine causes of problems and implement corrective actions. Here are several examples.

Automated tracking systems for certified copies. A team of employees investigated customer complaints regarding the methods used to track the 150 to 350 requests per week for certified copies and abstracts of title. The paper method consisted of making erratic and inconsistent entries of requests on several note pads. Later, employees were swamped with 70 to 100 phone calls from customers inquiring about the status of their requests. Both employees and customers were frustrated with the resulting, ineffective method for determining whether a request had been received, processed, or completed.

The team determined the root cause of the problem to be the lack of a reliable tracking system. In response, team members developed an automated tracking system for requests that allows employees to tell customers the status of their requests accurately and quickly. The tracking system ensures that the goals for filling requests are met, identifies outstanding requests, saves time, and guarantees the integrity of the request records. Clearly, the new tracking system benefits both customers and the organization. In fact, by solving this process problem, the number of days needed to provide certified copies was reduced from 10 to five, thereby reducing the number of status calls.

Public information telephones. The employees and manager received direct customer feedback from phone calls and from complaint letters on the difficulties of getting through to the public information office. The agency's solution was to double the number of phone lines from five to 10. Customers greatly appreciated the improved access.

Interdepartmental responsiveness. Patent examiners had registered numerous complaints regarding the insufficient responsiveness of the department charged with correcting patent drawings. In response, that department formed itself into a team. Team members brainstormed the problem and came up with new procedures to better respond to requests for files. The employees grouped themselves into subteams, each to be responsible for a particular customer group of patent examiners. Each subteam gave its phone numbers to its customer group to permit direct access. This approach has resulted in a reduction of the number of calls put on hold and the number of nonreturned calls. Customer groups have become more familiar with the team servicing them, and employees feel responsible for their customers. Overall, better communication, understanding, and cooperation between customers and suppliers have resulted. Prior to the change, the director received one to two complaints a week regarding the lack of responsiveness; four months into the implementation of the change, no complaint calls had been received.

Timeliness from customer viewpoint. In several cases, employees have revised their goals and measurement systems to meet customer requirements and improve communications. Prior to customer involvement, each unit measured timeliness within its own unit. For years, the service of providing certified copies of patent and trademark documents was measured from the date the request and all relevant office documentation was received in the branch until the service was rendered. As a result of the customer-focus workshop and the new focus on the customer's perspective, the timeliness measurement was changed to start with the date the request was received in the Patent Trademark Office.

Another example of the new, customer-focused view of timeliness can be seen in the mailing of filing receipts for newly filed patent applications. The historic goal was 22 days. Recognizing the importance to customers of receiving an early filing receipt so they can protect their patents in foreign countries, PSA reduced the goal to 18 days. In turn, it has made many improvements to the processing of newly filed patent applications, and is meeting the new goal this year.

Their quality focus has led employees to look at the *way* they do their work rather than at the outputs of the process. Before they started their quality efforts, they attempted to assure quality by measuring each individual's errors and stressing production volumes. They could see, however, that this was not producing the results they wanted. By concentrating on customer needs, employees now focus on making systemic improvements to the process and preventing errors.

A successful example of this change can be seen in the areas responsible for preexamination processing of patent applications and for recording patent and trademark assignments. The shift in employee focus is from corrective to preventive action and to doing it right the first time. As work is being done, employees and supervisors sample the work, looking for the *types* of errors being made. This method allows employees to catch errors early in the process and reduces the need for later corrections in response to inspection of final products or customer complaints. Even more important, employees analyze errors to determine their root cause and take actions to eliminate them. An important component of this method is the retraining of employees and the provision of direct feedback on errors.

The agency spent a great deal of time reviewing processes. As one supervisor said, "There were many times supervisors and employees complained about the many meetings they attended. But as time passed, doubt about things getting better changed in everyone's mind. They even said, 'Things have changed, haven't they?'"

The TEAMWORK journey has taught many lessons. Although its vision and goal have not changed, the organization has made many adjustments in the spirit of continuous improvement. Employees have also learned about what has worked well. These lessons will continue to guide them.

Don't assume you need a fail-proof way to do it before you begin. There is no magic package to implement quality management. From the beginning, the best ways to proceed were sought. But people didn't always agree on what was best. For example, some people believed firmly in Deming, some in Juran. Some felt team membership should be voluntary; others thought it should be mandatory. Some felt teams should define their own problems; some thought management should. Members spent much time debating best approaches. Here is what they learned: Do what you think is best for your organization, and move ahead once you have established your vision. Take small, organized steps in that direction. Evaluate your process often. A technique they frequently used was to step back, take a critical look at an activity, and ask, "what's gone well and what hasn't?" In the end, they continue to do those things that went well and improve those things that did not go well.

Prepare the way for change. Managers, supervisors, and other employees need to understand the reason for change, the direction in which the organization is going, and the strategy for getting there. Focusing on the need for change is a very important first step. They followed this strategy when they launched TEAMWORK, and it prompted others to buy in. Now they follow this strategy for all changes and initiatives. If the members of the organization acknowledge the need for change, they will more easily support change.

Keep the philosophy/key principles short and simple. The philosophy should be easy for employees to understand and to remember. The early drafts of TEAMWORK's key principles included eight principles, each accompanied by explanatory paragraphs. Senior managers realized that even they could not recall what they had written. Despite the large amount of time they had spent carefully crafting all the language, senior management went back to the drawing board. It consolidated and simplified the philosophy into four simple key principles.

Prepare managers and supervisors before involving employees. Managers and supervisors must understand and be prepared for their leadership roles in fostering a participatory environment for continuous improvement. When they researched the quality management efforts of other organizations, they uncovered a common problem—bypassing middle management and going first to employees. This approach does not work. Management must be prepared to support employee ideas before employees are asked to give them. For this reason, senior management made sure that all managers and supervisors were trained in quality management skills before employees were trained and involved.

Involve the union at the beginning. A cooperative relationship is key to fostering a participatory environment for quality management. Organizations that have bypassed union involvement have encountered problems. In contrast, senior management involved the union early on by getting its support and recommendations for the first employee survey and the TEAMWORK goal and key principles. The union was involved in the launching of TEAMWORK with all employees and in the quality action team (QAT) council from its creation.

Avoid making activities and systems too bureaucratic. The emphasis should be on simplification of processes. The initial process for monitoring team progress was cumbersome, with an inordinate amount of time spent documenting what was done versus *doing*. In response, the QAT council discontinued the requirement for teams to copy and forward agendas and minutes weekly to the team facilitator, QAT coordinator, and director. The council learned that teams had been spending *hours* trying to perfect their minutes to suit the needs of such a diverse audience. The QAT council simplified reporting by providing teams with a record book, and with one-page standardized forms, so teams can chart their progress. As an incentive for keeping good records, teams who do so are eligible to apply for the QAT medallion.

Give teams a clear focus. Teams should perform with a clear understanding of organizational goals and customer needs. They also should work on "bite-size," not "world-peace," issues. PSA began its effort with three pilot teams before it initiated the officewide customer-focus sessions with all employees. Pilot team members did not have the benefit of understanding who their customers were and how their work related to office goals. As a result, some of the problems they chose to work on were too broad and unrelated to improving the work process.

Establish meaningful measurements. "You can't tell how far you've come unless you know where you've been." Before TEAMWORK, while employees had many measurements, not all were meaningful in showing how they were meeting customer requirements. For example, no measures existed on in-process quality—the extent to which work was being done right the first time. Furthermore, several early teams had not established baseline data. Therefore, after implementing their recommendations, they had no means of determining the extent to which the changes had a positive impact. The organization now has a system for measuring its 45 key products and services in terms of customer satisfaction and in-process quality. The team training now emphasizes the importance of and the various methods for collecting and measuring data.

Maintain good communications. Managers, supervisors, and other employees must be kept informed to encourage their participation in quality efforts. Senior management learned that merely giving everyone copies of the goal and key principles does not send a real message. The more effective communication occurs with continuous demonstration and discussion of what the goals and principles mean and how they affect decisions and priorities. For example, the assistant commissioner now holds regular meetings with all managers and supervisors. The management meetings are usually constructed as workshops, where managers and supervisors focus on a particular issue and brainstorm ideas or concerns. The assistant commissioner also holds all-employee meetings, and a monthly newsletter keeps everyone current on TEAM-WORK activities.

Give quick recognition. Recognize employees. Through the employee survey, employees expressed the desire for more nonmonetary awards and recognition. Such rewards do not have to be elaborate. Certificates, recognition in newsletters, graduation ceremonies, and letters of appreciation go a long way in boosting morale.

Don't make quality management "another thing to do." Quality management should be viewed as a better way of doing things. Getting this message across has been a real hurdle in implementing quality management or TEAMWORK. Managers and supervisors evaluated their initial training as outstanding, but they found it difficult to spend the time in training while their work was piling up. In response, more real-life problems are now being used during training so that managers and supervisors can immediately apply what they are learning to their on-the-job problems.

The assistant commissioner is also reinforcing the message that TEAMWORK is not just "another thing to do" but is the way to manage. She does this in two ways: by basing all performance elements for senior managers on their demonstrated commitment to quality management principles and by publicizing successes. As they see the positive impacts of inculcating TEAMWORK principles throughout day-to-day work activities, managers, supervisors, and other employees are gaining confidence that this really is a better way of doing work.

PSA is continuing to change its management philosophy and organizational culture. It is moving from a style of traditional management toward a new style of leadership for quality management. Employee participation and teamwork are the keys to doing the right thing right the first time. The strategic plan includes actions to sustain and expand on a growing momentum. The numbers of employees who could be trained to be on teams has been limited by the number of trainers and the number of training rooms available. Thus, the strategy includes increasing numbers of trainers, training space, and types of training given to employees.

Team-building and problem-solving skills will increase involvement and effectiveness of employees. PSA is moving toward total involvement by having all people who work together in a unit form natural work teams that meet regularly to review their work processes and identify and remove barriers that prevent quality service. Moreover, PSA has expanded its benchmarking efforts, continued assessments through customer and employee surveys, and is exploring ways to realign traditional performance-appraisal systems to support a quality management environment.

When PSA first embarked on this new venture, the participants could not imagine the extent of its benefits (see Figure 5.3). Now that they see the early impact on their organization, they are intensifying their commitment to involve all employees, all customers, and all suppliers in the daily practice of TEAMWORK, their vision of quality management.

- Time required to process patent application filing receipts for external customers reduced from 36 to 18 days. In-process errors were reduced by over 50 percent, and public requests for corrections were reduced by 81 percent.

- Decreased assignment processing time from over 100 days to meet goal of 20 days. Reduced the error rate by 50 percent.

- Improved mail-processing productivity by over 63 percent, realizing savings of about $1 million.

- Improved customer perception of contracting and small purchasing staff's responsiveness to customer needs from 72 percent in FY 89 to 93 percent in FY 91.

- Saved over $1 million by implementing more efficient patent printing processes.

Figure 5.3. Patent and Trademark Office quality results.

U.S. Department of Labor—Wage and Hour Division, San Francisco

The Wage and Hour Division (WHD) was created as an agency within the Department of Labor in 1938, to enforce the Fair Labor Standards Act (FLSA). This law was passed during the Depression to address poor working conditions for many of the nation's wage earners.

The San Francisco Region is one of 10 regions within the Wage and Hour field network. Its Wage and Hour Division exercises autonomous budgetary, enforcement, and administrative responsibilities in the states of California, Nevada, Arizona, and Hawaii, along with the territories of Guam and American Samoa. The San Francisco WHD operates with a staff of 140, including 90 wage and hour investigators. With 19 office sites covering hundreds of thousands of square miles and serving a population base of some 35 million people, and with the full spectrum of employment-protection issues, the staff is never at a loss for requests for assistance.

In the early 1980s the San Francisco Region explored participatory management concepts and experimented with quality circles and special purpose project teams. It trained managers in the principles of quality leadership and encouraged them to find ways of improving effectiveness through employee involvement. Although these approaches produced some significant results, the efforts seemed fragmented. An organized system for innovation and empowerment seemed missing. The Region became convinced that quality management would provide the systematic approach it needed.

Now several years into the quality journey, the WHD quality program has taken shape as a blend of employee empowerment, continuous improvement of processes, and customer focus. In fact, the Wage and Hour Division in San Francisco was one of the 1992 Quality Improvement Prototype Award winners. The evolution of its belief in and commitment to this framework for success is contained in the following principles.

- External and internal customers define quality. It is their challenge to determine customers' expectations and meet or exceed these requirements. This is particularly important in government organizations, which often focus on internal goals at the expense of their customers.

- Employee empowerment is the key ingredient to the success of a quality program. Empowerment is accomplished by getting employees involved in everything through a participatory approach to management. The theory is that the people doing the work are in the best position to provide ideas on both the needs of the customer and the ways to improve delivery systems to accomplish objectives. The act of empowering employees improves morale, motivation, and productivity. The ideas generated by empowered people enhance the effectiveness of organizations.

- Team efforts must be fostered to allow organizations to tap human resources and effectively cope with the complexity of today's issues. By bringing together people with unique perspectives and technical skills, organizations are able to thoroughly evaluate the many options available, assess the consequences, and arrive at more effective decisions.

- The most effective way to enhance the quality of an organization's products and services is to improve its work processes. In asking why events occur rather than asking who caused them to happen, organizations come to realize that the quality of goods and services is dictated by the internal work processes—processes that can be controlled and improved.

The philosophy for implementing quality management within the San Francisco Region has as its foundation the belief that leadership does not flow from job titles or rank but permeates every level of the organization. Thus, quality leaders have involved every employee in managing processes that control the way they conduct business. In turn, each employee is empowered to exercise the leadership necessary to influence these processes in the direction of continuous improvement.

The quality management policy is to create and sustain an organizational culture that delivers quality services, as defined by all customers, through the continual improvement of processes. The critical strategy utilized in translating this policy from an abstract statement to operational reality is the full empowerment of all individuals in every level of the organization to influence and improve the processes they work with.

This policy is communicated and reinforced throughout the organization by "Quality Model," a visual representation of the core elements necessary to the quality journey. The model represents each individual's ownership and stake in the concepts it symbolizes. It also represents the collective direction for all organizational effort and is described through the Wage and Hour mission, its chosen values, its strategic vision for the future, and the areas in which it has chosen to focus improvements. Every component and individual in the region is able to connect his or her job responsibilities to the quality management model.

The quality management improvement process model seeks to reinforce and institutionalize the concept of customer-driven continual improvement of all work processes. A 10-step improvement process provides the structured and uniform vehicle that allows it to take place. It is the systematic design plan from which all improvements flow. By utilizing this structure, SFR ensures that all teams will follow a scientific approach, consider the needs and expectations of customers, and use objective data to make decisions. SFR's analysis of its current processes in the context of customer input, matched with its accurate and relevant measurement systems, are important components of this step-by-step approach to quality enhancement. Its 10-step improvement process is described here.

Step 1—Pinpoint
During this step, teams establish criteria for selecting the area of work and the inherent process that will be the focus of their improvement efforts through subsequent planning and action steps. In targeting the area of improvement, the teams seek to link in with other organizational pinpoints.

Step 2—Process study
During this step, team members develop and share key knowledge of the process selected for improvement—how it originates in terms of suppliers and inputs, how the work actually gets done, what the process produces or what service it provides, and what customers benefit from

the products or services. Since quality can only be defined by the customers of a process, identifying the customers and validating their needs and expectations define quality for the organization and the work process pinpointed for improvement.

Step 3—Measures
During this step, teams identify the critical points in the process where measures should be or are being made to track performance and to identify and quantify changes in the process performance. The teams identify measures that can validate the effectiveness of improvement efforts. They also determine how measures will be made and by whom.

Step 4—Baseline
During this step, teams determine and analyze how the process should work in terms of the measures selected in step 3.

Step 5—Goal
During this step, teams establish goals and targets for improvement in terms of the measures set in preceding steps.

Step 6—Action plan
During this step, teams plan the specific actions, identify the participants, and spell out the timetables for accomplishing the desired improvement.

Step 7—Feedback plan
During this step, teams determine which participants need what information, including the current measures, to stay fully informed about the implementation of changes and its effects.

Step 8—Recognize plan
During this step, teams describe what improvement results should be recognized and how contributions to the effort will be rewarded.

Step 9—Kickoff plan
During this step, teams lay out the process for implementing the action plan, including how they will effectively communicate each step to all participants as a means of obtaining their support for the initiative.

Step 10—Managing continuous improvement
During this step, teams lay out their responsibilities for insuring that plateaus of improvement achieved during the action plan are maintained and expanded within the organization. This step also serves as a springboard back into step 1, insuring the continuum of the improvement efforts.

Employee empowerment, strategic planning, and ongoing customer focus have come to represent the critical ingredients of the San Francisco Region's quality journey. While each of these ingredients has generated individual successes, together they form the path to the region's future.

The Wage and Hour Division, from its quality management effort, learned several lessons.

- Lesson 1: Whatever people's initial reaction to quality management, you can't push them into it. You need to be patient and give quality management a chance to prove itself.

- Lesson 2: Managers are important members of the teams. However, management domination of a team will be counterproductive to employee empowerment and quality efforts.

- Lesson 3: The 10-step process and group techniques should serve only as guides, important tools to reach a quality goal. They aren't blueprints.

- Lesson 4: Quality management is a process for improving the quality of work. Quality management is supposed to help investigators do cases and alleviate the backlog. Employees need to integrate quality management projects into their general program and priorities.

With the introduction, training, and belief in quality management, new relationships have developed among employees in the San Francisco Region. Management has learned the value of relinquishing control, and the empowered staff has responded in significant ways. An environment of mutual trust and respect, one where every work process is subject to constructive challenge, has been promoted. In turn, the public and the taxpayers have benefited. They receive more efficient and professional service than ever before.

Of course, there will always be problems to resolve, but they now have a viable approach to resolving those problems . . . together.

U.S. Department of Veterans Affairs

The Department of Veterans Affairs in Philadelphia also won the 1992 Quality Improvement Prototype Award. As articulated in its vision statement, it aims "to be the finest providers of services in the Department of Veterans Affairs and to be recognized as such; to have a culture which respects both their customers and their staff and which earns the trust of veterans and their families." To achieve the mission—to strive toward its vision—members of the organization must do the right things right the first time.

Senior management at the VA Regional Office and Insurance Center first began investigating the principles of quality management in 1987. Managers tried to learn as much about the topic as they could by reading 'the works of experts such as Deming, Juran, and Tom Peters. Several managers attended quality awareness seminars, and they began to look closely at private and public organizations that were especially noted for the quality of their service.

They soon realized that there was considerable room for improvement, not only in the accuracy and timeliness of the products and services they delivered, but also in the processes they used to develop and deliver them. Managers learned that they had tremendous opportunities to better understand and meet the needs and expectations of their customers—opportunities they were not then taking advantage of.

In September 1988, several senior managers attended a seminar conducted by Juran called "Making Quality Happen." The concepts they learned at this seminar now form the foundation of their quality management process. Their process is centered around Juran's quality trilogy, which has three basic elements: quality planning, quality control, and quality improvement (see chapter 3). They have found that this process fits all levels and functions of their organization.

During *quality planning,* managers determine the needs of customers and then develop the products, processes, and services that will meet those needs. During *quality control,* they evaluate their performance, compare that performance to their goals, and then act on the differences. Their *quality improvement* program involves the systematic process of creating beneficial change.

Managers realized early on that their structured approach to quality could not grow and mature in a vacuum; they needed to create an environment in which their customers came first and in which customers satisfaction was their goal. They needed an organization that would support and foster these concepts, that would provide the resources needed to learn and practice the varied components of the quality process, and that would provide the leadership and direction for the implementation of quality management.

The impetus for creating and sustaining an environment dedicated to quality is provided, first and foremost, by the quality council. The quality council created both a mission statement and a policy statement. The mission statement reads as follows: "The Philadelphia VA Quality Council will direct the station's quality planning, control, and improvement activities. The Council will be responsible for institutionalizing an ongoing, systematic process of continuous improvements in the delivery of the benefits, services, and information that the Philadelphia VA provides to its internal and external customers."

The policy statement reads as follows: "The Quality Council recognizes that most improvements in the quality of service provided by the Philadelphia VA will result from improvements in the administrative processes management has established to deliver benefits and services to the Philadelphia VA's internal and external customers, and by providing employees with the tools they need to do their jobs."

Shortly after its inception, the council established groups throughout the station to help focus everyone's attention on quality and quality improvement, to assist in the development and implementation of a quality plan, and to coordinate and monitor efforts associated with the quality process.

The type of organization the council established was specifically designed to focus on the issue of quality. A critical aspect of this focus is to keep all employees informed of and involved in the quality process. Every one of the employees (or members) has been introduced to the principles and concepts of quality management through a two-hour orientation and awareness program. This program, developed by a committee, addresses such issues and questions like these.

- What is quality?

- Why do we need a quality improvement process?
- Who benefits from having a quality improvement program?
- How do we implement such a program?

Using a script supported by color slides and video clips, a lead team presents the orientation to all division members. A member of the quality council provides introductory remarks, and managers provide specific examples from their own areas of responsibility to support the general concept. The presenters also discuss the office's and division's goals and objectives and invite the division members to be a part of the overall improvement process.

The orientation, however, is only a starting point. The focus on quality is maintained through regularly scheduled staff meetings, supervisors' meetings, and division employee meetings. The employee newsletter, *The Vet Gazette,* regularly features articles on QI teams, the quality planning process, training, and the accomplishments of teams, groups, or individuals.

Special activities are also used to help promote quality improvement. For example, the council sponsored a quality fair and other activities for National Quality Month. All employees were invited to the quality fair to view instructional videos, and a wealth of quality literature and information was provided to all participants. A lunchtime gathering, called a Lunch-N-Learn, offered a presentation on a QI team success story. Moreover, the entire building observes "Quality Day" every year. A day-long program includes a discussion by members of the quality council, called "State of our Quality"; workshops for QI team members; and a panel discussion.

With a structure in place to support and sustain an environment for quality, the council turned its attention to specifics—producing a quality product. Management knew that quality did not mean exhorting employees to do better. It did mean providing them with the training, tools, and techniques for improvement. Moreover, it meant developing, understanding, and employing specific processes, practices, and policies to lead them toward continuous incremental improvement.

The teams use a problem-solving technique called the *QI Story.* This is a systematic, data-driven process that takes a team from identifying a problem and its root causes, through developing and implementing measures for dealing with the problem, to the standardization of those measures throughout the organization. The steps for the QI process are summarized here.

Step 1: Reason for improvement. Identify a theme and the reason for working on it.

Step 2: Current situation. Select a problem and set a target for improvement.

Step 3: Analysis. Identify and verify the root causes of the problem.

Step 4: Countermeasures. Plan and implement countermeasures that will correct the root causes of the problem.

Step 5: Results. Confirm that the problem and its root causes have been decreased and the target for improvement has been met.

Step 6: Standardization. Prevent the problem and its root causes from recurring.

Step 7: Future plans. Plan what to do about any remaining problems and evaluate the team's effectiveness.

The Philadelphia VA now has more than 60 of these employee QI teams. They are working on such diverse issues as the quality of correspondence, file mail procedures, customer surveys, computer program manuals, customer inquiry referrals, programming documentation, and release of information to veteran clients. More than 30 percent of the teams are cross functional and interdivisional in nature.

They do not believe that there is an ideal or precise formula for quality management or its implementation. They do believe, however, that they can learn from numerous sources, including federal agencies, private organizations, and consultants and that each agency needs to choose and develop what it believes best fits its own organization.

The teams could not have dedicated the resources necessary to implement quality management without the commitment from senior management to quality and the quality process. Without that commitment—in word and in deed—there can be no sustained effort.

It is impossible, however, to do everything at once, and all of the elements of quality management cannot be learned and implemented at the same time. Once quality management has been defined and a general approach developed, its implementation must be phased in so that everyone is comfortable with and understands the changes that are taking place.

All employees must be kept informed about the quality process. This begins with the basic orientation, which explains what their own organization means by quality management and how quality management will affect each member of the organization. It continues with formal training sessions, information-sharing group meetings, recognition of successes, news of other teams' accomplishments and frustrations, and so on. This is all part of employees' involvement, participation, and empowerment.

They have learned the value of self-assessment and the PDCA cycle, meaning that they *p*lan what they are to do, they *d*o what they have planned, they *c*heck and evaluate what they did, and they *a*ct on the lessons they have learned. The PDCA cycle is part of their four overall principles of quality.

- Respect for people
- Customer satisfaction
- Management by fact
- Plan-do-check-act (PDCA)

They are proud of their experiences with quality management, and they hope that their customers are pleased with what they have done.

U.S. Department of Agriculture—Forest Service

The Easternal Regional Office of the U.S. Department of Agriculture's Forest Service, located in Milwaukee, Wisconsin, knows that success in quality management does not just happen! Hard work and determination on the part of the Forest Service's entire team have made revolutionary quality improvement and culture change possible.

The Eastern Region provides leadership for the 17 national forests in the 20-state northeastern area. The Eastern Region team now has several years of organizational quality improvement experience and the quality results to show for its efforts. In fact, the Eastern Region may be unique among the Forest Service regions—and even among other federal agencies. Through its own leadership, it has reinvented operations. First, the Eastern Region substantially downsized its own management staff (reducing the total number of management leaders) and then passed the dollar savings on to the national forests in the region, which, in turn, were able to provide improved quality services to their customers—the public. In effect, then, the Eastern Region truly reinvented its operations to the benefit of the public. In hard economic times, this organization found a way to work smarter rather than more bureaucratically.

The Eastern Region's quality journey began when the chief of the Forest Service initiated a national pilot study to evaluate a more open management culture for several Forest Service units. The effort was intended to encourage and implement workers' innovative ideas for reducing the agency's bureaucratic processes. One of the pilot study sites was the Eastern Region's Mark Twain Forest in Missouri. The chief established several guidelines for the study.

- No special treatment for the pilot units

- Personnel ceilings eliminated

- Line-item budgets no longer required

- Dollars saved could be applied to other priorities

- Pilot units given maximum flexibility to operate within legal limitations

The pilot study proved a bureaucracy-busting success at the Mark Twain National Forest and at other pilot units, which also realized significant increases in productivity and quality. Today, due to the pilot efforts, the Mark Twain National Forest continues to be a leader in creativity, cost-effective operations, and customer service. Moreover, the Mark Twain pilot lit a spark for constructive change within the Eastern Region of the Forest Service.

Based on the success of this effort, a new initiative was authorized called *Project Spirit*. The essence of this new management philosophy was to convince employees, by management leadership and actions, that they "can as individuals make a difference." The additional flexibility provided through Project Spirit began the change in traditional bureaucratic government management at the national forests. It gave people at all levels more freedom to make changes that improved the quality of their work.

Since the beginning, more than 12,000 useful ideas have been submitted by Eastern Region employees. These ideas have eliminated outdated rules, streamlined procedures, and improved the overall quality of the employees' work life. These improvement, in turn, have translated into better, more responsive service to customers. For example, just one proposal for streamlining a procurement process used in paying vendors was implemented nationally at an estimated savings of a half-million dollars annually. Also, changing a form for firewood permits resulted in $1000 of savings annually. Moreover, this savings occurred in every one of the 70 ranger districts in the region. Finally, a method of processing balsam-fir-bough permits through the Automated Timber Sale Accounting System saves about $7000 annually. Bottom-up ideas for change continue to be raised today, but they are more often accepted and implemented on the spot rather than being elevated and approved through a more traditional, formal bureaucratic process.

Clearly, Project Spirit became more than just a souped-up employee suggestion program. It provided the catalyst for wholesale changes in the organization. As a new culture took shape in the Eastern Region, the underlying quality philosophy helped to empower individuals, recognize their efforts, and encourage their initiatives in finding solutions. The collective talents of every employee made the difference in the Eastern Region. Regional Forester Butch Marita captures the new Eastern Region philosophy this way: "The best ideas come from our employees. They know the jobs. They know what works. Give people individual responsibility to make changes, and then get out of the way."

The team-based nature of the Eastern Region's organization also created an openness that is not normally found in a government hierarchical organization. Moreover, its use of teaming dramatically accelerated the use of cross-functional teams in virtually all work activities. The benefits have been awesome. Today, almost all substantive issues are dealt with in a team environment. Teamwork will no doubt remain the Eastern Region's most powerful device for conceiving new ideas and resolving issues.

To further improve its quality and unleash the potential that exists in every employee, the Eastern Region shifted from a traditional, hierarchical "command-and-control" organization to a "shared leadership" model, in which all people are encouraged to become leaders regardless of their position. Rather than letting quality be defined by the traditional hierarchy of supervisory layers, each individual is encouraged to try new ways of improving quality and productivity. Decisions are no longer vested in the top leaders but are most often achieved through consensus of team members from various levels. With shared leadership has come greatly enhanced decision making and more personal responsibility and accountability by each individual for producing a quality product or service.

Senior managers have also fundamentally changed their role and, in essence, changed the traditional characteristics of a Forest Service regional office by forming a strategy team. The strategy team is now composed of five senior managers and two regional foresters, who have become the change agents throughout the Eastern Region. The persistence, determination, passion, and entrepreneurial spirit of these individuals and other champions in the Eastern Region have made the impossible idea of changing the Forest Service bureaucracy a reality. Prominent in their vision are strategies for achieving an ecological approach to natural resources management and an approach to human resources management that supports the diversity and spirit of the people within the organization.

But as in most organizations, the bottom line is the key, and this is where the Eastern Region can show positive results and accomplishments. Since 1989, the Eastern Region has demonstrated a reduction in its overhead and expenditures, and it has capped its growth. Remarkably, the Eastern Region's budget actually shrank through its own efforts. In the past four years, the Eastern Region has cut over 40 positions. This has saved over $3 million. These dollars, in turn, have been redistributed to activities that directly improve the national forests and improve the quality of service to their customers.

And what has the Forest Service learned? That it's time to dismantle the traditional bureaucracy and move away from a control-oriented, risk-averse organization. The Forest Service's Eastern Region made sure that bureaucracy and other forms of inefficiency didn't get in the way of doing things.

There aren't any magic bullets, or quick fixes, for shaping a new quality-focused organizational culture and philosophy. Moreover, there aren't canned solutions, all-powerful guru cult philosophies, or secrets. The Eastern Region's management system is based on a commonsense approach. It created a mission-driven organization that focuses on strategic issues and applies guiding principles tailored to its own unique needs. In turn, the mission and principles helped management stay focused on valuing its people for their ingenuity, creativity, and quality performance.

State Quality Leaders
During the past several years, state governments have recognized the role they can play in improving quality at the local level. State programs have focused on the following goals.

- Improving quality within state government agencies

- Encouraging and supporting their business community to adopt quality management practices

- Encouraging business entrepreneurs to recognize that the quality of the state's work force can attract new jobs to the state

Local organizations that are looking for quality role models may find state programs less intimidating than the national quality efforts. Today, state-sponsored programs are being adopted by every government department (education, safety, administration, for example), and outside government, by small, medium, and large businesses that are encouraged by state quality programs.

The Quality Revolution in Arkansas
Shelby A. McCook, state quality coordinator for the Arkansas Advisory Council is proud of the quality management program started by then-Governor Bill Clinton in 1990. In fact, Arkansas's quality management program is a national leader in applying quality management principles to state government agencies.

- Arkansas was the first to apply quality management principles throughout state government.

- Arkansas was first to pass a law with provision for all state agencies to get involved.

- Arkansas was first to have large numbers of state employees in a quality management education program.

When Governor Bill Clinton attended Batesville's Arkansas Quality celebration in February 1988, he became convinced that quality management was also essential for state government. Realizing the potential for spurring economic development through quality management, he was already a strong supporter of the quality improvement efforts of manufacturers and communities. But at the celebration, he came to understand how the principles of quality management can work in all types of settings, including state government.

A team of Arkansas hourly workers presented to former Governor Clinton a well-thought-out solution to a problem, admitting that they had had a hard time getting started on the project because no one had ever asked them to think before. Responding to these workers' efforts, Governor Clinton accepted Arkansas Eastman Company's offer to loan an executive to the state for a year to help the government establish a quality management program. In January 1990, after several months of planning, six pilot agencies and the governor's office started their quality journey. By August 1990, state government's interagency training program began conducting ongoing classes. During the summer of 1991, all field offices of state agencies received an orientation on quality management. A quality advisory council was set up to advise the governor and ensure consistency in the spread of quality management throughout government.

This program was established in state government with a small investment of dollars. Only two salaried employees were added—a quality management training coordinator and one instructor. Other personnel working on the program assumed these duties while continuing to perform their regular work assignments. By staffing in this manner, three distinct advantages evolve: (1) the program is unlikely to be adversely affected by revenue shortfalls; (2) the responsibility for practicing quality management principles is more likely to be assumed by all state employees because training and team activities are incorporated into their regular duties, and (3) the likelihood of having the program discontinued during a change of administration is reduced.

Training became the responsibility of an established interagency training program of the Office of Personnel Management. The quality management training was simply added to an already well-managed training program with a good track record. Most of the training material was developed in-house, according to the unique needs of state employees. The courses are continually evaluated. Improvements can be made quickly, since control is within state government.

Here are some results to date.

- Because of an improved purchasing system, the Arkansas National Guard is saving over $30,000 a year on storage batteries.

- By improving the vendor registration process, a division of the Department of Finance and Administration reduced postage expense by $29,000 and offset other operating expenses by $121,000.

- Using quality management project teams, the Department of Human Services reduced patients' waiting-room time in pediatric clinics.

- A Department of Finance and Administration team reduced by four weeks the amount of time required to process an income tax refund.

- Another team reduced from three weeks to three days the time required for vehicle licensing by mail.

- The Department of Education eliminated 24 reports, allowing teachers and administrators to be more productive, while reducing paper flow from school districts to the department by 88 reams of paper a year and effecting a significant savings in postage.

To support the state effort, legislation was passed to accomplish the following:

- Assure that no state employee will lose employment because of efficiencies resulting from quality management projects.

- Provide a mechanism for agencies to transfer or reallocate funds saved through quality management projects.

- Establish a quality management training fund.

- Create a quality management board to oversee these activities. Three members of the five-member board must be from private industry and active in the Arkansas quality task force.

Quality management in Arkansas can be compared to the ever-expanding ripples created by a pebble thrown into a pond. Originating with the intention of improving the state's manufacturing core, the quality efforts have quickly spread to state government and to other types of organizations through community-based quality initiatives. The terminology of quality management—*systems, customers, variability, involvement*—can be used in any setting. They also can be used by disparate groups working together to solve problems outside the workplace—problems affecting children, education, health care, and the economy. Fortunately for our country, the Arkansas experience with the quality management movement will not be unique for long.

Community-Based Quality Initiatives

Jan Partain coordinates the Arkansas Quality Management Task Force, the first statewide effort of its kind in the nation. The program operates through the Established Industries Division of the Arkansas Industrial Development Commission. In addition, Partain is on the board of the Community Quality Coalition, a national group that institutes local quality initiatives throughout the United States.

In the *National Productivity Review*,[1] Partain summarized, as follows, the community-based quality program in Arkansas. Like their counterparts all over the country, manufacturers in Arkansas needed help learning some important new terms such as statistical process control, participatory management, and continuous improvement. Heeding their requests for assistance, in November 1986 the Arkansas Industrial

Development Commission (AIDC), the state's economic development agency, assembled a group of managers from Arkansas companies, members of professional associations, and representatives from educational institutions and government agencies to help create the Arkansas Quality Management Task Force.

The task force's mission was "to create a common awareness and understanding of the potential for increasing productivity through quality management as a means for Arkansas businesses to survive and grow as world-class competitors." It defined quality management as "a customer-oriented philosophy of management that utilized total employee involvement in the relentless daily search for improvement of quality of products and service through the use of statistical methods, employee teams, and performance management."

Task force activities are coordinated by the Established Industries Division of the Arkansas Industrial Development Commission (AIDC). It receives guidance from a private-sector steering committee and has a data bank of over 1400 people who have contacted the office. This fully state-funded service charges no fees for its services.

A mainstay of the task force's services is an active schedule of seminars featuring experts as well as managers of local industries. Subsidized by AIDC, these seminars are priced to be accessible to as many people as possible, with a standard $40 to $90 registration fee. In the last five years, the task force has sponsored more than 30 seminars on such topics as these.

- Customer service
- Employee involvement
- Statistical process control
- Quality teams
- Performance management
- The Malcolm Baldrige National Quality Award
- Competitive benchmarking
- The ISO 9000 series

Other educational opportunities offered in Arkansas include national award-winning conferences on team development given by the

University of Arkansas's Continuing Education Division, with AIDC and Zenger Miller as co-sponsors. The Arkansas Quality Council, composed of the state's five American Society for Quality Control sections, is also a key participant.

The task force has held three Governor's Quality Conferences, by-invitation-only events aimed at top managers. These seminars featured hard-hitting messages designed to convince leaders of their unique obligations in implementing quality management.

Another valuable service of the task force is the *Quality Management Newsletter*. This bimonthly publication, which is sent to over 3600 people in Arkansas and across the United States, highlights the activities of companies, schools, and community initiatives and provides seminar and course information. In addition, AIDC and Westark Community College's Center for Quality and Productivity stock a resource center containing books, videos, and software for preview or purchase. The Arkansas State Library also has an extensive holding of these resources, which can be loaned to any public library across the state.

Many people call the task force office seeking information about trainers, curriculum packages, consultants, speakers, and benchmarking contacts. AIDC has developed a *computerized clearinghouse* to handle these requests, to refer callers to other task force members who have experience in specific areas, or to help groups find speakers for events.

One of the most important services that the task force offers, however, is its support of community-based quality initiatives, an effort hailed by many as the most important economic development activity in the state. Thus, AIDC plays a multiple role in helping Arkansas cities.

1. As a promoter, AIDC encourages towns to become part of the Quality First network, because locally based programs are an integral part of economic development, a mainstay for existing companies, and an attraction for new industries.

2. As a documenter, AIDC records the curriculum, trainers, tuition, advisory committee, history, and outstanding events peculiar to each city's program. The team projects were reported in a standardized format, courtesy of colleagues in the Madison (Wisconsin) Area Quality Improvement Network.

These reports are entered into a computerized data base and are available for teams all over the state.

3. As an ex-officio member of Quality First advisory councils, AIDC can share the cumulative experiences of other towns. Still, it never forces rigid or intrusive methods, because each community is unique and must develop its own program according to its needs and resources.

4. As a funder, AIDC provides small grants to Arkansas towns as seed money. Arkansas training programs are based heavily on volunteer efforts, and once they get underway, they are self-supporting through tuition.

5. As a perpetuator, AIDC sponsors an annual community workshop in which towns that are both old and new can network.

The 18 community initiatives now active in Arkansas are part of a national phenomenon. The first community-based quality management programs were developed in the mid-1980s in places as diverse as Philadelphia, Pennsylvania; Lawrence, Massachusetts; Spartanburg, South Carolina; and Kingsport, Tennessee. Since then, at least 70 more towns, coast-to-coast, have joined the ranks. These community initiatives are based on the desire of people to share their enthusiasm about this new way of working—and to encourage others to treat customers better. The other goals of these programs are to

- Create and retain jobs
- Expand existing industry
- Recruit new industry
- Improve worker morale
- Reduce costs and inefficiency
- Develop a loyal customer (taxpayer) base

Communities are also learning how to nurture a powerful synergy that can offer promising solutions to many of the problems our society faces.

A community-based initiative represents the united effort of leaders from business, education, and government who have the common goal of building a strong economic future. They realize that the future is ensured only through the continuous improvement of the quality and value of the products and service provided by each of their organizations. Such initiatives include the following activities.

1. Awareness sessions to teach managers the philosophy of quality management and to prepare them for their new role. These sessions are important so that executives can support the teams that they will later send to be trained.

2. Ongoing roundtable meetings in which these leaders can compare notes about successes or disappointments and continue to learn.

3. Sessions that highlight local companies and their experiences or consultants with special expertise.

4. Training classes for four- to six-member teams from a variety of organizations. The employees on these teams learn to apply quality management philosophy and problem solving to work-related projects.

5. Celebrations in which the teams present the results of their projects. The improvement in day-to-day work processes, the money that has been saved, and the enthusiasm of the teams all prove the effectiveness of this training and lead to future participation.

A community-based initiative is generally guided by leaders from local industry or educational institutions and is frequently sponsored by the city's chamber of commerce or industrial development foundation. These people form an advisory group or steering committee that creates the awareness of the quality management concept and determines how to implement it.

Quality First programs get the quickest start when truly committed local businesses or industries guide their efforts. Because of their experience in quality management, these companies are true believers and demonstrate both the necessary enthusiasm and discipline. They also provide a source of trainers.

The local chamber of commerce or industrial development foundation often provides a home base for the program. The Quality First initiative fits in naturally with the economic development goals of the chamber. The local university or community college can also provide support for a community's Quality First program and, as a result, usually adds quality management to its standard course offerings.

The participants in the classes may represent large and small manufacturers, service companies, retailers, schools, hospitals, banks, or government. Every sector of the community is welcome. And the shared experiences are remarkable: when employees of the local car dealership, fast-food outlet, hospital, and factory realize that the same concepts can apply to all of them, an unexpected bond is formed.

The first community initiative in Arkansas began in Batesville in July 1987, when managers of the Arkansas Eastman Company called together an advisory committee composed of representatives of area industries, Arkansas College, the chamber of commerce, the mayor, and AIDC. The program began with an all-day orientation for local leaders, during which members of the advisory committee set out the benefits of such a program from their particular vantage points. The audience then heard the basics of quality management and were asked to consider sending teams of employees to training that fall.

Batesville uses the Transformation of American Industry curriculum, which was developed by Jackson (Michigan) Community College and Ford Motor Company. Trainers from Arkansas Eastman teach the 56-hour course, usually in seven eight-hour sessions. The course costs $750 for a four-member team. At the end of each round of training, everyone in town is invited to a celebration in which the teams present the results of their improvement projects. This lively event usually ensures new enrollment for the next round of instruction.

The diversity of organizations enrolled in Batesville's first training session proved that quality management could be applied to any setting. At the first celebration, projects ranged from ConAgra's attempt to improve methods for frying chicken to city government's attempt to reduce vehicle downtime. Martin Lumber Company, a small firm that supplies pallets for Campbell Soup, learned it could meet the high quality demands of its customer and save money at the same time. The $1/16$ of an inch per board per pallet the company saved through improved sawing operations amounted to enough lumber to build eight homes.

In Batesville, the local college has now added quality management courses to its regular offerings, and nearby public schools are seeing exciting results due to quality management practices. Here are some other examples of how Arkansas communities are spreading the word on quality.

- The city of Searcy started its quality management drive in the fall of 1988 under the guidance of a management professor from Harding University. Assisted by the quality manager of Vickers, Inc., he uses his own curriculum in an 18-hour course that costs $125 per person (less for small-business people when it is provided through the auspices of the Small Business Development Center). Searcy started its seventh round of training last fall, and now estimates that over $11 million has been saved by project teams representing a variety of companies, including banks, steel tubing manufacturers, industrial laundries, and ice cream makers.

- In January 1989, a management professor at Texarkana College launched a community effort in Texarkana. In addition to offering a 36-hour course based on the Transformation of American Industry curriculum, the school holds Deming breakfasts each month for local executives. A special course was conducted for school superintendents and college presidents. Texarkana, which began its sixth round of training last fall, has trained organizations ranging from hospitals to an ammunitions plant. Its Carpenter Steel Company attained such outstanding results that it was able to refund money to a customer.

- In early 1989, Russellville began its quality program. There, Arkansas Tech University leads an active advisory group and offers excellent support to the local chamber of commerce and industries such as Dow Chemical and ConAgra. Russellville's year-round agenda of opportunities is constantly growing. Early projects enabled a construction company to reduce worker compensation insurance premiums and Arkansas Tech to cut the cost of undergraduate catalogs.

- In Forrest City, the education sector took the lead in the absence of an industry with deep quality management experience. The local community college, the vo-tech school, and the public school have provided excellent examples of ways to contribute to quality management. Forrest City Public Schools have redesigned their management to follow the criteria for the Malcolm Baldrige National Quality Award and recently established of the Educational Quality Center. Faculty and staff are working on projects to improve reading, student attendance, food service, and energy consumption. School board members have learned to use quality management criteria for making decisions.

- Employees of Skil Corporation and Darling Store Fixtures have pooled their knowledge and enthusiasm with local chamber of commerce directors and other city leaders to provide a quick start to ongoing programs in Paragould, Pocahontas, and Walnut Ridge. In these towns, the genuine interaction between education and industry has been extremely beneficial, as each sector discovers common problems and solutions. This relationship was especially powerful in nearby Blytheville, where teams from industry worked with educators on projects to improve student test scores and attendance.

- Pine Bluff's "Quest for Quality" program was kicked off with a series of four breakfasts featuring respected local leaders who discussed components of quality management and outstanding results from its implementation. The town's major employer, International Paper Company, directed a series of activities during October, National Quality Month.

- A sister International Paper plant in nearby Camden is providing trainers for that community's "From Camden with Pride" program, which offers separate classes for manufacturers, health-care workers, service providers, and educators.

- El Dorado's "Quality Edge" program got underway in January 1992. To ensure wide participation, the steering committee planned an extensive publicity campaign consisting of one-on-one recruiting appeals, a series of articles in the local media, and speeches to local civic clubs and other groups. Great Lakes Chemical Company has taken a leading role, developing a standard speech with supporting transparencies that any steering committee member can use.

The underlying theme of industry's eagerness to share the new way of managing is also evident in the curriculum and consultant support given in other towns, such as the Green Bay Packaging Company in Morrilton, the Sara Lee Corporation in Clarksville, and Baxter Healthcare Corporation in Mountain Home.

Minnesota Quality Leaders

During the last two years, the Minnesota Quality Award (see chapter 4) has been presented to EMD Associates, Hutchinson Technology, and Zytec. Zytec went on to win the 1992 Baldrige award. The trend for major companies such as IBM to encourage their subcontractors to raise quality levels is demonstrated in all three of these award-winning subcontractors of IBM located in Minnesota.

Of course, some organizations resist the outside customer's requirements for enhancement of their quality. They believe that the only reason they are "doing" quality management is because their customer or higher level organization has required them to change. So be it! In some cases, top management must dictate change rather than wait for change-resistant organizations to see the light. The ripple effect in Minnesota of IBM Rochester winning the Baldrige award and the positive attitude shown by Minnesota business leaders demonstrate the synergy possible where quality improvement is encouraged.

EMD Associates, Inc.

EMD Associates is a full-service electronics design and manufacturing company. Founded in 1974, the company currently employs more than 800 workers at two facilities in Winona, Minnesota. EMD assembles electronic components on printed circuit boards (PCBs) using high-speed, automated, pick-and-place equipment. Customers incorporate the PCB assemblies into their final products. EMD also offers its customers a full line of engineering design services ranging from product design and development to prototype builds.

EMD has determined that the most important factors in maintaining and building customer relationships are product quality, technology, partner relationships, on-time delivery, flexibility, service, and price. The company's principal strategies for responding to these requirements are

1. To develop strong leadership in all areas of the business

2. To empower all co-workers through full deployment of EMD's quality vision and goals, team building, education, and shared ownership

3. To continuously improve quality by measuring performance of key processes and taking the appropriate actions

EMD is dedicated to fostering open communication, teamwork, commitment, and flexibility. One result of its commitment to quality and customer service has been sales growth from $8 million in 1986 to more than $100 million in 1992, at a time when the industry growth rate has been 15 percent. EMD's senior management, called the Team of 20, includes the two principal owners and co-CEOs, Daniel M. Rukavina and David H. Arnold; department managers; and critical specialists. EMD formed the Team of 20 in 1989 to provide a working platform for developing a group of leaders who would spearhead company growth.

EMD's flat organizational structure encourages cooperation among departments while demanding broad leadership from the Team of 20. Members of the Team of 20 collaborate to manage issues that extend beyond departmental responsibilities, meeting monthly to discuss strategic business and quality issues. The team welcomes and values the contributions of its co-workers, promoting open communication and cooperation through a team management style.

EMD's senior managers maintain and reinforce a stable customer base, with 20 customers representing 95 percent of the company's annual revenue. The company has chosen active participation on at least one Customer Team as the primary means of keeping the Team of 20 (and all EMD co-workers) focused on the customer.

Members of the Team of 20 create quality values and set expectations by participating in customer teams and in three of EMD's most important quality activities: quality training, quality improvement teams (QITs), and the strategic planning process.

Senior management communicates EMD's quality values to outside organizations in a variety of ways, most notably through Team of 20 member involvement in 17 associations, councils, boards of directors, colleges, and nonprofit organizations. EMD's quality values express senior management's understanding of the Deming theory of leadership.

EMD Quality Values

1. All co-workers must understand the quality chain reaction and why a focus on quality improvement assures long-term profitability and job survival.

2. All co-workers must understand the concept of extended process, internal/external customer, and costs of producing defects.

3. All co-workers must understand that quality requirements are defined by internal/external customers, and that the degree to which external customer requirements are understood and exceeded is dependent on their degree of meeting internal customer needs.

4. All co-workers must understand that the EMD design and manufacturing systems are responsible for 90-plus percent of the defects produced (not the co-workers) and that they must work as a team in an orderly fashion to improve their systems.

These quality values serve as a basis for daily operations. They are reinforced by EMD's vision, mission, environment, principles, strategic quality vision, and quality philosophy.

- **EMD company vision**

    Products bearing the mark "Made by EMD Co-workers" recognized worldwide as the best

- **EMD company mission**

    To understand and exceed the customer's expectations by providing the world's best design and manufacturing services and solutions

- **EMD desired environment**

  Customers, workers, and suppliers creating an environment of innovation and continuous improvement that encourages partnership and fosters human creativity, trust, and pride of ownership

- **EMD principles**
  - Recognize the collective human values of customers, suppliers, and co-workers
  - Share company profits with all co-workers through profit sharing and ESOP participation
  - Be responsive to the needs of the community and the environment
  - Conduct all aspects of business with high ethical standards of honesty, integrity, and fairness

- **EMD strategic quality vision**
  - Empowered and involved co-workers who bring life and energy to the EMD quality philosophy by personally accepting responsibility for satisfying all external and internal customer needs
  - Educated co-workers who embrace the EMD teamwork strategy in order to achieve continuous quality improvement
  - Enlightened leaders who serve the needs of their customers, co-workers, and suppliers through reverence for the individual, active listening, and openness to change
  - Satisfied customers who consider EMD to be an extension of their own company and who work with them to create mutually rewarding partnerships that utilize their full service engineering and manufacturing capabilities

- **EMD quality philosophy specific to electronic product design and manufacturing**

  Minimum quality requirements must be defined by customers. EMD must exceed all requirements through leading simultaneous improvements in the following:

  1. Product design (function, manufacturability, testability, component quality)

  2. Manufacturing processes (process design, testing, auditing)

3. Business processes (JIT, supplier certification and improvement programs, capable business support services)

4. Workplace environment (communication, education, training, team development)

EMD communicates its quality values through several methods, including buttons, posters, mugs, and calendars; the monthly company newsletter; semiannual company meetings; and review with co-workers in QITs and training.

EMD uses its system for leadership and strategic planning to integrate its quality values into day-to-day quality leadership and management. The system translates customer and quality requirements and objectives into manager, supervisor, departmental, and individual requirements and objectives. It makes each EMD co-worker responsible for clarifying and taking responsibility for his or her role in achieving EMD's mission and objectives.

At its annual planning retreat, the Team of 20 sets one- and five-year QCS (Quality/Cost/Scheduling) objectives and financial objectives (profit, company growth, and technology) with the customer needs assessment and corporate vision in mind. Intradepartmental teams, each consisting of 10 members from the department and five cross-functional members, create departmental objectives and the measures or means to achieve them. The Team of 20 reviews the departmental objectives, which are then deployed to each department. Individual worker or team objectives are created from the departmental objectives. Each worker in the company receives QCS goals and action plans specific to his or her department. Before the next planning retreat, the intradepartmental teams summarize and present progress on the previous year's goals and problems or barriers to achieving these goals to the Team of 20.

EMD also reviews company and work-unit quality plans and performance through its customer teams, quality planning committee (QPC), and senior management. QITs hold weekly reviews of their individual process-related quality goals. The QPC is a cross-functional, operational body charged with reviewing progress on ISO 9001 certification, Baldrige improvement plans, and other system improvement action plans. Senior management reviews monthly quality performance data on selected customer assemblies compared to expected performance data, the quality improvement plans and results of the customer teams, and the line-return reject ratio for each customer assembly.

Hutchinson Technology

Hutchinson Technology, Inc., (HTI) was founded in 1965. HTI is a leader in precision manufacturing, producing over 100 products for use in disk drives, medical devices, and other electronic-related applications. Its major product line, Suspension Assemblies, positions magnetic read/write heads just a few millionths of an inch above the spinning disks in rigid disk drives. Headquartered in Hutchinson, Minnesota, HTI employs more than 3200 people. Hutchinson Technology has a second manufacturing facility in Sioux Falls, South Dakota, and has foreign sales offices in Minneapolis, Korea, Singapore, and the Netherlands.

Hutchinson's quality vision incorporates the following values.

- Customers—promising value and customer satisfaction

- Products and processes—promising to set new standards of quality excellence

- Employees—promising to promote creativity and encouraging involvement, teamwork, and employee development

- Suppliers and communities—promising to extend teamwork to them and guaranteeing forthright relationships

Quality performance is a way of life at Hutchinson Technology. It is integrated into all aspects of the business—from customers to suppliers—to insure long-term economic success.

Judy Conrad, National Quality Award manager at Hutchinson Technology, believes that the Minnesota Quality Award and the Malcolm Baldrige National Quality Award are excellent tools to help an organization benchmark its attitude and level of quality performance. She believes that the extended level of feedback provided by applying for the awards is one of the most valuable benefits of the award process.

Kathleen Skarvan, spokesperson for Hutchinson Technology, noted that "involvement with the National Quality Award and the Minnesota Quality Award provided an excellent opportunity to inexpensively benchmark our company. The award process also pulled together all total quality management activities as we at HTI assessed our own efforts."

The Minnesota Quality Award provides an excellent process for self-assessment. Offering an award exclusive to Minnesota provides an opportunity for businesses to assess their quality efforts rigorously while raising the competitiveness of their state.

According to Skarvan, "The benefits from applying for the awards are too numerous to list. We've used the feedback to prioritize and formally mobilize our efforts to improve. For example, feedback on category 7.0, Customer Focus and Satisfaction, indicated that it was not clear how HTI ensures objectivity and validity of customer satisfaction data. This comment caused us to evaluate this area and plans were developed to close this gap. This process continuously improves our business.

"HTI's market, rigid disk drive, is very demanding; we have to be good to survive. We have always tried to improve all facets of the business, and the quality awards provided another means to continue our improvement."

New York Governor's Excelsior Award Leaders

The New York Governor's Excelsior Award (see chapter 4 for details) is the first to award state agencies and educational institutions for quality performance. In response, during the past two years, the educational community has begun to become aware of and aggressively implement quality management principles and priorities. The New York leadership in this area is now being followed by other state government organizations.

The Kenmore–Town of Tonawanda Union Free School District and the New York State Police are just two of the recent award winners in New York.

Kenmore–Town of Tonawanda Union Free School District

This combined school district is located in Kenmore and the town of Tonawanda, New York, suburban areas of Buffalo with a population of approximately 92,000. It is a public school system that provides educational services for more than 8,000 students from kindergarten through

12th grade. The staff consists of 36 administrators, approximately 650 teachers, and more than 600 support staff. Kenmore employees are represented by the Kenmore Administrators' Association, the Kenmore Teachers' Association, and the Kenmore–Town of Tonawanda School Employees' Association.

Kenmore School District networks with school districts from Rhode Island to Colorado. In addition, Kenmore has served as a role model, having hosted educators from Canada, Germany, the former Yugoslavia, India, Ceylon, Japan, and Thailand in order to share their educational experiences.

To support its commitment to lifelong learning, the school district has developed one of the largest continuing community education systems in New York State. In 1981, the district developed its highly successful School Improvement Program, which focuses on quality and recognizes increased student learning as an ultimate goal. This program promotes autonomous school-based planning teams. The teams are fully empowered to meet the needs of different constituencies, including students, teachers, parents, and the community.

The district's aggressive approach to partnerships enables it to implement successful programs to meet the diverse needs of its constituents. This approach includes a significant amount of external community involvement and strong partnerships with local businesses and industries.

Nine of the schools in the district have been recognized as New York State Schools of Excellence. In addition, two of the elementary schools were cited as National Schools of Excellence in 1990–1991.

New York State Police
The New York State Police is a division of the Executive Department. Since its inception as a full-service police agency in 1917, it has been responsible for controlling crime and providing highway safety and related services to the citizens of New York State. This state agency also supports the state's criminal justice system and more than 500 local and county police agencies.

The New York State Police division employs approximately 2400 troopers assigned to the Uniform Force Division. The Bureau of

Criminal Investigation is the detective branch and has 912 investigators and senior investigators. The remaining 677 employees are administrative and support staff. It is the largest full-service state police agency in the nation. Its work force is represented by the Police Benevolent Association of New York State Troopers, Inc., the Civil Service Employees' Association, and the Public Employees' Federation.

Leadership at all levels is strong, top-down, very visible, and committed to clear organizational quality values that are communicated successfully to all employees. The overall pride and professionalism demonstrated by employees are exceptional.

The state police know their constituents well and continually strive to serve them. Their proficiency is founded on rigorous quality training programs. Troopers and support staff demonstrate an intrinsic sensitivity to constituency needs. The expected standards for constituent contact are well-defined, carefully assessed, vigorously supported, and universally understood by all employees. In short, the New York State Police care about the citizens they serve.

This agency has extensive systems in place to ensure the success and quality of their programs and services, both inside and outside the agency.

Follow by Example

Clearly, government organizations must recognize the potential benefits of applying quality management to their day-to-day processes. Unfortunately, many individuals in government have not yet recognized the need for internal and external customer identification, customer satisfaction, and continuous improvement. The success stories that we have just described show that government can improve by applying quality management to your organization. If your peers can do it, why can't you follow their leadership example?

Notes

1. Permission to edit and use "Creating a Grassroots Quality Revolution in Arkansas" provided by Jan Partain.

6   Quality Management
Self-Assessment

*Look for the ways you trip yourself up—how you get
in your own way without meaning to. It will help
you anticipate where problems and setbacks will likely
occur.*

Tom Peters and Nancy Austin
A Passion for Excellence

This chapter provides a method for you to assess the current practices,
policies, procedures, and attitudes throughout your organization as they
relate to quality management. It also provides an opportunity for you to
check your progress by occasionally reevaluating your performance. In
short, these questions show WHY your organization needs to adopt
quality management. This self-assessment asks questions concerning
four aspects of your organization.

- Climate. People's perceptions of their organization and/or
  work units

- Processes. The organization's or work unit's policies, practices, and procedures

- Management tools. The specific techniques used to promote
  quality management improvements throughout the organization or work units

- Outcomes. Mission accomplishment

Some questions ask you to consider the *entire organization* in your
response, and others ask you to think only about your *immediate work*

unit. The definitions of these two terms need to be clear in your mind before you begin this self-assessment so that your responses will be consistent.

Decide which organization and work unit you wish to examine. For example, you may be in charge of a department. The department may contain three divisions. The divisions, in turn, may be composed of several subunits. Depending on your interest, you may designate the department as the *organization,* and one of the three divisions as the *work unit.*

Another term you will encounter is *customer,* defined here as anyone who receives the work that you, your work unit(s), or your organization performs. Note that customers can be another organization, another work unit, or any organization member. The traditional notion of customer as someone outside your immediate organization or work unit that uses or buys your product or service can also apply. In all cases, consider that your customer relies on and judges the quality of the work that you do.

The source of this evaluation structure is the "Quality and Productivity Self-Assessment Guide," a public domain DoD report. You may reproduce this chapter to aid in your or your team's use of this self-assessment tool.

To conduct this quality management self-assessment, complete the following worksheets for each self-assessment element (climate, processes, tools, outcomes). There are 215 self-assessment questions, which you can answer in approximately 15 minutes. The scoring rationale follows the questions.

Assessment of Organizational Climate

The following list of statements is presented for your evaluation and ranking. There are no wrong answers. Circle the number that best indicates the extent of your agreement with the statement. The values for the following portion of the questionnaire are as follows: (1) strongly disagree, (2) disagree, (3) somewhat disagree, (4) somewhat agree, (5) agree, and (6) strongly agree.

	Strongly Disagree*	Strongly Agree*

1. People in this organization are aware of its overall mission.   1 2 3 4 5 6

2. In general, this organization's customers believe that we care about what they think. 1 2 3 4 5 6

3. People in this organization are aware of how their jobs contribute to the organization's mission.   1 2 3 4 5 6

4. It's in everyone's best interests that this organization be successful.   1 2 3 4 5 6

5. People in this organization are aware of how the organization's mission contributes to higher level missions and objectives.   1 2 3 4 5 6

6. In general, this organization's customers would not go elsewhere even if it were possible.   1 2 3 4 5 6

People in this organization

7. Try to plan ahead for changes (such as in policy) that might impact our mission performance   1 2 3 4 5 6

8. Try to plan ahead for technological changes (such as new developments in computer software) that might impact our mission performance   1 2 3 4 5 6

9. Regularly work together to plan for the future   1 2 3 4 5 6

10. See continuing improvement as essential   1 2 3 4 5 6

11. Care about what will happen to the organization after they are reassigned   1 2 3 4 5 6

*Legend: (1) strongly disagree, (2) disagree, (3) somewhat disagree, (4) somewhat agree, (5) agree, (6) strongly agree.

	Strongly Disagree*				Strongly Agree*	

12. Creativity is actively encouraged in this organization.   1 2 3 4 5 6

13. Innovators are the people who get ahead in this organization.   1 2 3 4 5 6

14. The quality of our work is second only to mission accomplishment as the overriding focus of this organization.   1 2 3 4 5 6

15. Every member of this organization is concerned with the need for quality management.   1 2 3 4 5 6

16. Continuous quality improvements within this organization can lead to more productive use of our resources.   1 2 3 4 5 6

17. People in this organization know how to define the quality of what we do.   1 2 3 4 5 6

18. Every member of this organization needs to contribute to quality improvement.   1 2 3 4 5 6

People in this organization

19. Live up to high ethical standards   1 2 3 4 5 6

20. Like to do a good job   1 2 3 4 5 6

21. Emphasize doing things right the first time   1 2 3 4 5 6

The leader(s) in this organization (people at the highest level)

22. Are committed to providing top-quality services/products/work   1 2 3 4 5 6

23. Regularly review the quality of work produced   1 2 3 4 5 6

*Legend: (1) strongly disagree, (2) disagree, (3) somewhat disagree, (4) somewhat agree, (5) agree, (6) strongly agree.

	Strongly Disagree*			Strongly Agree*		
24. Ask people about ways to improve the work produced	1	2	3	4	5	6
25. Follow up suggestions for improvement	1	2	3	4	5	6

The leader(s) in this organization (people at the highest level)

26. Set examples of quality performance in their day-to-day activities	1	2	3	4	5	6
27. Regularly review the organization's progress toward meeting its goals and objectives	1	2	3	4	5	6
28. Attempt to find out why the organization may not be meeting a particular goal/objective	1	2	3	4	5	6

People in my work unit

29. Turn to their supervisors for advice about how to improve their work	1	2	3	4	5	6
30. Know their supervisors will help them find answers to problems they may be having	1	2	3	4	5	6
31. Are challenged by their supervisors to find ways to improve the system	1	2	3	4	5	6

The supervisors in my work unit

32. Make continuous improvement of our work top priority	1	2	3	4	5	6
33. Regularly ask our customers about the quality of work they receive	1	2	3	4	5	6

*Legend: (1) strongly disagree, (2) disagree, (3) somewhat disagree, (4) somewhat agree, (5) agree, (6) strongly agree.

	Strongly Disagree*				Strongly Agree*	
34. The structure of our organization makes it easy to focus on quality.	1	2	3	4	5	6
35. The way we do things in this organization is consistent with quality.	1	2	3	4	5	6
36. People in my work unit understand how a quality emphasis leads to more productive use of resources.	1	2	3	4	5	6
37. People in my work unit can describe the organization's quality and productivity policy.	1	2	3	4	5	6
38. People in my work unit believe that quality and productivity improvement are their responsibility.	1	2	3	4	5	6
39. People in my work unit take pride in their work.	1	2	3	4	5	6
40. People in my work unit share responsibility for the success or failure of our services/products.	1	2	3	4	5	6
41. People in my work unit believe that their work is important to the success of the overall organization.	1	2	3	4	5	6
42. We have good relationships between departments in this organization.	1	2	3	4	5	6
43. Co-workers in this organization cooperate with each other to get the job done.	1	2	3	4	5	6
44. A spirit of cooperation and teamwork exists in this organization.	1	2	3	4	5	6

*Legend: (1) strongly disagree, (2) disagree, (3) somewhat disagree, (4) somewhat agree, (5) agree, (6) strongly agree.

	Strongly Disagree*				Strongly Agree*	
45. We have good relationships with other organizations that we work with.	1	2	3	4	5	6
46. Supervisors in my work unit request employee opinions and data.	1	2	3	4	5	6
47. People in my work unit are involved in improving our services/products/work.	1	2	3	4	5	6
48. We have the appropriate personnel in my work unit to get the job done properly.	1	2	3	4	5	6
49. The work goals or standards in my work unit are generally fair.	1	2	3	4	5	6
50. The supervisors in my work unit do a good job of setting work expectations.	1	2	3	4	5	6
51. People in my work unit are friendly with one another.	1	2	3	4	5	6
52. People in my work unit enjoy their co-workers.	1	2	3	4	5	6
53. We have the right tools, equipment, and materials in my work unit to get the job done.	1	2	3	4	5	6
54. The materials and supplies we need in my work unit are delivered on time as ordered.	1	2	3	4	5	6
55. The distribution of work among the people in my work unit is well balanced.	1	2	3	4	5	6
56. In my work unit, we have enough time to perform our jobs in a professional manner.	1	2	3	4	5	6

*Legend: (1) strongly disagree, (2) disagree, (3) somewhat disagree, (4) somewhat agree, (5) agree, (6) strongly agree.

	Strongly Disagree*					Strongly Agree*
57. My work unit is structured properly to get the job done.	1	2	3	4	5	6
58. People in my work unit are rewarded for good work.	1	2	3	4	5	6
59. People in my work unit are paid fairly for the work they do.	1	2	3	4	5	6
60. Attempts are made to promote the people in my work unit who do good work.	1	2	3	4	5	6
61. People in my work unit receive promotions because they earned them.	1	2	3	4	5	6
62. Supervisors in my work unit give credit to people when they do a good job.	1	2	3	4	5	6
63. There are penalties for people in my work unit.	1	2	3	4	5	6
64. People in my work unit are given quick recognition for outstanding performance.	1	2	3	4	5	6
65. People in my work unit know who their customers are.	1	2	3	4	5	6
66. People in my work unit care about our customers.	1	2	3	4	5	6
67. There are effective communication channels between departments in this organization.	1	2	3	4	5	6
68. People in my work unit do not have to rely on the grapevine or rumors for information.	1	2	3	4	5	6

*Legend: (1) strongly disagree, (2) disagree, (3) somewhat disagree, (4) somewhat agree, (5) agree, (6) strongly agree.

	Strongly Disagree*					Strongly Agree*

69. People in my work unit have ample opportunity to exchange information with their supervisors.   1 2 3 4 5 6

70. People in my work unit get the facts and the information they need to do a good job.   1 2 3 4 5 6

*Legend: (1) strongly disagree, (2) disagree, (3) somewhat disagree, (4) somewhat agree, (5) agree, (6) strongly agree.

Assessment of Processes

The statements in the following sections are varied in format. In each case, circle the number to the right of each statement that most closely represents your perception of your organization.

	Yes	No	Not Sure

This organization has

71. Used surveys of some/all of its members in order to determine whether improvements in quality are needed | 2 | 1 | 1

72. Used formal interviews with some/all of its members in order to determine whether improvements in quality are needed | 2 | 1 | 1

73. Informally asked some/all of its members for their opinions about whether improvements in quality are needed | 2 | 1 | 1

74. Asked senior management for their opinions about whether improvements in quality are needed | 2 | 1 | 1

	Yes	No	Not Sure
75. Analyzed data concerning goal/objective accomplishments in order to determine whether improvements in quality are needed	2	1	1
76. Relied on "higher level" directives in order to determine whether improvements in quality are needed.	2	1	1
77. asked established team members to report periodically	2	1	1

This organization is (or might become) committed to quality improvement because

	Yes	No	Not Sure
78. We are mandated to do so by a higher authority.	2	1	1
79. The people at the top level of this organization are/were dissatisfied with the quality being achieved.	2	1	1
80. We want to improve an already acceptable quality record.	2	1	1
81. We want to maintain a specified level of service in the face of budget reductions.	2	1	1
82. The people we serve deserve our best efforts.	2	1	1

	Yes	No	Don't Have Policy
This organization has a quality improvement policy that			
83. Is written	2	1	1
84. Has specific goals and objectives	2	1	1

	Yes	No	Don't Have Policy
85. Everyone in the organization has seen	2	1	1
86. Is taken seriously by people	2	1	1
87. Holds people accountable for success/failure	2	1	1

	Yes	No	Does Not Apply
Responsibility for quality improvement			
88. Is accepted by senior management	2	1	1
89. Is accepted by middle management	2	1	1
90. Is accepted by almost all organizational members	2	1	1
91. This organization has a separately identified office that oversees its quality improvement efforts.	2	1	1
92. Quality improvement concerns are discussed/monitored at least on a quarterly basis.	2	1	1
93. Managers at all levels have clearly defined roles in our quality improvement process.	2	1	1
94. This organization uses teams to monitor quality improvement projects.	2	1	1
95. Managers at all levels are responsible for the success or failure of our quality improvement efforts.	2	1	1
96. This organization has a data base or tracking system for relevant quality information.	2	1	1

	Yes	No	Not Sure
In order to determine what our customers think about our products/services, we			
97. Conduct surveys on a regular basis	2	1	1
98. Ask customers informally	2	1	1
99. Monitor complaints	2	1	1
100. Ask our employees who have contact with our customers	2	1	1
The leaders at the top level in this organization			
101. Have agreed upon a definition of quality improvement	2	1	1
102. Have set long-term goals concerning quality improvement	2	1	1
103. Have set short-term objectives concerning quality improvement	2	1	1
104. Have defined performance measures to monitor progress toward reaching objectives and goals	2	1	1

	Almost None*					Almost All*
How many work units within this organization						
105. Know how the organization defines quality improvement?	1	2	3	4	5	6
106. Have set long-term goals concerning quality improvement?	1	2	3	4	5	6
107. Have set short-term objectives concerning quality improvement?	1	2	3	4	5	6

*Legend: (1) almost none, (2) very few, (3) some, (4) quite a few, (5) most, (6) almost all.

	Almost None*				Almost All*	
108. Have defined performance measures to monitor progress toward reaching their objectives and goals?	1	2	3	4	5	6

How many organizational members

109. Can specify, if asked, what goals or objectives they are working toward?	1	2	3	4	5	6
110. Were invited to participate in setting goals or objectives related to their work?	1	2	3	4	5	6
111. Know how the goals/objectives they are working toward relate to their work unit's mission?	1	2	3	4	5	6
112. Know how performance measures relate to monitoring their accomplishment of goals and objectives?	1	2	3	4	5	6

*Legend: (1) almost none, (2) very few, (3) some, (4) quite a few, (5) most, (6) almost all.

	Yes	No	Not Sure
Long-range planning in this organization includes			
113. Integration of quality improvement planning into general business planning	2	1	1
114. Prioritizing quality improvement issues	2	1	1
115. Customer input	2	1	1
116. Employee input	2	1	1
117. Quality improvement implementation strategies for all work units	2	1	1
118. A means for monitoring quality improvement effectiveness over time	2	1	1

	Yes	No	Not Sure
In terms of setting organizational improvement priorities, we have considered or evaluated			
119. Changing our business strategy	2	1	1
120. Improving our work methods or procedures	2	1	1
121. Improving our employee utilization	2	1	1
122. Revising or instituting training programs	2	1	1
123. Acquiring recent technological improvements (equipment, materials)	2	1	1

	Strongly Disagree*			Strongly Agree*		
124. The structure of this organization supports its efforts to carry out its mission.	1	2	3	4	5	6
125. Organizational members have the information they need to do their work.	1	2	3	4	5	6
126. This organization has a realistic schedule for replacing outdated equipment.	1	2	3	4	5	6
127. This organization's members have been adequately trained to use the equipment they have.	1	2	3	4	5	6
128. Before equipment is bought by or issued to this organization, plans have been made concerning how it will be used and who will use it.	1	2	3	4	5	6

*Legend: (1) strongly disagree, (2) disagree, (3) somewhat disagree, (4) somewhat agree, (5) agree, (6) strongly agree.

	Strongly Disagree*					**Strongly Agree***
129. Efforts are made to update work methods in this organization (for example, the way work is organized and the tools or materials used to accomplish it).	1	2	3	4	5	6
130. People in charge of similar work units frequently share information about their work methods and practices.	1	2	3	4	5	6
131. Updating work methods can be key to quality improvement.	1	2	3	4	5	6

Organization members with good ideas are likely to

132. Formally submit them through a suggestion system	1	2	3	4	5	6
133. Tell their supervisors	1	2	3	4	5	6
134. Be asked periodically what they think	1	2	3	4	5	6

*Legend: (1) strongly disagree, (2) disagree, (3) somewhat disagree, (4) somewhat agree, (5) agree, (6) strongly agree.

	Yes	**No**	**Not Sure**
135. This organization has a suggestion program.	2	1	1
136. This organization has conducted brainstorming sessions that included lower level organizational members.	2	1	1
137. This organization has used teams to gather information or solve problems.	2	1	1

	Strongly Disagree*				Strongly Agree*	
138. Creative thinking is rewarded in this organization.	1	2	3	4	5	6
139. Taking risks is rewarded in this organization.	1	2	3	4	5	6
140. Managers at all levels have the authority to try a promising new approach.	1	2	3	4	5	6
141. A promising new approach is likely to be approved quickly for a trial.	1	2	3	4	5	6
142. The future strength of this organization is dependent on the continuing growth of its members through appropriate training.	1	2	3	4	5	6

*Legend: (1) strongly disagree, (2) disagree, (3) somewhat disagree, (4) somewhat agree, (5) agree, (6) strongly agree.

143. Circle the response number next to the *one* statement that best represents your organization.

Most nonsupervisory members have direct input in setting goals or expectations for their work.   6

Most nonsupervisory members have indirect input through representatives in setting goals or expectations for their work.   4

Most nonsupervisory members can negotiate with management after they are assigned goals or expectations for their work.   3

Most nonsupervisory members have no input about goals or expectations for their work.   1

144. Circle the response number next to the *one* statement that best represents your organization.

Most organizational members attend mandatory in-house training programs to learn about quality management improvement techniques.   6

Most organizational members attend in-house training programs on a voluntary basis to learn about quality management improvement techniques.   5

Most organizational members attend outside seminars to learn about quality management improvement techniques.   4

Most organizational members review resources (books, tapes) that are available in-house to learn about quality management improvement techniques.   3

None of the above.   1

	Yes	No	Not Sure
In order to tell how well we are doing as an organization, we monitor data about			
145. Our efficiency	2	1	1
146. Our effectiveness	2	1	1
147. Our productivity	2	1	1
148. The quality of our services/products/work	2	1	1
149. The timeliness of our work	2	1	1
150. Our innovativeness	2	1	1
151. The quality of working life for our members	2	1	1
152. Our finances	2	1	1

	Yes	No	Don't Collect Data
The performance data that this organization collects			
153. Are tracked over time	2	1	1
154. Are compared with goals, standards, or objectives	2	1	1
155. Are compared with data from other similar organizations	2	1	1
The performance data that this organization collects			
156. Are evaluated at least quarterly	2	1	1
157. Are used to identify problems/barriers	2	1	1
158. Are evaluated by a team or task force	2	1	1

	Yes	No	Not Sure
159. Are used to identify opportunities for quality improvement	2	1	1
160. Organizational members are informed about how this work unit stands in relation to goals, objectives, or standards.	2	1	1
Top-performing managers at all levels in this organization			
161. Can expect a monetary bonus or award	2	1	1
162. Can expect an award	2	1	1
163. Can expect to be recognized by leaders at the top level	2	1	1
164. Can expect to be told they are doing a great job	2	1	1

	Yes	No	Not Sure
165. Can expect increased responsibility	2	1	1
Top-performing organizational members:			
166. Can expect a monetary bonus or award	2	1	1
167. Can expect an award	2	1	1
168. Can expect to be recognized by leaders at the top level	2	1	1
169. Can expect to be told they are doing a great job	2	1	1
170. Can expect increased responsibility	2	1	1
171. The performance appraisals of managers at all levels include quality improvement criteria.	2	1	1
172. The performance appraisals of organizational members include quality improvement criteria.	2	1	1

Management Tools Assessment

This organization has

	Yes	No	Not Sure
173. Used surveys to assess employees' opinion about the organization's practices or policies	2	1	1
174. Used surveys to gather information about what in the organization needs improving	2	1	1
175. Used surveys to assess the outcomes of its work	2	1	1
176. Used surveys to assess the quality of its work	2	1	1

	Yes	No	Not Sure
177. Used surveys to assess employee opinions about the goals/objectives they are working toward	2	1	1
178. Called groups of individuals together to define or clarify the organization's mission and/or work	2	1	1
179. Called groups of individuals together to define long-term organizational-level goals and/or long-term work unit-level goals	2	1	1
180. Called groups of individuals together to define short-term organizational objectives and/or short-term work unit objectives	2	1	1
181. Called groups of individuals together to identify obstacles to goal/objective accomplishment	2	1	1
182. Called groups of individuals together to define performance measures to track progress toward goal attainment	2	1	1
183. The organization uses statistical process control charts or graphs to track data over time.	2	1	1
184. This organization uses diagrams or flowcharts to highlight potential causes of problems.	2	1	1
185. This organization has evaluated its office and work space design.	2	1	1
186. This organization has a high quality information resource library.	2	1	1
187. This organization has arranged workshops to promote quality management awareness among its members.	2	1	1

	Yes	No	Not Sure
188. This organization has published newsletters containing quality improvement information.	2	1	1
189. This organization has posted information about quality improvement on bulletin boards.	2	1	1
190. This organization has held contests to reward the most improved work units.	2	1	1
191. This organization has attempted to inform and involve everyone in quality improvement.	2	1	1
192. This organization has used team-building techniques to improve group members' relationships.	2	1	1
193. This organization has established improvement teams (groups of individuals who come together to solve quality management-related problems).	2	1	1

Organizational Assessment

	Strongly Disagree*			Strongly Agree*		
194. Work delays are uncommon in this organization.	1	2	3	4	5	6
195. Once a job or project gets started, it's usually finished without undue delay.	1	2	3	4	5	6
196. There is little waste of materials and supplies.	1	2	3	4	5	6

*Legend: (1) strongly disagree, (2) disagree, (3) somewhat disagree, (4) somewhat agree, (5) agree, (6) strongly agree.

	Strongly Disagree*				Strongly Agree*	
197. People make efforts to reuse or salvage excess materials and supplies whenever possible.	1	2	3	4	5	6
198. Tools and/or equipment are maintained and operated at peak efficiency.	1	2	3	4	5	6
199. Our tools and/or equipment rarely require repair.	1	2	3	4	5	6
200. This organization has sufficient personnel to accomplish its mission.	1	2	3	4	5	6
201. The personnel turnover rate is low.	1	2	3	4	5	6
202. Working conditions (noise, heat, light, cleanliness) in this organization are excellent.	1	2	3	4	5	6
203. Work facilities (bathrooms, cafeterias, conference rooms) are excellent.	1	2	3	4	5	6
204. Organizational members are well trained.	1	2	3	4	5	6
205. Organizational members receive the guidance and assistance they need to accomplish their work.	1	2	3	4	5	6
206. This organization's materials and supplies are well accounted for without unexplained losses.	1	2	3	4	5	6
207. This organization's materials and supplies meet quality specifications.	1	2	3	4	5	6

Organizational members rarely need to

208. Shift work priorities in order to get jobs done	1	2	3	4	5	6

*Legend: (1) strongly disagree, (2) disagree, (3) somewhat disagree, (4) somewhat agree, (5) agree, (6) strongly agree.

	Strongly Disagree*			Strongly Agree*		
209. Redo a job or task	1	2	3	4	5	6

The organization's customers

210. Are satisfied with the quality of our work	1	2	3	4	5	6
211. Seldom complain	1	2	3	4	5	6

The organization's customers

212. Are satisfied with the quantity of our work	1	2	3	4	5	6
213. Are satisfied with the timeliness of our work	1	2	3	4	5	6

The organization's customers

214. Find minimal errors in our work	1	2	3	4	5	6
215. Find our work consistent	1	2	3	4	5	6

*Legend: (1) strongly disagree, (2) disagree, (3) somewhat disagree, (4) somewhat agree, (5) agree, (6) strongly agree.

Scoring Self-Assessment

The following scoring worksheets provide a way to evaluate your self-assessment. Transfer the value of your responses to the questions or sets of questions as indicated by the worksheet groupings. Then divide by the number shown on the form. Carry out the division to two decimal points. For example, say you responded 6, 5, 4, 3, 2, and 1 to questions 1 through 6. On the Climate Scoring Worksheet, then, you would write 21 in the blank for "Awareness of strategic challenge," divide 21 by 6 (the value indicated), and enter 3.50 in the blank in your score column.

Following each worksheet, a scoring summary table shows the target score for each category. Transfer your worksheet scores to the corresponding category in the table. In our example, you would write 3.50 in the "Your Score" column next to "Awareness of strategic challenge."

By comparing your scores with the target scores, you can evaluate how you and your organization perceive quality management. If your score is equal to or lower than a target score, you need to improve your approach to quality management in that area. Study the quality management principles and practices described in chapter 7 to discover ways you can significantly improve your quality.

	Climate Scoring Worksheet	**Your Score**
Awareness of strategic challenge	Add response numbers from questions 1–6 and place total in space at right.	____ ÷ 6 = ____
Vision for the future	Add response numbers from questions 7–11 and place total in space at right.	____ ÷ 5 = ____
Innovation	Add response numbers from questions 12–13 and place total in space at right.	____ ÷ 2 = ____
Quality policy/philosophy	Add response numbers from questions 14–18 and place total in space at right.	____ ÷ 5 = ____
Value systems/ethics	Add response numbers from questions 19–21 and place total in space at right.	____ ÷ 3 = ____
Strategic Focus =	Total of scores (questions 1–21)	____ ÷ 21 = ____
Top management involvement	Add response numbers from questions 22–25 and place total in space at right.	____ ÷ 4 = ____
Visible commitment to goals	Add response numbers from questions 26–28 and place total in space at right.	____ ÷ 3 = ____
Role in quality improvement process	Add response numbers from questions 29–31 and place total in space at right.	____ ÷ 3 = ____

Your Score

Concern for improvement	Add response numbers from questions 32–33 and place total in space at right.	_____ ÷ 2 = _____
Systems/structure for quality improvement	Add response numbers from questions 34–35 and place total in space at right.	_____ ÷ 2 = _____
Leadership and Management	Total of scores (questions 22–35)	_____ ÷ 14 = _____
Awareness of quality issues	Add response numbers from questions 36–37 and place total in space at right.	_____ ÷ 2 = _____
Attitudes/ morale	Add response numbers from questions 38–41 and place total in space at right.	_____ ÷ 4 = _____
Cooperation	Add response numbers from questions 42–45 and place total in space at right.	_____ ÷ 4 = _____
Involvement	Add response numbers from questions 46–47 and place total in space at right.	_____ ÷ 2 = _____
Perceptions of work environment	Add response numbers from questions 48–50 and place total in space at right.	_____ ÷ 3 = _____
Social interactions	Add response numbers from questions 51–52 and place total in space at right.	_____ ÷ 2 = _____
Task characteristics	Add response numbers from questions 53–57 and place total in space at right.	_____ ÷ 5 = _____
Consequential constraints	Add response numbers from questions 58–64 and place total in space at right.	_____ ÷ 7 = _____

			Your Score
Work Force	Total of scores (questions 36–64)	_____ ÷ 29 =	_____
Customer orientation	Add response numbers from questions 65–66 and place total in space at right.	_____ ÷ 2 =	_____
Communications	Add response numbers from questions 67–70 and place total in space at right.	_____ ÷ 4 =	_____

Copy the result for each category to the spaces in Tables 6.1, 6.2, 6.3 or 6.4, respectively. If any score is lower than or equal to the target score, it means that some practices typically considered helpful for quality management may be absent from your organization.

Table 6.1.   Summary of climate scores.

Category	Your Score*	Target Score
Awareness of strategic challenge	_____	3.50
Vision for the future	_____	3.50
Innovation	_____	3.50
Quality policy/philosophy	_____	3.50
Value system/ethics	_____	3.50
Top management involvement	_____	3.50
Visible commitment to goals	_____	3.50
Role in quality improvement process	_____	3.50
Concern for improvement	_____	3.50
System/structure for quality improvement	_____	3.50
Awareness of productivity/quality issues	_____	3.50
Attitudes/morale	_____	3.50
Cooperation	_____	3.50

*From the Climate Scoring Worksheet   *(continued)*

Table 6.1.   (continued)

Category	Your Score*	Target Score
Involvement	_____	3.50
Perceptions of work environment	_____	3.50
Social interactions	_____	3.50
Task characteristics	_____	3.50
Consequential constraints	_____	3.50
Customer orientation	_____	3.50
Communications	_____	3.50
Total (average your score by adding the values in this column and dividing by 20)	_____	3.50

*From the Climate Scoring Worksheet

	Process Scoring Worksheet	**Your Score**
Job analysis	Add response numbers from questions 71–77 and place total in space at right.	_____ ÷ 7 = _____
Higher authority	Add response numbers from questions 78–82 and place total in space at right.	_____ ÷ 5 = _____
Quality emphasis	Add response numbers from questions 83–87 and place total in space at right.	_____ ÷ 5 = _____
Top management leadership	Add response numbers from questions 88–96 and place total in space at right.	_____ ÷ 9 = _____
Customer/ service activities	Add response numbers from questions 97–100 and place total in space at right.	_____ ÷ 4 = _____

		Your Score
Define improvement	Add response numbers from questions 101–104 and place total in space at right.	_____ ÷ 4 = _____
Unit goals	Add response numbers from questions 105–108 and place total in space at right.	_____ ÷ 4 = _____
Organization goals	Add response numbers from questions 109–112 and place total in space at right.	_____ ÷ 4 = _____
Quality planning	Add response numbers from questions 113–118 and place total in space at right.	_____ ÷ 6 = _____
Planning strategy	Add response numbers from questions 119–123 and place total in space at right.	_____ ÷ 5 = _____
Organizational streamlining	Add response numbers from questions 124–125 and place total in space at right.	_____ ÷ 2 = _____
Investment/ appropriate technology	Add response numbers from questions 126–128 and place total in space at right.	_____ ÷ 3 = _____
Methods/ process improvement	Add response numbers from questions 129–131 and place total in space at right.	_____ ÷ 3 = _____
New ideas	Add response numbers from questions 132–134 and place total in space at right.	_____ ÷ 3 = _____
People-oriented input	Add response numbers from questions 135–137 and place total in space at right.	_____ ÷ 3 = _____
Track progress	Add response numbers from questions 138–144 and place total in space at right.	_____ ÷ 7 = _____

Your Score

Measurement | Add response numbers ___ ÷ 8 = ___
from questions 145–152 and
place total in space at right.

Feedback | Add response numbers ___ ÷ 3 = ___
from questions 153–155 and
place total in space at right.

Evaluation | Add response numbers ___ ÷ 4 = ___
from questions 156–159 and
place total in space at right.

Results | Place response number ___ = ___
from question 160 in
space at right.

Awards | Add response numbers ___ ÷ 10 = ___
from questions 161–170 and
place total in space at right.

Personnel | Add response numbers ___ ÷ 2 = ___
evaluations | from questions 171–172 and
place total in space at right.

Copy the result for each process category to the space in Table 6.2. After you have placed your scores in the appropriate spaces, please refer to the adjacent column for score interpretation. If your score for any category is lower than or equal to the target score, you may want to review your quality management program.

Table 6.2. Summary of process scores.

Category	Your Score	Target Score
Job analysis	___	1.50
Higher authority	___	1.50
Quality emphasis	___	1.70
Top management leadership	___	1.55

(continued)

Table 6.2. (continued)

Category	Your Score*	Target Score
Customer/service activities	_____	1.60
Define improvement	_____	1.60
Unit goals	_____	3.50
Organization goals	_____	3.50
Quality planning	_____	1.50
Planning strategy	_____	1.50
Organizational streamlining	_____	3.50
Investment/appropriate technology	_____	3.50
Methods/process improvement	_____	3.50
New ideas	_____	3.50
People-oriented input	_____	1.40
Track progress	_____	3.50
Measurement	_____	1.50
Feedback	_____	1.40
Evaluation	_____	1.50
Results	_____	1.00
Awards	_____	1.50
Personnel evaluations	_____	1.50
Total (average your score by adding the values in this column and dividing by 22)	_____	2.12

*From the Process Scoring Worksheet

Management Tools Scoring Worksheet		Your Score
Assessments	Add response numbers from questions 173–177 and place total in space at right.	_____ ÷ 5 = _____

Your Score

Definition of tools	Add response numbers from questions 178–182 and place total in space at right.	＿＿	÷ 5 =	＿＿
Measurement/ process analysis	Add response numbers from questions 183–185 and place total in space at right.	＿＿	÷ 3 =	＿＿
Awareness/ communication	Add response numbers from questions 186–190 and place total in space at right.	＿＿	÷ 5 =	＿＿
Organizational development	Add response numbers from questions 191–193 and place total in space at right.	＿＿	÷ 3 =	＿＿

Copy the result for each management tools category to the space in Table 6.3. After you have placed your scores in the appropriate spaces, please refer to the adjacent column for score interpretation. If your score for any category is lower than or equal to the target score, you may want to review your quality management program.

Table 6.3. Summary of management tools scores.

Category	Your Score*	Target Score
Assessments	＿＿	1.30
Definition of tools	＿＿	1.50
Measurement/process analysis	＿＿	1.50
Awareness/communication	＿＿	1.50
Organizational development	＿＿	1.50
Total (average your score by adding the values in this column and dividing by 5)	＿＿	1.46

*From the Management Tools Scoring Worksheet

Organizational Outcomes Scoring Worksheet   **Your Score**

Work flow/delays	Add response numbers from questions 194–195 and place total in space at right.	_____ ÷ 2 = _____
Waste	Add response numbers from questions 196–197 and place total in space at right.	_____ ÷ 2 = _____
Tools/ equipment	Add response numbers from questions 198–199 and place total in space at right.	_____ ÷ 2 = _____
Staffing	Add response numbers from questions 200–201 and place total in space at right.	_____ ÷ 2 = _____
Facilities	Add response numbers from questions 202–203 and place total in space at right.	_____ ÷ 2 = _____
Training	Add response numbers from questions 204–205 and place total in space at right.	_____ ÷ 2 = _____
Supplies/parts	Add response numbers from questions 206–207 and place total in space at right.	_____ ÷ 2 = _____
Organization/ group structure	Add response numbers from questions 208–209 and place total in space at right.	_____ ÷ 2 = _____
Customer quality survey	Add response numbers from questions 210–211 and place total in space at right.	_____ ÷ 2 = _____
Quantity	Add response numbers from questions 212–213 and place total in space at right.	_____ ÷ 2 = _____

Your Score

Reliability   Add response numbers   _____ ÷ 2 = _____
from questions 214–215 and
place total in space at right.

Copy the result for each organizational outcome category to the space in Table 6.4. After you have placed your scores in the appropriate spaces, please refer to the adjacent column for score interpretation. If your score for any category is lower than or equal to 3.50, you may want to review your quality management approach.

Table 6.4.   Summary of organizational outcomes scores.

Category	Your Score*	Target Score
Work flow/delays	_____	3.50
Waste	_____	3.50
Tools/equipment	_____	3.50
Staffing	_____	3.50
Facilities	_____	3.50
Training	_____	3.50
Supplies/parts	_____	3.50
Organization/group structure	_____	3.50
Customer quality survey	_____	3.50
Quantity	_____	3.50
Reliability	_____	3.50
Total (average your score by adding the values in this column and dividing by 11)	_____	3.50

*From the Organizational Outcomes Scoring Worksheet

Computerized Analysis

This chapter is an edited version of the DoD Quality and Productivity Self-Assessment Guide. If you want more members of your organization to conduct this self-examination so that you can compare your impressions of organizational quality, consider purchasing an automated version of the analysis, available for use on an IBM PC-compatible computer. The software can be obtained from DPPO, Two Skyline Place, Room 1404, 5203 Leesburg Pike, Falls Church, Virginia 22041, 703-756-2346. Contact Lee Wexel for price and availability of the latest version of the software.

Assessment Leads to Action

This chapter has presented an armchair approach to assessment of your organization's perceived level of quality. It has provided a scoring methodology that alerts you to the strengths and weaknesses in your quality management efforts. The total scores are really not important. But your response to each category and the impression you now have about the potential to improve your quality, your service, and your performance are very important.

In chapter 7, the key quality management principles and practices that can significantly improve your organization's quality are briefly described.

7 How to Significantly Improve Your Quality

A journey of a thousand miles must begin with a single step.

> *The Way of Lao Tzu*

Adopt a Quality Management Strategy

Quality management means that you are meeting your internal and external customer requirements by doing the right things right the first time. To provide high-quality products and services, management must have an obsession with quality and perfection that pervades all facets of the organization. The driving force behind quality management is customer satisfaction.

Quality management begins with a strategic decision, a decision that must be made and fully supported by your top management. That decision, simply put, is the decision to perform as a quality organization. Quality management concentrates on quality performance—in every facet of your organization—as the primary strategy to achieve and maintain better government. It requires taking a systematic view of your organization and looking at how each part relates to the whole process. In addition, it demands continuous improvement as a way of life.

The quality management methodology is based on four concepts. These concepts state simply that an organization must have (1) quality management systems; (2) quality products, services, and technology; (3) quality people; and (4) a combined focus of all management, products, and people on customer satisfaction.

Quality management is the integration and synergy of quality management initiatives developed by Crosby, Deming, Juran, Ishikawa, and Camp. The concepts, principles, and practices developed by these people provide a point of departure for your organization's specific needs.

Quality Management Activities

Getting started with improvement would be easy if we didn't have so much work to do! But we have so much work to do precisely because we have not recognized the importance of quality management and the benefits of continuously improving every system and process. We must get our systems under control and eliminate the sources of unnecessary and unproductive work.

Getting started and sustaining the early quality improvement initiative are the most difficult tasks in quality management. They require us to make time in our already tight schedules to do something that we perceive to be an additional task. We must modify many of our long-held notions about what good management is all about in exchange for the promise of improvement. It is sometimes surprising that anyone is willing to take these first steps; however, many have already done so and are being richly rewarded. By ultimately gaining real control over our work processes instead of permitting them to control us, we will make large gains.

Those who have blazed the trail toward continuous improvement have left us a legacy of lessons learned. Many have had false starts, traveled down dead-end roads, and had to start over. If we have learned one consistent lesson from those who have led this effort, it is that there is no universal strategy for success. The road to continuous improvement must be appropriately tailored, optimized, and personal. A general set of actions, however, characterizes most successful efforts. Those actions are presented here as a suggested general strategy for starting your quality management journey.

While this section speaks directly to you, many actions apply equally to your organization as a whole. The elements of this general strategy are listed somewhat in order of recommended implementation. The experience of many organizations is that focused application of specific improvement techniques and tools promotes continuous improvement. In this chapter, the elements presented first provide a foundation that is essential to successful process improvement efforts and to creating a culture of continuous improvement that will have long-term success and ultimately be self-sustaining. Some elements are necessary only during the initial phases, but most should become routine.

The basic, core elements of quality management fall into 19 areas of activity: customer satisfaction-driven quality; leadership demonstration; awareness building; continuous improvement; improved communication; employee participation and development; continuous presentation of your vision; management by fact; faster response; long-range outlook; demonstrated success; teamwork development; partnership development; design quality; training; building of trust and respect; adoption of quality management as a way of life; application of quality process to suppliers; responsibility. Each area encompasses a number of actions.

Customer Satisfaction-Driven Quality

Quality is judged by the customer. All product and service attributes that contribute value to the customer and lead to customer satisfaction and preference must be the foundation for an organization's quality management system. A customer's perception of value, satisfaction, and preference may be influenced by many factors in the customer's overall service experiences. These factors include the organization's relationship with customers and whether that relationship helps build trust, confidence, and loyalty. This concept of quality management includes the service and product attributes that not only meet basic customer requirements but also enhance those attributes and differentiate them from competing offerings. Such enhancement and differentiation may be based upon new offerings, combinations of product and service offerings, rapid response, or special relationships.

Customer-driven quality management is thus a strategic concept. It is directed toward customer retention. It demands constant sensitivity to emerging customer and market requirements, and measurement of the factors that drive customer satisfaction and retention. It also demands awareness of developments in technology, and rapid and flexible response to customer requirements.

Such requirements extend well beyond merely reducing defects and errors, meeting specifications, and reducing complaints. Nevertheless, defect and error reduction and elimination of causes of dissatisfaction contribute significantly to the customers' view of quality and are thus also important parts of customer-driven quality. In addition, the organization's success in recovering from defects and errors (making things right for the customer) is crucial to building customer relationships and to customer retention.

Leadership Demonstration

Quality management depends on people more than anything else, and people lead or are led; they are not managed. In other words, quality management depends on effective leadership, and you must provide that leadership. By taking the initiative, providing an example, and showing the way, you can lead your subordinates and inspire your peers to follow your example. As the noted management consultant Peter Drucker said, "You need a critical mass of 30 percent, then the rest of your organization will follow their lead." Top leadership is essential, but quality management leaders are needed at all organizational levels. Effective leadership does not necessarily depend on your place in the organization but rather on your enthusiasm and your visible commitment to the process of continuous improvement.

Your organization's senior leaders must create a customer orientation, clear and visible quality management values, and high expectations. Reinforcement of the values and expectations requires substantial personal commitment and involvement from management. Moreover, the leaders' basic values and commitment need to include areas of public responsibility and citizenship. Further, the leaders must take part in the creation of strategies, systems, and methods for achieving excellence. These systems and methods need to guide all activities and decisions of the organization.

The senior leaders must commit to the growth and development of the entire work force and should encourage participation and creativity by all employees. Through their regular, personal involvement in visible activities, such as planning, communications, review of the organization's quality management performance, and recognition of employees for quality management achievement, the senior leaders serve as role models reinforcing the values and encouraging leadership at all levels.

Awareness Building

Building awareness—an understanding of what quality management is and why it is important to you and your organization—is one of the first and perhaps most important steps in implementing quality management. Every person in the organization must become aware of the need to improve, of the promise offered by quality management, of the various methodologies, and of the tools and techniques available for improvement efforts. Awareness is the key that opens the door to quality management's potential.

Continuous Improvement

Continuous process improvement is the basis of quality management. Perfection is an ultimate, unattainable goal, but this ideal provides the vision for continuous improvement efforts. To begin, you must view everything your organization does in terms of interrelated processes. As you do, process improvement should become your organization's way of life because goals and objectives are realized through process improvement. Your own focus should be to improve all the processes you own and remove all those barriers under your control that hinder others from improving their own processes. The only true measure of your performance over time is the degree of process improvement you effect.

Process standardization is a means of defining a process and ensuring that everyone understands and employs it in a consistent manner. It is difficult to improve something that is not well defined. Process standards communicate the current, best-known way of performing a process and ensure consistent process performance by a variety of individuals. With a standard, people have a way to know that they are doing their jobs correctly, and you have a means of assessing their performance objectively. Process standards provide the baseline from which to continuously improve the process. The people doing the work should maintain and update standards as they improve their processes so that the standards always reflect the current, best-known means of doing the work.

Achieving the highest levels of quality management requires a well-defined and well-executed approach to continuous improvement. The term *continuous improvement* refers to both incremental and breakthrough improvement. A focus on improvement needs to be part of all operations and of all work unit activities of an organization.

You can make improvements and enhance value to your customer in several ways: (1) by introducing new and improved services and products; (2) by reducing errors, defects, and waste; (3) by improving responsiveness and cycle time performance; (4) by improving productivity and effectiveness in the use of all resources; and (5) by improving the organization's performance and leadership position in fulfilling its public responsibilities and serving as a role model in corporate citizenship. Thus, improvement is driven not only by the objective to provide better service and product quality, but also by the need to be responsive and efficient. Both confer additional advantages. To meet all these objectives, the process of continuous improvement must contain regular cycles of planning, execution, and evaluation. This requires a basis—preferably a quantitative basis—for assessing progress and for deriving information for future cycles of improvement. Such information should provide direct links between desired performance and internal operations.

Improved Communication

As you build awareness throughout your organization, begin to establish lines of communication both horizontally and vertically. Honest, open communication is probably the single most important factor in successfully creating a quality management environment. It will take time, but it can lead to trust and mutual respect, and it can sometimes be the only thing that keeps the effort alive. If people keep talking to one another, they can work through problems, overcome barriers, and find encouragement and support from others involved in quality management efforts.

Employee Participation and Development

An organization's success in meeting its quality and performance objectives depends increasingly on work force quality and involvement. The close link between employee satisfaction and customer satisfaction creates a "shared fate" relationship between organizations and employees. For this reason, employee-satisfaction measurement provides an important indicator of the organization's efforts to improve customer satisfaction and operating performance.

Improving organizational performance requires improvements at all levels of an organization. This, in turn, depends upon the skills and dedication of the entire work force. Thus, organizations need to invest in the development of the work force and to seek new avenues to involve employees in problem solving and decision making. Factors that bear upon the safety, health, well-being, and morale of employees need to be part of the organization's continuous improvement objectives. Increasingly, training and participation need to be tailored to a more diverse work force and to more flexible work organizations.

Continuous Presentation of Vision

Constancy of purpose establishes a common direction for all organizational elements and ensures that efforts at all levels contribute to achieving broad objectives relevant to the entire organization. Communicating your vision of the organization's goals and objectives throughout the organization is essential to focusing improvement efforts for the common benefit. Your behavior and attitudes must reinforce this constancy of purpose, and you must be conscious of the unspoken signals you send your subordinates.

Management by Fact

To pursue quality and achieve operational performance goals, an organization must have reliable information, data, and analysis. Facts and data needed for quality improvement and quality assessment concern many subjects including customers, service and product performance, operations, markets, competition, supplier performance, employees, and costs and finances. The next step, analysis, refers to the process of extracting larger meaning from data to support evaluation and decision making at various levels within the organization. Such analysis may entail using data to reveal information—such as trends, projections, and cause and effect—that might not be evident without analysis. Facts, data, and analysis support a variety of organization purposes, such as planning, reviewing organizational performance, improving operations, and comparing organizational performance with that of competitors or with "best practices" benchmarks.

A major consideration relating to use of data and analysis to improve performance involves the creation and use of *performance indicators*.

Performance indicators are measurable characteristics of products, services, processes, and operations the organization uses to evaluate and improve performance and to track progress. The indicators should be selected to best represent the factors that lead to improved customer satisfaction and operational performance. A system of indicators tied to customer and/or organizational performance requirements represents a clear and objective basis for aligning all activities of the organization toward common goals. Through the analysis of data obtained in the tracking processes, the indicators themselves may be evaluated and changed. For example, indicators selected to measure product and service quality may be judged by how well improvement in quality correlates with improvement in customer satisfaction.

Faster Response

Success in competitive markets increasingly demands ever-shorter cycles for new or improved product and service introduction. Also, faster and more flexible response to customers is now a more critical requirement of management. Major improvements in response time often require work organizations, work processes, and work paths to be simplified and shortened. To accomplish such improvement, more attention should be given to measuring time performance. This can be done by making response time a key indicator for work unit improvement processes. Other important benefits are derived from this focus as well: response time improvements often drive simultaneous improvements in organization, quality, and productivity. Therefore, it is beneficial to consider response time, quality, and productivity objectives together.

Long-Range Outlook

Achieving quality leadership requires organizations to have a strong future orientation and a willingness to make long-term commitments to customers, employees, suppliers, and the community. Thus, during planning activities, employees need to determine or anticipate many types of changes, including those that may affect customers' expectations of products and services, technological developments, changing customer segments, evolving regulatory requirements, and community/societal expectations. Plans, strategies, and resource allocations need to reflect these commitments and changes. A major part of the long-term commitment relates to the development of employees and suppliers, and to fulfilling public responsibilities and serving as a citizenship role model.

Demonstrated Success

The success or failure of your initial quality efforts and projects can greatly affect how easily you can get your organization to adopt quality management ideas. Thus, it pays to choose these early efforts carefully, looking for opportunities that (1) have a good chance of success; (2) are visible throughout the organization, and preferably, to important external customers; and (3) can significantly improve the lives of workers and managers alike. The trick is to find something that is neither so large that you are doomed to failure nor so small that no one will notice if improvements are made.

Teamwork Development

Teamwork is the engine that drives many improvement efforts. Creating teams allows you to apply diverse skills and experience to your processes and problem solving. Teams provide an underlying basis of experience and history for your improvement effort and are a vehicle through which you allow all individuals to participate in that effort. Not only must individuals cooperate within teams, the teams must cooperate throughout the organization. An atmosphere of teamwork should permeate your organization, affecting not only formal team efforts but also each individual's interaction in the organization.

Often, encouraging teamwork involves teaching people who already work together to consciously act as a team. These natural work groups exist as permanent teams whose objective is the continuous improvement of the processes they own.

Partnership Development

Organizations should seek to build internal and external partnerships to better accomplish their overall goals. Internal partnerships might include those that promote labor-management cooperation, such as agreements with unions. Agreements may also initiate employee development, cross training, or new work organizations, such as high-performance work teams.

Examples of external partnerships include those with customers, suppliers, technology transfer, and educational organizations. An increasingly important kind of external partnership is the strategic partnership, consortium, or alliance. Such a partnership might offer an organization entry into new products or services.

Design Quality

Quality systems should place strong emphasis on design quality. Problem and waste prevention can be achieved through building quality into products and services and into the processes through which they are produced. In general, costs of preventing problems at the design stage are much lower than costs of correcting problems that occur *downstream*. Design quality includes the creation of fault-tolerant (robust) processes and products.

A major issue in the competitive environment is the design-to-introduction (product generation) cycle time. Meeting the demands of rapidly changing markets requires that companies carry out stage-to-stage coordination of functions and activities from basic research to commercialization in order to provide services or products cheaper, better, and faster.

Consistent with the theme of design quality and problem prevention, continuous improvement and corrective action need to emphasize interventions *upstream*—at early stages in the processes. This approach yields the maximum overall benefits of improvements and corrections. Such upstream intervention also needs to take into account your suppliers.

Training

If you expect to implement quality management yourself and expect your subordinates to follow suit, you must ensure that adequate time and training resources are available to support your effort. Quality management does not depend on additional people or money; rather, it relies on the availability of time for individuals and groups to pursue improvement efforts and on the availability of training and education to develop needed skills and experience in quality management improvement tools and techniques. You must make those time and training resources available for yourself and your people; doing so is one way for you to demonstrate your commitment to the improvement effort.

While awareness is the way you get your quality management effort moving, education and training help accelerate the effort dramatically. Provided in the right place at the right time, education and training allow you to develop needed skills both in yourself and throughout the organization. With training, employees develop experience in the techniques necessary to implement quality management. That experience is the first step to making quality management a part of your day-to-day work life. And, of course, technical training and education are essential to improving each employee's job skills. Education and training must be comprehensive, intensive, and unending.

Building of Trust and Respect

Employees who trust their managers and who are trusted and respected in turn can provide the edge that organizations need to provide superior services or products. Workers are in a position to have the best, most up-to-date knowledge about how well processes are working, what problems have arisen, and how things could be better. If their opinions are respected, they will share their knowledge and creativity with management—the only way to ensure continuous improvement.

Trust and respect are essential for individual participation. Without such elements in an atmosphere, people will not take actions or make recommendations they perceive to be risky. Simply put, quality management is a process that depends on every person being unafraid to take chances and unworried about risking self-esteem. You must be open and honest with your people and establish reliable and accessible channels of communication that are available to everyone in the organization. If people broach ideas, they should be praised; if they identify problems in the process or system, they should be thanked; when they contribute, they should be recognized; when they fail, they should be supported; and when they succeed, they should be rewarded. As their leader, you are responsible for creating an atmosphere of trust and support, and you are responsible for maintaining each individual's sense of self-worth and self-esteem.

Adoption of Quality Management as a Way of Life

By making continuous improvement a part of your daily routine, you will integrate it into all aspects of your work. Continuous improvement only approaches maturity when it is applied routinely to all your organization's work. Routine application entails using the process-improvement cycle in all areas, collecting data and using those data to assess process suitability, removing roadblocks to your improvement efforts and those of others, and continuously improving your knowledge and expertise in process improvement. Ideally, continuous improvement should be your normal approach to doing your work; it must become your way of life.

Application of Quality Process to Suppliers

Your organization's ability to improve its processes depends in part on the materials and services that enter those processes. To the extent that you procure materials and services from other organizations, then, your continuous improvement effort depends on those suppliers. Expanding your improvement culture to all your suppliers will help ensure that the quality of your process inputs is sufficient to meet your own improvement objectives. You can expand your culture of continuous improvement by working more closely with your suppliers, helping them get their own improvement efforts underway, building mutual trust and respect, and generally becoming a better customer yourself.

Responsibility

An organization's quality management system objectives should address responsibility and citizenship. *Responsibility* refers to an organization's business ethics and its protection of public health, public safety, and the environment.

Health, safety, and environmental considerations need to take into account the organization's operations as well as the life cycles of its products and services. Organizations need to address factors such as waste reduction at its source. Quality management planning related to public health, safety, and environment should anticipate adverse impacts that may arise in a facility's management, production, distribution, transportation, and use and disposal of products. Plans should seek avenues to avoid problems, to provide forthright organizational response if problems occur, and to make available information needed to maintain public awareness, safety, trust, and confidence. Including public responsibility areas within a quality management system means not only meeting all local, state, and federal legal and regulatory requirements, but also treating these and related requirements as areas for continuous improvement beyond mere compliance.

Citizenship refers to leadership and support—within reasonable limits of an organization's resources—of publicly important purposes, including the above-mentioned areas of corporate responsibility. Such purposes might also include education, resource conservation, community services, improvement of industry and business practices, and the sharing of nonproprietary quality-related information.

Improve Your Quality

This chapter has described the concepts and principles involved in implementing the quality management methodology. By tailoring these concepts and principles to your unique operation, you can significantly improve your quality, increase productivity, and provide better service to your customers.

8   Quality Management Planning

Every great president in our history had a policy of his own, which eventually won the people's support.

> Harry S Truman
> *Memoirs—Years of Trial and Hope*

You Need a Plan

Governmental organizations all too often have jumped to implement new, hot, buzzword solutions to their problems. As a result, they have tended to spend too little time, thought, and energy on developing their organizations' policy and planning needs to implement their actions. The Japanese, in contrast, spend half their effort building consensus, developing understanding of their customers' needs, reviewing options for implementation, and only then thinking through all the steps needed to implement a change or process. In government, we tend to spend less than one-third of our efforts on planning, then jump into the implementation phase and continue to fight fires to resolve the errors and inconsistencies that with proper planning we could have avoided. The concept of doing things right the first time depends on realistic, thorough planning and management leadership.

This chapter, on planning, and chapter 9, on implementation of your quality management effort, are one. Described in these two chapters are a total of 17 planning and implementation steps for your review, modification, and adoption in your own unique quality management program.

This chapter describes the 10 planning steps (see Figure 8.1) needed to help you identify your policy and plans for implementing a quality management program in your organization.

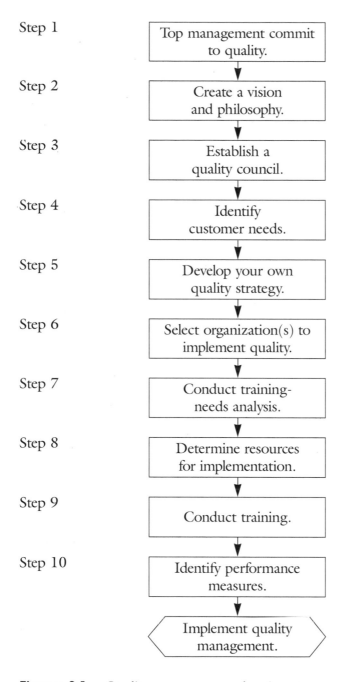

Figure 8.1. Quality management planning steps.

Step 1: Commit to Quality

Simply put, quality management is a new way for organizations to do business. Since the methods by which an organization conducts its business are clearly the prerogative of top management, top management must be convinced of the merits of quality management. Top management's recognition of the need for improvement and its willingness to learn more is the first step toward implementation.

I cannot overstate the importance of the role of top management. Leadership is essential during every phase in the development of your organization's quality management program, and it is particularly vital at the initial stages of planning. In fact, indifference and lack of involvement by top management are frequently cited as the principal reasons for the failure of quality management improvement efforts.

To be successfully implemented, quality management requires not only the vision, planning, and active involvement of top management, it also requires their practical support through provision of necessary resources—time, money, and personnel. Delegation and rhetoric are insufficient.

John A. Betti, former Ford Motor Company executive and former under secretary of defense for acquisition, said that "commitment to quality must start at the top. But as we at Ford learned, commitment in itself is not enough. Along with commitment must be dedication and involvement. Actions not words produce results."

To obtain top management's commitment you need to educate senior managers regarding how government can be enhanced by quality management. Further, you need to encourage them to learn the basic philosophy, principles, and practices (chapter 1, 2, and 3) involved in making your organization's policy one that focuses on quality management.

The bottom line is that top management must enthusiastically participate in changing your organization's culture. Without top management's active participation as the champions of quality management your organization will not obtain the full scope of benefits possible. Table 8.1 identifies some of the culture changes that your top management needs to understand and address to achieve improved quality.

Table 8.1.   Examples of quality management cultural changes.

Category	Previous state	New culture
Mission	Maximum return on investment (ROI)/management by objectives (MBO)	Ethical behavior and customer satisfaction; climate for continuous improvement; ROI a performance measure
Customer requirements	Incomplete or ambiguous understanding of customer requirements	Use of a systematic approach to seek out, understand, and satisfy both internal and external customer requirements
Suppliers	Unidirectional relationship	Partnership
Objectives	Orientation to short-term objectives and actions with limited long-term perspective	Deliberate balance of long-term goals with successive short-term objectives
Improvement	Acceptance of process variability and subsequent corrective action assigning blame as the norm	Understanding and continually improving the process
Problem solving	Unstructured individualistic problem solving and decision making	Predominantly participatory and interdisciplinary problem solving and decision making based on substantive data
Jobs and people	Functional, narrow scope; management controlled	Management and employee involvement; work teams; integrated functions
Management style	Management style with uncertain objectives, which instills fear of failure	Open style with clear and consistent objectives, which encourages group-derived continuous improvement
Role of manager	Plan, organize, assign, control, and enforce	Communicate, consult, delegate, coach, mentor, remove barriers, and establish trust
Rewards and recognition	Pay by job; few team incentives	Individual and group recognition and rewards, negotiated criteria
Measurement	Orientation toward data gathering for problem identification	Data used to understand and continuously improve processes

Source: Department of Defense.

Step 2: Create a Vision and Philosophy

A key step in the quality management process is the creation of a common understanding among top managers about what they want the organization to look like in the future and what principles will guide the actions they take to achieve the desired future. These agreements will become the basis for formal statements of the organization's vision and values.

The vision is a clear, positive, forceful statement of what the organization wants to be in five, even 10 years. It is expressed in simple, specific terms. The vision allows the organization to stretch and aim for a higher goal. The vision must be powerful enough to excite people and show them the way things can be. A well-crafted vision statement supported by action can be a powerful tool for focusing the organization toward a common goal.

Whatever form the vision and guiding principles take, they must be communicated throughout the organization frequently and with conviction. The timing and method of communication provide an opportunity for creativity by top management. Moreover, the vision must be followed soon by a concrete plan of action so that employees do not dismiss the vision as a hollow slogan.

Step 3: Establish a Quality Council

Developing an organizational structure that will institute, sustain, and facilitate expansion of your quality management improvement effort is an essential element for success. The structure is the vehicle for focusing the energy and resources of the organization toward one common goal—continuous improvement of the products and services it provides to your customer. Successful organizations tailor their structure so that it maximizes strong points and accommodates their unique mission, culture, and approach for improving quality. This tailoring accounts for some of the differences in the way organizational charts are drawn and for variations in the nomenclature used to describe the quality management organization. In spite of these differences, several common practices emerge that merit examination.

Virtually every organization that has successfully introduced the quality management approach has formed a quality council of top managers during the early stages of implementation. This team is also sometimes called the executive steering committee (ESC), executive steering group (ESG), or executive quality council (EQC).

By establishing a quality council, top management provides identity, structure, and legitimacy to the quality management improvement effort. It is the first concrete indication that top management has recognized the need to improve and has begun to change the way the organization conducts business. The direction this change will take becomes clear when the quality council publishes its vision, guiding principles, and mission statement.

The quality council is chaired by the organization head or deputy and members include the top management team. The quality council is responsible for launching, coordinating, and overseeing the quality management improvement effort.

An example of one organization's quality management structure comes from the Defense Contract Management District Northeast in Boston. As part of its Quality Improvement Prototype Award application, DCMDN presented a description of its unique "Structure for Success," as depicted in Figure 8.2.

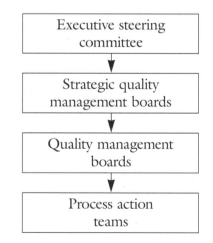

Source: Defense Contract Management District Northeast, Boston, Quality Improvement Prototype Award Application, 1993.

Figure 8.2. Defense Contract Management District Northeast's "Structure for Success."

In order to implement its strategy, a "Structure for Success" was established which maximizes employee involvement at all levels. The executive steering committee (ESC), at the top of the structure, provides leadership and direction for the organization. At the next level, four strategic quality management boards (SQMB) work on the organization's targets. To ensure communication between these two groups, members of the ESC act as sponsors and linchpins on each QMB. Below the QMBs are the process action team (PATs), designated by the QMS, to carry out one task. When the task is completed, the PAT is disbanded. Members from each QMB and QMB act as sponsors and linchpins for the PATs in the same manner as the ESC members. Because every team is composed of employees from different levels and different departments, the "Structure for Success" promotes cooperation across departments. This structure has helped DCMDN change from a bureaucratic organization to a quality management organization interested in the views and opinions of its employees.

Quality councils also can be used to link your quality management organization together. Vertical linkage is accomplished by having a member of a top-level quality council serve as chairperson of a lower-level (second-tier) council. A member of that council, in turn, chairs a lower-level (third-tier) council or leads a subordinate-level team. Horizontal linkage is accomplished by having members of different functional departments (for example, personnel, administration, service, finance) serve together on cross-functional teams. These teams are sometimes called total quality management boards. This quality management council structure offers a number of benefits to your organization.

- It helps the organization stay focused on pursuing the same goals rather than on having functional departments working at cross purposes.

- It fosters better teamwork and less internal competition.

- It improves communication throughout the organization and better understanding of how all the pieces fit together.

- It improves the ability to replicate ideas and standardize solutions that have applicability to processes in other departments of the organization.

Step 4: Identify Customer Needs

Quality means that your organization is meeting your customers' expectations. *Customers* can be co-workers (internal customers) or end users (external customers) of your services or products. *Expectations* are your customers needs and wants. Meeting customer expectations through application of quality management principles is the key to your productive future.

You can use the customer-supplier model described in chapter 10 to determine what your customers want, need, or expect. Only through interaction between the supplier (you) and the customer can you answer these questions.

The customer-supplier model was designed to help you analyze your customers' needs. It involves four key steps.

- Define your process or task.

- Define your value-added contribution to that process.

- Define your customer's expectations—that is, negotiate specific requirements and define appropriate feedback measurements.

- Communicate with your supplier and negotiate your requirements and feedback mechanisms just as you did with your customer.

To define requirements and feedback, consider the following points.

- Requirements are the most critical characteristics of your output, as defined by your customer.

- Feedback from your customer communicates the degree to which your output conforms to the requirements negotiated with your customer.

Taking these simple steps will significantly improve the quality of your work as it is defined by the most important person in the process: your customer.

Step 5: Develop Your Own Unique Quality Management Strategy

There is no *one* right way to implement quality management successfully in your organization; no guaranteed recipe for success. The process proposed in this book is a synthesis of approaches used successfully by federal, state, and local government and service businesses. It is offered only as a guide in developing strategies and associated plans to carry out these strategies. The intent of a flexible approach is to capitalize on an organization's strong points and allow energy to be focused on key improvement opportunities.

Because the missions, cultures, and management styles of organizations vary so greatly, it would be inadvisable to attempt to develop one *ideal* plan or organizational structure for implementing quality management. Furthermore, it would be useless to graft the experience of one organization wholesale onto another, without tailoring it to meet the unique needs of that second organization.

The best plans are those that result in action—action that improves the processes of the organization and results in better services and products for the customer. A simple plan that generates action and gets results is better than an elaborate plan that collects dust. Some initial quality management strategic actions might include the following:

- Create a team to review the quality management concept and define a unique strategy for your organization.
- Conduct customer surveys and identify benchmarks to be reflected in quality indicators.
- Create quality teams to address specific operating problems.
- Define your own unique quality management problem-solving process.
- Define your own quality management improvement plan.

It is a good idea, too, for your organization to begin the process of identifying customers, their requirements, and quality indicators for services or products. Such activities might occur in the organizational components where quality management will be implemented initially, or on a more wide-scale basis in anticipation of future quality management implementation.

Step 6: Select Organization(s) to Implement Quality Management

At the outset of a quality improvement effort, most organizations implement quality management either organizationwide or with one or more pilots. It is also possible to tailor a combination of the two approaches to fit particular circumstances. In any case, each organization must make the decision after realistically assessing a number of factors including the following:

- The size and complexity of the organization
- The ability of the organization to change
- The resources (time, money, and people) that can be allocated to introduce and sustain the effort
- The level and intensity of support for quality management throughout the organization

Implementing quality management on a broad scale across a large organization is a major undertaking. It requires significant allocations of time, money, and people, and for most organizations, requires substantive operational and cultural changes. The larger the organization, the more massive the change.

Some advantages to broad-scale implementation are as follows:

- It promotes consistent implementation. Each organizational element uses the same quality management philosophy, language, and training and is guided by the same vision and core principles.
- It demonstrates strong commitment at the very top level of the organization. This can facilitate the removal of barriers *between* organizations.
- The quality management organizational structure can be cascaded throughout an organization, providing linkage between the corporate headquarters and operating units for improved communications.
- It provides for economies of scale (such as when procuring consultant services or developing in-house training support). For example, a large training contract is generally less expensive per person than a series of smaller contracts.
- It allows the organization to capitalize on its staff offices to support implementation. For example, statistical specialists located at the management level can be used to provide technical assistance to operating units.

You are encouraged to study closely your peers' efforts before undertaking a similar venture.

Some organizations have found the following advantages to starting pilot efforts rather than total organization adoption.

- Initial expenditures of resources are less.

- Development of new produces or services allows organization to start from "greenfield" and create new quality culture from the start.

- Resistance to change is minimized by targeting locations where local champions reside. Alternatively, the effort can be planned for success by targeting locations that have demonstrated adaptability to change by participating successfully in previous pilot efforts.

- Early successes can be used to galvanize support in other parts of the organization. Skeptics can be converted by seeing that the pilot effort can work in their organization.

- Early failures can be turned into lessons learned, without major disruptions throughout the parent organization.

- The pilot effort can be used as a model for broad-scale implementation.

- Pilot efforts are consistent with the Plan-Do-Check-Act (PDCA) approach to improvement (see chapter 5).

Step 7: Conduct Training-Needs Analysis

Chapter 6 provides a self-assessment methodology that encourages the analysis of your organization's quality status. This self-assessment provides a baseline analysis that can be used to identify when and where you need additional quality training.

Once you have progressed to using the appropriate quality award criteria (chapter 4) either through in-depth self-assessment or application for a quality award, the ongoing learning about your organization's needs will also be an extremely valuable tool in improving your training.

Step 8: Determine Resources for Implementation

Your quality management plan must disclose how the effort will be funded, where the required time will come from, how it is to be accounted for, who will provide what personnel, and what facilities will be used for quality management. Obviously, these resource decisions must be coordinated with all those affected by the decisions. This part of the plan may be the hardest to develop because quality management will now be competing with other requirements for organizational resources. One must keep in mind that quality management is to become a way of life in the organization—in fact, the new way of managing. In reality, quality management is not competing for mission resources because it will be an integral part of the future corporate mission. This part of the plan may be the first big test of management's commitment to quality management. Thus, milestones for providing the identified resources should also be included in the plan.

Step 9: Conduct Training

Training is essential to the success of your quality management initiative. Thus, during the early stages of implementing your quality management effort, attention should be given to developing a detailed plan for training.

In addition to providing training on specific quality management principles and practices such as statistical quality control, continuous process improvement, benchmarking, use of data, and process analysis, most organizations will also need to cover such related areas as participatory management, group dynamics, and team development. The ideal training program will target the specific needs of each group—top management, middle managers, supervisors, and other employees in various team groups—and will deliver training "just in time," meaning only as it is needed for smooth transition to the next step in your quality management program.

All employees must better understand their jobs and their roles in the organization and how their jobs will change. Such understanding goes beyond the instruction given in manuals or job descriptions. Employees need to know where their work fits into the larger context:

how their work is influenced by workers who precede them and how their work influences workers who follow.

The organization's training plan should be an outgrowth of your unique quality management implementation strategy and should be directed to the organizational units or projects where top management has focused the implementation effort in the first year. To prevent surprises and delays in implementation, the training plan must include reasonably accurate estimates of the schedule and required resources.

Step 10: Identify Performance Measures

Earlier, we discussed measuring the success of your quality improvement efforts operationally—in terms of your customers' perceptions of you, your employees' satisfaction, and everyone's productivity. These techniques measure the success of your organization. However, these key performance indicators are also critical to measuring the success of all quality management activities. Thus, the objective of every quality management program must be to identify performance measures for your organization, and then continue to improve on these key measures of success. It is also important, though, to measure the success of the quality management process itself, and of the progress each organization makes in implementing its quality management improvement plan.

Document Your Quality Plan

Write down your plan for quality management adoption in your organization. Moreover, create a living plan that reflects the continuous improvement of your operations and quality management efforts. Make this plan available to your managers and personnel to assure that your goals and approach are communicated throughout your organization. Chapter 9, "Implementation of Quality Management," describes the process for documenting quality management in your organization.

Sell Your Plan

Tom Peters and Robert Waterman, Jr., writing *In Search of Excellence*, stressed the need for leadership in improving your quality. They describe the fired-up quality management champion this way: "Not a blue-sky dreamer, nor an intellectual giant. The champion might even be an idea thief. But, above all, he's the pragmatic one who grabs onto someone else's theoretical construct if necessary and bullheadedly pushes it to fruition. . . . Champions are pioneers, and pioneers get shot at. The organizations that get the most from champions, therefore, are those that have rich support networks so their pioneers will flourish. This point is so important it's hard to overstress. No support system, no champions. No champions, no innovations."

Quality management champions can sell their program by

- Visibly supporting the company's quality management strategy
- Insisting on the team approach
- Measuring success by customer satisfaction
- Building feedback loops within the organization and to suppliers and customers
- Meeting the organization's goals
- Walking the talk—continuously

The implementation of quality management is just beginning in federal and state governments. Champions of quality management have the opportunity to introduce benefits that will create a fundamentally different approach to "government as usual."

9 Implementation of Quality Management

Practice is the best of all instructors.

Publilus Syrus
Maxim 439

The Seven Critical Implementation Steps

This chapter delineates the critical steps for implementing a quality management program in your organization (see Figure 9.1). To begin the process, top-level management must make the decision as shown in step 11, to change its operations by implementing their quality management plan.

In step 12, you need to examine how your services and/or products compare with those of your peers. The discussion here of step 12 describes the Xerox Corporation's approach to benchmarking, which your organization could use as a model to determine where change is needed. As described in step 13, you must embed the continuous improvement concepts throughout your organization. This will represent a major change in how your organization operates in the 1990s and beyond. Step 14 describes the need to monitor and evaluate your progress in improving your quality performance. After you monitor, of course, you can tell your supervisors of your success, but more important, let your people know how they have contributed to the improvement operation of your organization (step 15). Recognize their success. As you begin to demonstrate success and convince the doubters, you must also continue to learn from feedback. In other words, you must revise or adjust your quality management program to meet the changing needs of your organization, as noted in step 16. And, finally, you must continue to improve (step 17).

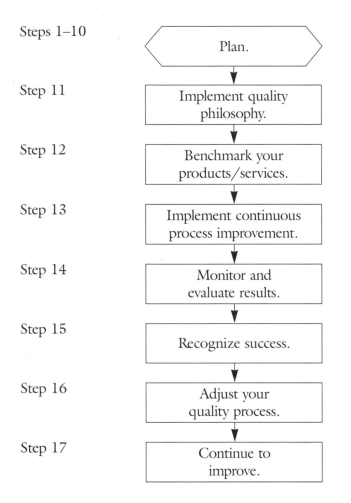

Figure 9.1.   Quality management implementation steps.

Step 11: Implement a Quality Management Philosophy

To help you implement a quality management philosophy in your organization, apply an approach based on the plan-do-check-act (PDCA) cycle to each area of your quality improvement plan. AT&T's systematic approach to identifying quality improvement opportunities and resolving an organization's process problems is shown in Figure 9.2.

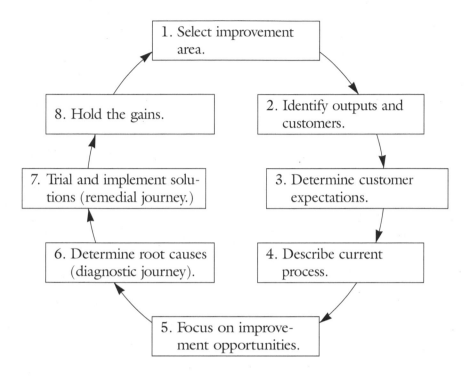

Source: AT&T, *Quality Improvement Process Guidebook* (Baskin Ridge, N.J.: AT&T, 1988), p. 29.

Figure 9.2. A quality management improvement cycle.

The quality management improvement cycle, whether AT&T's or the one you create for your organization, offers a common language and a problem-solving methodology for use throughout your organization. First, it facilitates communication about work underway among groups with similar interests. Second, it supports the basic quality value of managing by fact, by offering individuals and teams a disciplined problem-solving approach. The cycle embodies several basic quality management theories and principles, thus further assuring that managing by fact is accomplished through the use of the cycle. Third, the quality management improvement cycle increases the credibility of solutions that are developed in one part of the organization, allowing them to be readily replicated in other areas of the organization. Fourth, the cycle is important as a tool for managers who are responsible for quality improvement efforts in their organizations. It provides a framework for reviewing status of quality improvement projects. Finally, it can assist in tracking the effectiveness of solutions and in permanently eliminating root causes of quality problems.

The objectives of each step in AT&T's quality management improvement cycle, along with tools and techniques for achieving improvement, are shown in Table 9.1.

Step 12: Benchmark Your Products/Services

In 1979, Xerox pioneered a process called *competitive benchmarking*. At first, only a few of its operating units used this process, but today, benchmarking practices are used throughout Xerox. Other organizations look to Xerox as a benchmarking model.

In fact, Xerox's recent strong performance in regaining its competitive edge in the marketplace can be attributed largely to its benchmarking program. According to *DataQuest,* a research newsletter, "Xerox's benchmarking program deserves the lion's share of the credit for the organization's turnaround in recent years. A whole new way of doing business was inaugurated with the start of this program. Every group and system was dissected as Xerox searched for ways to become more competitive."

After studying the Japanese product-development system (with the help of its partner, Fuji Xerox), Xerox began to completely revamp the way its products were designed. Xerox has also sought out benchmarks for functions besides design. For example, L. L. Bean served as Xerox's benchmark for shipping operations, and Sears Roebuck provided a model for management of field distribution.

In this book, we have defined *benchmark* as a standard of excellence or achievement against which other similar things must be measured or judged. Simply speaking, benchmarking an activity involves the following process.

- Figuring out what to benchmark
- Finding out what the benchmark should be

Table 9.1. Tools and techniques for meeting quality management objectives.

Objectives	Key Activities	Tools and Techniques	Outputs
Identify a problem area and the reason for working on it.	• List possible problem areas. • Collect data. • Select problem area for improvement. • Schedule activities.	Brainstorming Interviewing Check sheet graph	• Problem area and rationale • Team project planning schedule
Identify outputs and customers.	• Identify outputs. • Identify customers.	Customer/supplier model	• List of outputs • List of customers
Understand customer requirements and degree of satisfaction.	• Identify characteristics, customer requirements, and priorities. • Establish measures and collect data. • Assess conformance to requirements and describe the gap.	Customer needs analysis, survey Check sheet Graph	• Description of the gap • Customer requirements and satisfaction level
Understand how things actually work and the performance necessary to meet customer requirements.	• Identify inputs and suppliers. • Chart the process. • Collect data. • Assess process performance and establish targets.	Customer/supplier model Flowchart Check sheet Graph	• List of inputs and suppliers • Flowchart of process in question • Targets for overall process in question

Source: AT&T, *Quality Improvement Process Guidebook* (Baskin Ridge, N.J.: AT&T, 1988), p. 46.

Table 9.1. (continued)

Objectives	Key Activities	Tools and Techniques	Outputs
Select opportunities to pursue.	• Identify contributing factors. • Select opportunities to pursue. • Write the problem statement.	Pareto diagram Problem selection matrix Problem statement matrix	• Prioritized list of potential problem areas • Clear, concise problem statement • Clear, concise objective statement
Identify root causes of the problem.	• Perform cause-and-effect analysis on the problem to the level of root causes. • Select actionable root causes. • Support potential root causes with data. • Select root causes with greatest probable impact.	Fishbone diagram Check sheet Pareto diagram Histogram Graph	
Develop, test, evaluate, and implement solutions.	• Develop and select potential solutions. • Develop an action plan. • Test, evaluate, and revise solutions. • Implement and monitor solutions.	Barriers and aids Solutions selection matrix Action plan Cost estimation	• Implemented solution and data on impact
Sustain improvement, consider replication, evaluate implementation, and plan future actions.	• Recommend required education and revised methods and procedures. • Establish tracking system to monitor results. • Recommend areas for replication. • Plan further actions, if necessary. • Evaluate implementation.	Graph Control chart Action plan	• Control at new performance level • Replication recommendations • Celebration • Plans for next project

- Determining how it's achieved

- Deciding to make changes or improvements in one's own organization's practices to meet or exceed the benchmark

These four steps—while sounding fairly simple—require thinking and analysis. They require that you know your own organization's processes and practices down to the smallest detail.

The Xerox benchmarking template, shown in Figure 9.3, is a guide, a mold, or a pattern for accomplishing the analyses required for benchmarking. Unlike a process model, the template is not strictly sequence-sensitive, nor does it focus on actions to take. Rather, it poses four questions that might be answered in different sequences (even though we've numbered the four quadrants for reference).

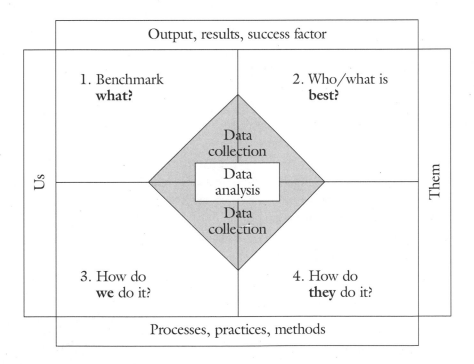

Source: Xerox Corporation, *A Guide for Benchmarking in Xerox*, NTIS Publication PB91-780106 (Springfield, Va.: NTIS, 1990), p. 69.

Figure 9.3.   Xerox benchmarking template.

First, notice the two vertical axes of the template—the us and them. The two quadrants to the left pose questions about your results or processes (us); the two quadrants to the right refer to the organization or process with which you are making the comparisons (them). The "them" may represent an outside organization or one within your own organization.

To begin a comparison, you must answer the questions, "Benchmark what?" and "Who or what is best?" In other words, what will you choose to compare yourself against? We will refer to this first comparison as the *upper-tier* comparison (see Figure 9.4). These top two quadrants suggest comparisons between outputs or results.

At the heart of the template is data collection and analysis. *Data* is just another name for *information*. You will need to have a plan for collecting information both about yourself and about the object of your benchmark study. Naturally, you will need the information to be in a form that allows comparison. Much of what you find in chapter 10 will guide you through the process of collecting good, usable information and will offer basic discussions about how to analyze and display your information.

If you went no further than the top two quadrants, you would have accomplished a competitive analysis. You would know what the benchmark is (today) and how you measured against it.

The lower-tier comparison represented in the bottom two quadrants (see Figure 9.5) constitutes true benchmarking—understanding the reasons for the differences and understanding what changes in process, practices, or methods must be undertaken to meet or exceed the benchmark.

For example, assume that your training department averages a 3.6 (out of a possible 5.0) participant-satisfaction rating on a particular course. You ask other divisions or departments that offer the same course for their participant-satisfaction rating and find that one division achieves a 4.2. You have completed the upper-tier study—establishing the benchmark and who has achieved it. Moreover, you have discovered that the gap between you and the benchmark is 0.6.

But only the lower-tier study results will allow you to make changes toward improvement. Lower-tier questions—"Why are their results better than ours?"—"How do they achieve that better score?"—are the ones that lead to change or improvement.

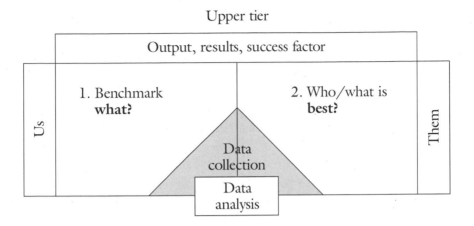

Source: Xerox Corporation, *A Guide for Benchmarking in Xerox,* NTIS Publication PB91-780106 (Springfield, Va.: NTIS, 1990), p. 69.

Figure 9.4.   Upper-tier benchmarking comparison.

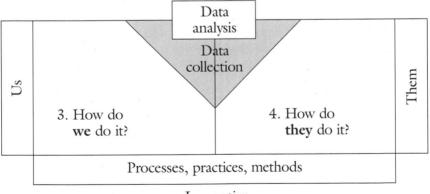

Source: Xerox Corporation, *A Guide for Benchmarking in Xerox,* NTIS Publication PB91-780106 (Springfield, Va.: NTIS, 1990), p. 69.

Figure 9.5.   Lower-tier benchmarking comparison.

The objective of benchmarking is change leading to improvement. Without change in processes, practices, and ultimately, results, benchmarking is an incomplete, academic exercise. You must increase your rating by 0.6 or more in order to achieve the benchmark status prescribed in the examples.

If your work processes are documented and measured, you will find benchmarking to be an extremely valuable (and not terribly difficult) activity. On the other hand, if you wander into a benchmark project without understanding your own process, you will find your lack of knowledge to be a barrier to your successful benchmarking attempts.

Determined to proceed anyway? Then be prepared for some hard work in the two "us" quadrants of the template.

Competitive benchmarking helps formulate real-world guides as to whether and how well you are meeting your customers' needs. If the results of a competitive benchmarking activity show that some other organization is meeting customer requirements better, then change in your quality efforts is clearly called for.

Competitive benchmarking is the continuous process of measuring your services, products, and practices against your toughest competitors or those organizations renowned as leaders. The process provides a better awareness of what competitors are doing, how they are doing it, and how well it is working.

I would encourage you to learn more about benchmarking. Xerox, as part of its technology-transfer commitment under the Malcolm Baldrige Award Program, has made available to the public its corporate bible on benchmarking. The report is called *A Guide to Benchmarking in Xerox,* part of the Leadership Through Quality Training Programs series. It is available through a partnership with the U.S. Department of Commerce, National Technical Information Services (NTIS), Port Royal Road, Springfield, Virginia, 22152. The NTIS document number is PB91-780106.

Step 13: Implement Continuous Process Improvement

Continuous process improvement addressees the creation of positive change in the way work is done. It includes the definition of work flow, strengthening of supplier-customer relationships, elimination of efforts that do not add value to your outputs, reduction of variation, and control of processes.

The continuous improvement concepts used in this book are from *An Introduction to the Continuous Improvement Process—Principles and Practices,* developed by LMI (see acknowledgments) under DoD contract MDA903-85-C-0139. We thank DoD and LMI for permission to use their material.

The quality management process improvement model shown in Figure 9.6 is a seven-step process. It begins with the activities needed to create an environment conducive to quality management and continues through selecting and improving a process, and finally moves to assessing the level of performance improvement, where the model cycles around to focus on the next process improvement effort. Here are the seven continuous process improvement steps.

1. Set the stage for process improvement.

    At the organizational level, setting the stage for process improvement involves everything the organization does to become aware of the need for improvement and to establish a commitment to the continuous improvement process. It includes basic education and training, goal setting, barrier reduction, and leadership. Setting the stage means the organization must create an environment in which continuous process improvement is encouraged and nourished. Management must have a clear vision of what it wants to accomplish and where it wants to go, and it must put in place support systems to help the improvement effort.

    At the team and the individual levels, setting the stage involves selecting and educating the team or the individuals and training them in the specific concepts, tools, and techniques they will need for the contemplated improvement effort. The team or individual should determine how to function in the overall organizational environment and should ensure that all individuals involved are determined to accomplish their perceived mission.

2. Select a process to improve.

    A team must identify potential candidates and, in conjunction with organizational and team objectives, select one process on which it will focus its improvement effort during each pass

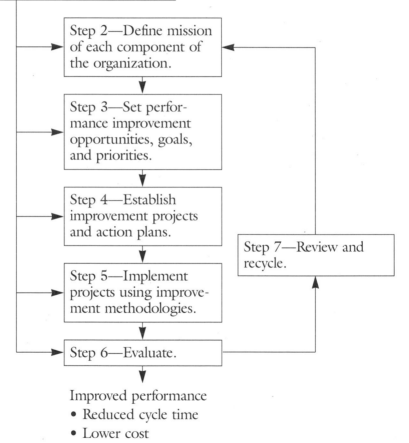

Step 1—Establish the management and cultural environment.
• Vision
• Long-term commitment
• People involvement
• Disciplined methodology
• Support systems
• Training

Step 2—Define mission of each component of the organization.

Step 3—Set performance improvement opportunities, goals, and priorities.

Step 4—Establish improvement projects and action plans.

Step 7—Review and recycle.

Step 5—Implement projects using improvement methodologies.

Step 6—Evaluate.

Improved performance
• Reduced cycle time
• Lower cost
• Innovation

Source: *Total Quality Management Guide*, Vol. 1, Office of the Deputy Assistant Secretary of Defense for Total Quality Management, DoD 5000.51-G, February 15, 1990, p. 96.

Figure 9.6.   Flowchart of continuous improvement strategy.

through the cycle. Selecting the improvement target involves identifying all the potential opportunities, setting priorities, and choosing the process that presents the most serious problem or offers the greatest opportunity for improvement. Once the process is selected, the team must identify its major problems and isolate their root causes. Using this background, the team may modify its plan for improvement, building on its objectives. Identifying measurement points is also necessary before beginning the continuous process improvement effort.

3. Define the process.

Once a process has been targeted for improvement, the team should define that process as clearly and completely as possible. Process definition involves determining the customers (both internal and external) and the suppliers of the process, documenting how the process is currently performed (usually through using a flowchart or diagram), and identifying measures of process performance. Documentation should be formal and consistent among all organizational processes. A sound process definition provides a consistent base from which to begin process improvement; without knowing where you are at a given moment, it is hard to determine how to get to your destination.

4. Standardize the process.

By standardizing a process, the team institutionalizes the current best way to perform that process. It creates a means for instructing people in their jobs within a consistent performance definition, provides a means for evaluating performance consistently, and provides a basis for evaluating the success of the improvement efforts. The team accomplishes all this by following the standardize-do-check-act cycle, which requires the team to first bring its measurement system under control, next identify and document the current method of performing the process (which becomes the process *standard*), and then communicate and promote use of the standard. Management ensures that individuals are trained to the standard, enables its use, and enforces that use (the *do* part of the cycle). Once the standard is in force, teams measure all process performance against that standard (check) and respond appropriately to deviations from it (act). Reducing performance variation by assessing the causes of deviation and eliminating them allows the teams to prevent recurrent deviation. The standard should always reflect the best current way of performing the process.

5. Tighten the process.

    Once a team has defined a process standard, it should tighten the process before actually attempting to improve it. Tightening is the maintenance work that makes process improvement efforts as effective as possible. Essential elements of this effort to tighten the process include ensuring that the process meets its stated and perceived requirements; cleaning and straightening the process work areas; eliminating unnecessary equipment; instituting total, productive maintenance; and establishing reliable, adequate data-collection systems.

6. Improve the process.

    Efforts to improve the process should follow the classic plan-do-check-act (PDCA) cycle in which a team *plans* an improvement, implements solution *(do)*, *checks* for improvement, and *acts* to institutionalize the improvements. The team's effort involves developing solutions that address stated requirements and conform to theories on problem causes. Data-collection and measurement methodologies must support the envisioned solution. Further, the team must be trained in the techniques necessary to carry out the plan. After it carries out its planned improvement, it should assess the data to determine how well its actual performance matches planned improvements. Successful improvement should be institutionalized; less-than-successful efforts require another pass through the improvement cycle.

7. Assess improvement performance.

    After an improvement has been implemented, a team should document the improved performance and the successful improvement effort thoroughly. That documentation allows others to benefit from the lessons the team has learned and brings recognition to the team's efforts. It also provides a road map for replicating successful improvement techniques. Documenting the improved process also requires the team to update its process definition and flow diagrams, and moreover, requires that process standards be rewritten to reflect the new standard of performance. Teams should set in place a means of continuously measuring performance level if such a system does not already exist. Recommending follow-up actions or subsequent improvement efforts is also appropriate.

The principles at the heart of the continuous improvement process include the following:

1. A constancy of purpose that provides a steady and consistent vision of where your organization is going

2. A commitment to quality that drives productive change in all the services and products you produce

3. A customer focus and customer involvement that ensures your improvement efforts are driven by meaningful purposes

4. Process orientation that addresses the means of work accomplishment and not just the outcomes

5. Continuous improvement that ensures dynamic and adaptive processes over time

6. System-centered management that ensures improvement of the whole and not just the parts

7. Investment in knowledge that leverages the effectiveness of the improvement process

8. Teamwork that leverages the knowledge and provides essential synergy

9. Conservation of human resources that preserves your organization's most valuable assets

10. Total involvement that brings the entire intellectual power of your organization to bear on improvement

11. Perpetual commitment that precludes giving up when the road gets a little rough

You apply these principles together in a logical and holistic manner to give substance and vitality to the continuously improving organizational culture. Of course, no single, correct formula can be used to achieve continuous improvement in all situations or all organizations. A core set of ingredients, however, is evident in most successful continuous improvement efforts and can be applied to your own effort. A number of the suggested readings at the end of this book examine in depth these principles and their supporting practices.

As noted earlier, your quality management effort will be unique in its details, but in general, it should move your organization toward satisfying these six criteria.

1. Exceeding your customers' requirements and expectations and being a high-quality supplier

2. Believing in people, working to eliminate barriers that prevent people from taking joy and pride in their work, and involving everyone

3. Tapping the power of individuals, multiplying that power through training and teamwork, and focusing that power on understanding and process improvement

4. Recognizing that most problems are in your management systems and are not due to particular individuals or circumstances, and providing leadership to continuously improve the systems

5. Making decisions based on data rather than on opinions or emotions; stimulating creative thinking; and seeking innovation in products, processes, and services

6. Focusing more on defect prevention than on defect detection

Step 14: Monitor and Evaluate Results

As part of their strategy for improvement, many organizations that have introduced quality management have conducted more in-depth assessments aimed at identifying the existing culture and management style of the organization. An assessment helps to identify those vital processes to be targeted for change and provides a baseline measurement for judging progress. Assessments can take a variety of forms and frequently involve identifying and surveying the organization's internal and external customers, managers, and employees. The following key considerations are often probed.

- What is the mission of the organization? What services and products are provided?

- Who are the internal and external customers?

- What measurement systems are presently in place?

- Does the organization measure its success in terms of meeting customer requirements and expectations?

- How well does the organization communicate with its customers and its suppliers?

- How much emphasis is placed on planning as opposed to fire fighting?

- How does the organization generate ideas for improvement? Does it focus on improvement in general or quality improvement specifically?

- What type of suggestion system is in place? How effective is it?

- What does the organization reward? Improvement in general or quality improvement specifically?

- To what extent is teamwork used, encouraged, and recognized?

- What is the nature of management's relationship with employees' unions?

- How well do functional units cooperate? Are turf battles endemic?

- Does the executive leadership have credibility in the eyes of middle and line managers? Front-line workers?

- What type of management style is employed? Is it directive or participative?

- How much discretion do employees have in making decisions? Is authority delegated to the lowest levels?

- What is the attitude toward training?

- What is the attitude toward quality work? Is the focus on quality of the end product or quality of the process?

- Are the organization's values, goals, objectives, policies, and procedures clearly stated and widely known?

- Does the organization have an abundance of priorities, or have a vital few been identified and articulated?

Step 15: Recognize Success

The success of quality management is determined, in large part, by the degree of importance the organization places on it. Recognition is one of the most important ways to reinforce a proactive, positive change in behavior as it relates to quality improvement. Recognition is given for the successful application of the quality management principles and practices. Your goal, then, is to create an environment in which change in the customer's interest is encouraged and then celebrated when it does occur. Recognition is a means to demonstrate respect and appreciation for all employees and the value they add to your business.

Traditionally, rewards have been based on the most numbers: most revenue brought in, most profitable new product, and so on. Quality management, of course, also rewards bottom-line numbers. But since continuous quality improvement is a process, quality management also recognizes and rewards those who demonstrate success with its processes and activities of quality management—in measurable or non-measurable ways.

Recognition and reward are not the same things. *Recognition* means noticing (recognizing) a person or group doing a good job. A manager may notice the good job at any point along its progress—not only when it is completed. Recognition usually takes the form of praise, either spoken or written. It may be as simple as a word of approval about the way an employee ran a team meeting, or as formal as a letter of commendation with copies sent to his or her management.

Recognition provides both motivation and support for employees; people work better when they feel their efforts are valued. Research has shown that such reinforcement can have a real and measurable impact on productivity.

To provide effective reinforcement, recognition should have the following characteristics.

- Be specific. If someone is told, "Good job on that report!" he or she is left not knowing which part of the report succeeded so well. Was it the succinct executive summary? the fact that it was turned in two days early? the thoroughness of the research? the potential value of the recommendations? or the nice printing job? Managers stand a better chance of having desirable actions repeated if they clearly specify the actions.

- Direct it at the right person. If the report came from a team, and one member has been out of town while it was being written, that person is not the one to recognize, even if he or she is the team leader. Who wrote the report?

- Be genuine!

- Be timely. Reinforcement given as close as possible to the time of the success is most effective.

- Recognize process, not just results. The results will be unique to only one situation. The quality management processes, on the other hand, are versatile enough to adapt to a wide variety of situations. It is the internalization of quality processes you wish to encourage; therefore, that is what you should reinforce with praise.

Reward is given at the completion of a job and should be tangible: usually mementos, merchandise, or cash. Rewards range from a simple plaque to a profit-sharing program. Rewards say, "You deserve to share in the tangible assets of your work," and as such, can be powerful motivators.

Quality management is bolstered by effective use of recognition and reward. All managers, at all levels, should continually identify those people doing a good job—and then devise ways to tell them so.

Your organization should bestow rewards and sponsor many recognition events. Same organizations use *teamwork days* or *team excellence awards*.

Teamwork days are recognition events designed to honor the achievements of quality teams. Teamwork days can be held on department, division, regional, or functional levels. In addition, the organization can sponsor annual teamwork days, at which everyone in the organization celebrates progress.

A teamwork day is like a cross between a professional conference, a trade fair, and a revival meeting. Teams create display booths, often with much ingenuity and exuberance, that showcase their accomplishments. Speakers discuss the organization's progress in becoming a quality management organization. People learn from each other, and the quality management transformation grows.

The *team excellence award* can be a cash award given to several teams each year as a reward for using quality management tools to achieve outstanding results. Generally, an organization will have more excellent teams than it can possibly reward. Recipients are chosen by senior staff after they successfully compete at division levels within their function. All teams reaching the status of *excellent* are recognized by a certificate.

What makes an excellent team? There are three criteria.

- Teamwork. How well does the team work together? Team members on an excellent team (1) all understand their purpose as a team, (2) start with a clear problem statement and/or desired output, (3) organize for maximum effectiveness, and (4) use interactive skills well and consistently.

- Use of quality tools and processes. Excellent teams (1) use applicable analytical tools, (2) identify several possible alternatives to solving their problem, and (3) evaluate the results of their actions.

- Results. The team project should (1) produce tangible results, (2) impact the external customer or those who support the external customer, (3) demonstrate an innovative approach, and (4) effectively maximize the cost of quality opportunities.

Recognition and reward must be woven into the very fabric of quality management. People who assume responsibility for continuous growth and meet customer requirements, are, in turn, motivated to grow further because the large role their efforts play is honestly recognized.

Step 16: Adjust Your Quality Management Process

Your quality management planning and implementation efforts must not be carved in stone. As you learn more about your organization's strengths and weaknesses, you may have to change your quality management efforts to reflect the feedback. If the results are not as expected, than you must develop a new approach for improvement, based on what you learned.

Step 17: Continue to Improve

Don't stop now! Continue to improve every facet of your organization's operation.

10 Quality Management Tools and Techniques

One picture is worth more than 10,000 words.

Anonymous Chinese Proverb

The Right Tool or Technique

This chapter provides the government manager with a primer on quality management tools, techniques, and methods. These generic tools can be used to improve any process and are presented here to let you know what they are, why they are used, and how to use them. Not all of the tools are appropriate for use in all applications.

Tools and techniques are essential for implementing the quality management improvement process. *Tools* will allow you to accomplish work, make meaningful measurements, and analyze, visualize, and understand information. *Techniques* help you organize and accomplish your quality management effort in a structured and systematic manner.

Graphic Tools

As the Chinese proverb asserts, a picture is worth many words *and* numbers. Graphic displays allow you to create a logical storyboard that most people can understand at a glance.

A number of factors can lead to the decision for using one particular graphic tool over another, including the unique application and an individual's or team's experience and preferences. Most graphic tools are oriented toward a certain type of activity, and each tool has its strengths and weaknesses. This section summarizes some of the common graphic tools used to implement the quality management

289

Table 10.1.   Use of graphic tools.

Graphic tool	Use when you need to . . .
Bar chart	Compare quantity of data in different categories to help visualize differences.
Cause-and-effect (fishbone) diagram	Systematically analyze cause-and-effect relationships and identify potential root causes of a problem.
Check sheet	Gather a variety of data in a systematic fashion for a clear and objective picture of the facts.
Control chart	Monitor the performance of a process with frequent outputs to determine if its performance is meeting customer requirements or if it can be improved to meet or exceed them.
Flowchart	Describe an existing process, develop modifications, or design an entirely new process.
Histogram	Display the dispersion or spread of the data under consideration.
Pareto chart	Identify major factors in a subject being analyzed and highlight the "vital few" in contrast to the "trivial many."
Scatter diagram	Show the relationship between two variables.
Time line chart	Visually display complex and quantifiable data; show changes in quantity over time.

methodology. Table 10.1 will help you decide when graphic tools are most appropriate for your need.

In the following sections, each graphic tool is briefly described to enhance the manager's understanding of its use under the quality management methodology.

Check Sheet

A check sheet provides a list of checkoff items that permit data to be collected quickly and easily in a simple, standardized format that lends itself to quantitative analysis. Check sheets are frequently used to collect data on numbers of defective items, defect locations, and defect causes. Figure 10.1 is a simple example of a check sheet.

Make a check sheet by laying out the categories of information you are concerned with and your collected data on a standardized form or grid. Determine your categories by asking such fact-finding questions as these:

- What happens?
- Who does it, receives it, or is responsible for it?
- Where does it occur—place?

Product: TRC receiver unit   Date: 09/09/93

Name: Hunt

Total examined: 200   Lot: 51

Defect type	Defect count	Subtotal
Chipped	ＨＨＴ ＨＨＴ ＨＨＴ	15
Off-color	ＨＨＴ ＨＨＴ ＨＨＴ ＨＨＴ ＨＨＴ	25
Bent	ＨＨＴ	5
	Grade total:	45

Figure 10.1. Simple check sheet.

- When does it occur—time of day or month; frequency?
- How does it happen, how much, or how long has it been happening?

Do not ask *why*. This will lead you to search for causes while still trying to determine whether a problem exists and what it looks like. The check sheet should be designed to facilitate the collection of as many different kinds of data as are useful. The team can brainstorm items and then refine the list. It is also helpful to gather a little data before designing your check sheet. You may determine the appropriate categories from this smaller sample. The check sheet should also clearly indicate who collected the data and where, when, and how it was collected. In a sample, the total population from which the data was gathered should also be indicated.

Bar Chart

Bar charts show a comparison of quantities by the length of the bars that represent them (such as frequencies of events in different locations, cost of different types of breakdowns, and so on). Bars may be horizontal or vertical.

Along with time lines, bar charts are among the most common of data displays. The time line differs from the bar chart in two ways that are worth noting. The obvious difference is that a bar chart uses height columns, while the time chart connects data points with a line. Visually, then, the bar chart emphasizes differences (or similarities) between the columns of various heights. The time chart, on the other hand, emphasizes the direction of change over time. The second difference is that the divisions along the horizontal line of the time chart are time (quantitative) intervals. The divisions along the horizontal axis of the bar chart are nominal categories.

Figure 10.2 is an example of a bar chart. It displays data regarding sales of household appliances. We can see that TVs were the item most frequently purchased in both 1980 and 1990, that microwaves have increased in popularity, but that ranges and refrigerators were purchased relatively infrequently in the two years being studied. The bar chart is really two bar charts superimposed: one for 1980 and one for 1990.

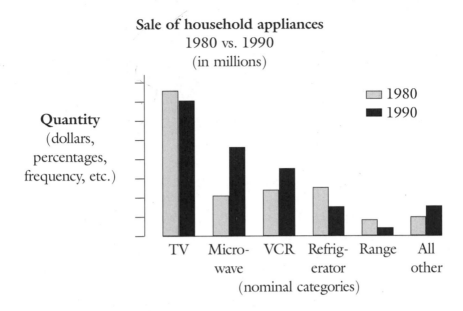

Source: Xerox Corporation, *A Guide to Benchmarking in Xerox,* NTIS Publication PB91-780106 (Springfield, Va.: NTIS, 1990), p. 69.

Figure 10.2.   Example of bar chart.

As with all graphic displays of data, the bar chart tells its story at a glance. The more data you have to analyze, the more important the use of graphics becomes. Bar charts make graphic comparisons easy to see.

To construct a bar chart, proceed as follows:

- Collect the raw data on a check sheet, if necessary. Refer to page 291 for more information on the check sheet.

- List the categories (usually words rather than numbers) across the horizontal scale at the bottom. You may set them in any sequence, such as in descending order or any other way that makes sense. Label all categories.

- To set the vertical scale to the left, find both the largest and smallest value from the data, and make sure the scale is broad enough to include both. Label both the scale and the intervals.

- Determine the quantity of each category and draw the bar accordingly. Generally speaking, bars should not touch or overlap. Bar charts can compare data for different years (as in Figure 10.2) or for different populations (for example, households with earnings under $50,000 and over $50,000).

- Give your bar chart a descriptive title. Include any legends that show what different patterns or colors represent.

Cause-and-Effect (Fishbone) Diagram

The cause-and-effect diagram is a graphic representation of the relationships between an effect (problem) and its potential causes. It is a useful tool in brainstorming, examining processes, and planning activities. The process of constructing a cause-and-effect diagram helps stimulate thinking about an issue, helps organize thoughts into a rational whole, and generates discussion and the airing of viewpoints. The cause-and-effect diagram documents the level of understanding about an issue and provides a framework from which to begin expanding that understanding.

Cause-and-effect diagrams can be used to explore a wide variety of topics, including the relationships between an existing problem and the factors that might bear on it, a desired future outcome and the factors that relate to it, or any event—past, present, or future—and its causal factors.

Cause-and-effect diagrams go by several names: fishbone diagrams, which describes how it looks, and Ishikawa diagrams for its inventor, the late Kaoru Ishikawa, a Japanese quality management leader.

The problem—or effect—appears in a box to the right (the *head* of the fish) as shown in Figure 10.3. To the left are the *bones* of the fish, on which causes are organized and displayed as categories. The entries are words, or nominal data.

In this example, the problem or effect is that the corn will not pop. The four factors that may be causing this are people, tools for popping corn, materials, and the method or process used. These are the four main bones for this example, but a different problem would suggest different major bones.

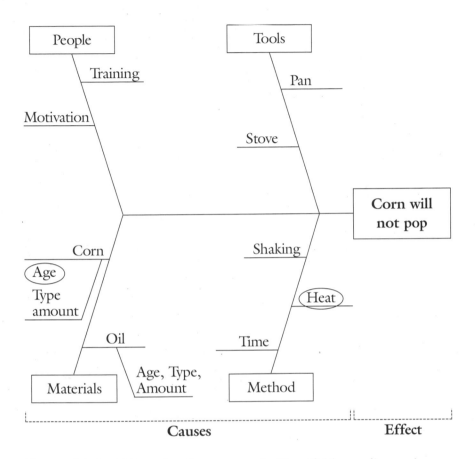

Figure 10.3.   Example of a cause-and-effect (fishbone diagram).

The fishbone diagram ensures that quality management analysis groups thoroughly examine all possible causes or categories. More important, it provides a process for groups to follow. And because the fishbone is a graphic display, it focuses the attention of the group on something concrete—something everyone sees and interprets in a more-or-less consistent manner.

To develop a cause-and-effect diagram, proceed as follows:

- Define the effect or current situation as clearly as possible. You can always go back and refine it later as you collect new data. Write the effect in the head of the fish.

- Begin by brainstorming causes and listing them on a flip chart in no particular order. When the group runs dry of ideas, they look for categories and similarities suggested by the list. These major categories, or themes, become the big bones.

- To encourage lots of ideas, ask "why? why? why?" When the answers begin to sound silly, you can stop.

- Draw the major bones and label them. You may decide on three, four, or more major themes. Use generic branches (people, methods, materials, machines) if helpful.

- Place the causes from the brainstorm list as small bones under the appropriate big bone.

- Allow the organization of the brainstormed causes to stimulate other ideas for causes. The group should be encouraged to add as many potential causes as they can think of. For each cause identified, ask, "What caused this?"

- Have the group highlight the cause(s) they believe to be contributing to the effect. In the popcorn example (Figure 10.3), the group has circled "age of corn" and "amount of heat" as the most likely causes.

- To verify causes, you will need to collect information to either accept or reject them.

- Work on most important causes (for example, apply design of experiments methods).

- Desensitize, eliminate, or control causes.

Control Chart

A control chart is used to monitor the performance of a process with frequent outputs. It provides a pictorial representation of an ongoing process and is based on four concepts.

- All processes fluctuate with time.

- Individual points in the process are unpredictable.

- A stable process fluctuates randomly, and groups of points from a stable process tend to fall within predictable bounds.

• An unstable process does not fluctuate randomly, and these fluctuations are generally out of the range of normal operations.

The control chart in Figure 10.4 displays data taken over time and also shows computed variations of those data. Control charts are used to show the variations in averages ($\overline{X}$), and range (R), and also the number of defects (PN), percentage defective (P), defects per variable unit (U), and defects per fixed unit (C). *A Guide to Total Quality Management Control* by Kaoru Ishikawa provides excellent guidance on using control charts. The control chart allows you to distinguish

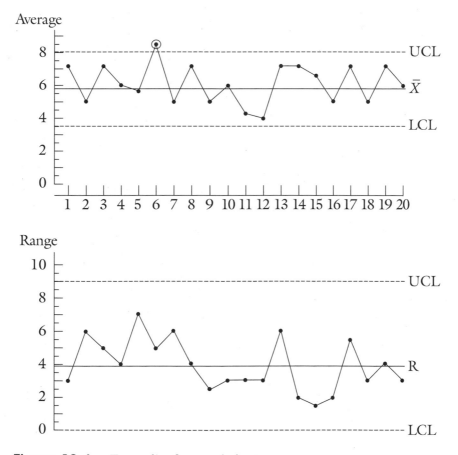

Figure 10.4. Example of control chart.

between measurements that are predictably within the capability of the process (common causes of variation) and measurements that are unpredictable and produced by special causes.

The upper and lower control limits (UCL and LCL) must not be confused with specification limits. Control limit averages can describe the natural variation of the process—that is, points within the limits generally indicate normal and expected variation. On the other hand, points outside the limits signal that something has occurred that requires special attention because it may be outside the built-in systematic cause of variation in the process. Each individual point out of the limits should be explained.

Control charts help you understand the inherent capability of your processes, bring your processes under control by eliminating the special causes of variation, reduce tampering with processes that are under statistical control, and monitor the effects of process changes aimed at improvement.

To construct a control chart, follow these basic steps.

- Determine the control limits, which are a function of sample size, to describe the expected variation of a process.

- Collect data.

- Plot data on the control chart to assess performance and identify points outside established control limits.

- Determine causes of points outside control limits.

- Identify ways to eliminate special causes and reduce normal variation.

After constructing your control chart, examine it to see where the data points are located. If your process is fairly consistent and stable, most of the data points should fall within the established limits. Control charts illustrate fluctuations within the process that occur in a nonrandom pattern. Points that fall outside one of the control limits should be reported or investigated.

Once you've created your control chart, you can continue to use it to determine whether your operations are staying within the operating limits you've established. As you add points, examine the chart for favorable or unfavorable out-of-control points, and look for special or assignable causes.

There are many types of control charts. The one you use depends on the type of data collected. Since choosing and developing control charts are rather complex processes, you may need to ask your quality management specialist for initial assistance.

Flowchart

A flowchart is a pictorial representation of the steps in a process. It is a useful tool for determining how a process really works. By examining how various steps in a process relate to one another, you can often uncover potential sources of trouble.

Flowcharts can be applied to anything from the flow of materials to the steps in making a sale or servicing a product. Flowcharts permit you to examine and understand relationships in a process or project. They provide a step-by-step schematic, or picture, that creates a common language, ensures common understanding about sequence, and focuses collective attention on shared concerns.

Several types of flowcharts are particularly useful in the continuous improvement process. Three frequently used charts are the top-down flowchart, the detailed flowchart, and the work-flow diagram. The top-down flowchart (Figure 10.5) presents only the major, or most fundamental steps, in a process or project. It helps you and your team to easily visualize the process in a single, simple flow diagram. Key value-added actions associated with each major activity are listed below the steps. You can construct a top-down flowchart fairly quickly and easily. You generally do so before attempting to produce detailed flowcharts for a process. By limiting the top-down flowchart to significant value-added activities, you reduce the likelihood of becoming bogged down in the detail.

The detailed flowchart (Figure 10.6) provides very specific information about process flow. At its most detailed level, every decision point, feedback loop, and process step is represented. Detailed flowcharts should be used only when the level of detail provided by the top-down or other simpler flowcharts is insufficient to support understanding, analysis, and improvement activity. The detailed flowchart may also be useful and appropriate for critical processes, where precisely following a

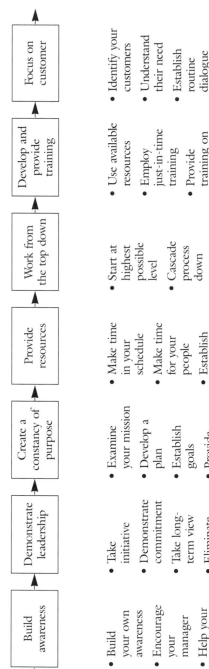

Figure 10.5.   Example of a top-down flowchart.

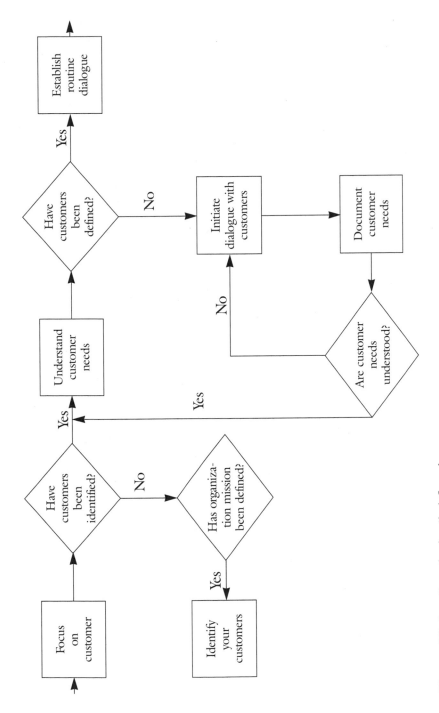

Figure 10.6. Sample detailed flowchart.

specific procedure is essential. The work-flow diagram is a graphic representation or picture of how work actually flows through a physical space or facility. It is very useful for analyzing flow processes, illustrating flow inefficiency, and planning process flow improvement.

Histogram

A histogram is a visual representation of the spread or dispersion of variable data (for example, the number of defects per lot). In histograms there is a tendency for many items to fall in the center of the distribution (central tendency), with progressively fewer items as you move from the center.

In a histogram, the data are represented by a series of rectangles, or bars, proportional in height to the frequency of the group or class represented, as shown in Figure 10.7. Since class intervals (but not number) will be equal in size, the rectangles are of equal width. The heights of

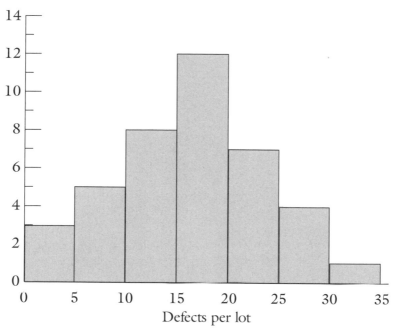

Figure 10.7. Example of a histogram.

the rectangles relative to one another indicate the proportion of data points in each class.

Histograms help to identify changes or shifts in processes as changes are made. Histograms show how measurements of a process or product can vary, and thus, they help in establishing standards. Once standards have been set, measurements can be compared to these standards.

To construct a histogram, proceed as follows:

- Collect the data you plan to chart and count the total number of data points.

- Determine the range of your data by subtracting the smallest data point from the largest.

- Keep the number of data bars in your graph between six and 12. To determine the width of each class interval (bar), divide the range by the desired number of bars.

- Place your class intervals (groupings of data) on the horizontal axis.

- Place your frequency or number scale on the vertical axis.

- Arrange the data points in ascending order.

- Draw the height of each bar to represent the number or frequency of its class interval using the scale on the vertical axis; each bar should be the same width with all data points included.

Pareto Chart

A Pareto chart is used when you need to discover or display the relative importance of data or variables (problems, causes, or conditions). It helps highlight the *vital few* in contrast to the *trivial many*. A Pareto chart may be used to examine the how, what, when, where, and why of a suspected problem cause. It also helps teams identify which problems, causes, or conditions are the most significant or frequent so they can work on these first.

Like most charts and graphs, the Pareto chart illustrates your data as of a specific time and date. Once your team has addressed the most significant problem, cause, or condition revealed by your Pareto chart, you can redraw it with new data and pick another area to improve.

In the late 1800s, Vilfredo Pareto, an Italian economist, found that typically 80 percent of the wealth in a region was concentrated in less than 20 percent of the population. Later, Joseph Juran formulated what he called the Pareto principle of problems: Only a vital few elements (20 percent) account for the majority (80 percent) of the problems. For example, only 20 percent of your equipment problems account for 80 percent of your downtime. Because this Pareto principle has proven to be valid in numerous situations, it is useful to examine your data carefully to identify the vital few items that most deserve attention.

The Pareto chart shown in Figure 10.8 is a bar chart in which the data are arranged in descending order of importance, generally by magnitude of frequency, cost, time, or a similar parameter. The chart is really

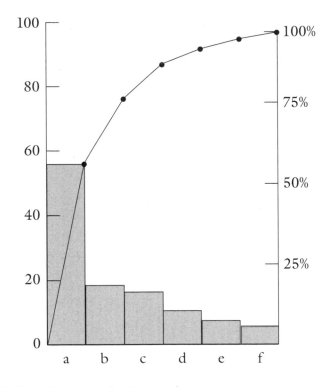

Figure 10.8. Example of a Pareto chart.

two charts in one—part bar chart and part pie chart. The bars are easy to see, but the ascending line that plots the cumulative height of the bars is really a pie chart unrolled.

To create a Pareto chart, proceed as follows:

- Select the most likely causes of a problem (from the cause-effect diagram).

- Collect the data on causes (using a check sheet, perhaps).

- Total the number of observations and calculate the percentages of each cause.

- Always set the right vertical scale from 0 to 100 percent.

- Make the left vertical scale the same height as the right scale; it begins with 0 at the bottom and ends with the number of observations at the top, directly across from 100 percent.

- Draw the columns using the left scale.

- Plot the first point at the upper-right corner of the first column.

- Calculate and add together the percentages of cause 1 and cause 2. Place the second point, corresponding to the sum, across from the right scale directly over the second column or bar. For the third point, add the percentage of cause 3 to the total of 1 and 2 and plot accordingly. The total of all the columns added together should be 100 percent, and the last point will be at the 100-percent point.

- Join the dots with a line.

Scatter Diagram

Scatter diagrams (Figure 10.9) and their related correlation analysis permit you to examine two factors at one time and determine the relationship that may exist between them. The graphic display can help you determine the possible causes of problems, even when the linkage between the factors is counterintuitive. The pattern or distribution of data points in a scatter diagram describes the strength of the relationship between the factors being examined. However, even a strong correlation does not necessarily imply a cause-and-effect relationship

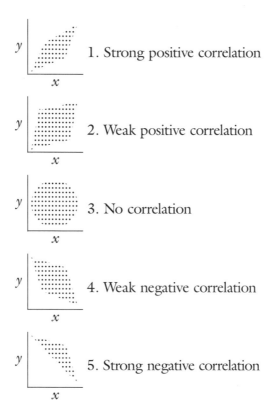

1. Strong positive correlation

2. Weak positive correlation

3. No correlation

4. Weak negative correlation

5. Strong negative correlation

Source: U.S. Government, *Introduction to Total Quality Management*, 1989, p. 16.

Figure 10.9.   Examples of scatter diagram correlations.

between the factors. Additional work may be required to uncover the nature of the indicated relationship.

The scatter diagram shows plotted points against two measures: one displayed on the vertical (y) axis, the other on the horizontal (x) axis. The visual pattern of the plotted points gives quick information about the presence of a relationship or correlation.

If you see a correlation (either positive or negative) between two measures, you can assume that if you can change the incidence of one measure, the other will move as well. For example, if telephone call duration is positively correlated to customer satisfaction (the longer the call lasts, the greater the customer satisfaction), then changing telephone call duration will produce a change in customer satisfaction.

To prepare a scatter diagram, proceed as follows:

- Collect data on the two selected measures for each occurrence.

- Draw the horizontal and vertical scales.

- Assign the horizontal (x) axis to the independent variable. The *independent variable* is the one you can have the most direct effect on, such as call duration. The dependent variable is the other variable, which depends on the first. The dependent variable is assigned to the y axis. Establish the interval scales for both and label.

- Plot each data point on the grid.

- To interpret the relationship, you can "eyeball" it, but a statistician can perform some quantitative tests on the data to give you a more accurate numeric indication of correlation.

Time Line Chart

The time line chart as shown in Figure 10.10 is a graphic display of changes over some period of time. The left scale is a quantity: percentages or simple counts of frequency. The horizontal line is divided into time intervals such as days of the week, months, or even an ordinal sequence such as first job, second job, and so on.

The line that joins the plot marks gives a moving picture of the fluctuations over time. Defect rates are reported on time lines in order to spot trends. For example, in Figure 10.10, note that during the study period, errors occurred least frequently first thing in the morning. Error rates peaked, however, around lunchtime and quitting time.

To prepare a time line chart, proceed as follows:

- Collect the raw data on a check sheet, if necessary.

- Develop time intervals (usually hours, days, or weeks). The intervals should be evenly spaced. Label each interval.

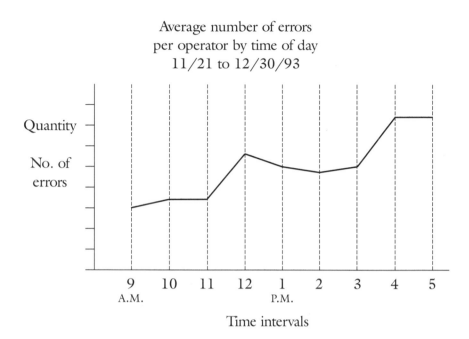

Figure 10.10. Example of time line chart.

- Draw a line to connect the quantities observed on each successive interval.
- Connect the points with a line.
- Add horizontal and vertical grid lines if the points are difficult to read, as shown in the figure.
- Title the chart to define the period of time over which the data were collected.

Techniques

This section summarizes some of the basic techniques used to implement the quality management methodology. Table 10.2 will help you decide which technique is most appropriate for your needs. Each of these techniques is briefly described to enhance the manager's understanding of its use under the quality management methodology.

Table 10.2. Use of quality management techniques.

Quality technique	Use when you need to . . .
Action plan	Explain implementation plans to management and workers and ensure an organized, objective implementation.
Barriers and aids	Analyze a situation and make use of available aids and/or overcome barriers that prevent implementation of a solution.
Benchmarking	Measure your processes/performance against those of your competitors.
Brainstorming	Generate, clarify, and evaluate a sizable list of ideas, problems, or issues.
Concurrent engineering (CE)	Shorten the design-to-development life cycle of a product.
Cost estimation	Determine the dollar impact when prioritizing and selecting improvement opportunities.
Cost of quality	Understand the hidden costs of a product or service.
Customer-needs analysis	Identify what customers expect of you, their requirements, and what you have jointly agreed to provide.
Customer-supplier model	Identify the total customer-supplier relationship and analyze and/or improve your work process.
Customer-supplier questionnaire	Assess your relations with your customers and suppliers.
Deming (PDSA) and Shewhart (PDCA) cycles	Implement a continuous improvement process.
Design of experiments	Reduce costs, stabilize production processes, and desensitize production variables.

Table 10.2.   (continued)

Quality technique	Use when you need to . . .
Interviewing	Broaden the team's foundation of knowledge and identify other people who are not on the team but who are sources of needed information.
Multivoting	Accomplish "list reduction" and set priorities quickly and with a high degree of group agreement.
Nominal group technique (NGT)	Reach consensus within a structured situation.
Problem-selection matrix	Prioritize improvement opportunities.
Problem-statement matrix	State specifically the improvement opportunity that the team is addressing.
Quality function deployment (QFD)	Transform customer wants and needs into quantitative terms.
Solutions-selection matrix	Select those potential solutions that best address the root causes of the problem.
Statistical process control (SPC)	Improve process performance.

Action Plan

The quality management team's action plan is a catalog of things that must be done to ensure a smooth and objective trial and implementation of the solution. Although the action plan may have different formats, it should answer who, what, when, where, and how and consider the barriers and aids for success. Figure 10.11 is a typical example of an action plan for assigning tasks.

To develop an action plan, proceed as follows:

- Have the team analyze the proposed improvement or solution.

- Break it down into steps.

		Prepared By _____ Date ____ Page ____ of ____			
TASK ASSIGNMENT RECORD		Loc'n/Proj. _____ Period ____			
No.	Task/project	Priority/ due date	Assigned to	Date assigned	Status/Remarks

Source: Florida Power and Light and *AT&T Quality Improvement Process Guidebook* (Baskin Ridge, N.J.: AT&T, 1988), p. 32.

Figure 10.11. Typical action plan.

- Consider the materials and numbers of people involved at each level.
- Brainstorm, if necessary, for other items of possible significance.
- Add items to the list until you think the list is complete.
- Create a form or log that helps document the plan.

Barriers and Aids

This technique pinpoints and analyzes elements that resist change (barriers) or push for change (aids). This focused brainstorming technique helps a team meet its objectives by planning to overcome barriers and making maximum use of available aids. Factors to consider are

- People
- Environment
- Hardware
- Dollars

Figure 10.12 describes some typical barriers and aids. To construct a barriers-and-aids analysis, proceed as follows:

- Identify the solution, task, change, or concern.

Barriers and Aids	
Forces pushing against quality improvement	Forces pushing for quality improvement
• Lack of dollars	• Team
• People shortage	• Personal commitment
• Vested interest/old attitude	• Management support
• Would the team stay together?	• Support of line manager
• Other priorities	• Communications
—Time	—With team
—Maintain work flow	—Outside team
—Complicated techniques	• New techniques
	• Increasing cost of failure
	• Good planning
	• Specific goals

Figure 10.12.   Typical elements of a barriers-and-aids analysis.

- Brainstorm a list of barriers (forces pushing against change).
- Brainstorm a list of aids (forces pushing for change).
- Rank listed items by level of significance: high, medium, or low.
- Match aids that balance or overcome barriers.
- List matching barriers and aids on a chart.
- List nonmatching barriers and aids, and brainstorm any off-setting factors.
- Use your rankings to identify items needing team action.
- Develop an action plan.

Note: It is not necessary to come up with an aid for every barrier.

Benchmarking

Benchmarking is a significant element of the quality management methodology that allows you to measure your processes against those of recognized leaders (Figure 10.13). It helps you to establish priorities and targets leading to process improvement. Benchmarking is conducted when you want to know where you stand with respect to your peer competitors.

To perform a benchmarking analysis, proceed as follows:

- Identify processes to benchmark and their key characteristics.

- Determine who to benchmark: organizations or processes.

- Determine benchmarks by collecting and analyzing data from direct contact, surveys, interviews, technical journals, and advertisements.

- From each benchmark item identified, determine the best-of-class target.

- Evaluate your process in terms of the benchmarks and set improvement goals.

Benchmarking was covered in greater detail in chapter 9.

Brainstorming

Brainstorming is a way of using a group of people to quickly generate, clarify, and evaluate a sizable list of ideas, problems, issues, and so on. In

Figure 10.13.   Comparative benchmarking.

this case, the emphasis is on quantity of ideas, not quality. It can be an excellent technique for tapping the creative thinking of a team. Brainstorming has three phases.

- During the *generation phase,* the leader reviews the rules for brainstorming, and the team members generate a list of items.
- During the *clarification phase,* the team goes over the list to make sure that everyone understands all the items. Discussion will take place later.
- Finally, during the *evaluation phase,* the team reviews the list to eliminate duplications, irrelevancies, or issues that are off limits.

To conduct a brainstorming session, proceed as follows:

- State the purpose clearly.
- Either have participants take turns in sequence or volunteer their ideas spontaneously.
- Allow only one thought at a time.
- Don't criticize ideas or allow participants to do so.
- Don't discuss ideas.
- Encourage participants to build on each other's ideas.
- Record ideas so that team members can see them.

Note: Brainstorming is a subjective technique that must later be substantiated by data.

Techniques such as multivoting or nominal group techniques (NGT) will generally be used next, to select those items that the team should pursue.

Concurrent (Simultaneous) Engineering

Concurrent (simultaneous) engineering is an approach where design alternatives, manufacturing-process alternatives, and manufacturing-technology alternatives are dealt with in parallel and interactively, beginning with the initial design trade-off studies.

Traditionally, quality and producibility analyses have occurred after the review of designs to assess the impact of proposed design features on manufacturing cost and to identify alternatives for the major production cost drivers. With concurrent engineering, the focus is on both product and process definition simultaneously.

This approach can be used to shorten the design-to-development life cycle and reduce costs by examining the interaction of functional disciplines from the perspective of a cross-functional process. The basic elements involved in applying concurrent engineering include the following:

- Use cross-functional teams, including design, quality, marketing, manufacturing, and support.

- Identify and reduce variability in production and use through careful selection of design parameters.

- Extend the traditional design approach to include such techniques as enterprise integration, design for assembly, robust design, computer-aided design, design-for-manufacture, group technology, electronic data interchange, and value analysis.

- See also the description of the following techniques:
  —Design of experiments
  —Quality function deployment

Cost Estimation

Cost estimation aids in selecting improvement opportunities. Quality management teams can determine problems with the largest dollar impact by estimating costs in one of two ways—the bottom-up approach or the top-down approach. Use these two approaches as follows:

- Bottom-up approach

  —Estimate how many times the problem occurs per unit (example: three times per week).

  —Estimate time and cost per unit to fix (example: 2 people × 3 hours × $17 per hour equals $102).

  —Calculate annual cost (without overhead expenses) by multiplying above factors by weeks worked (example: 3 people × $102 per week × 50 weeks per year equals $15,300 per year).

- Top-down approach

  —Estimate percentage of total labor or other expenditure.

  —Multiply estimate by budgeted annual cost to calculate amount spent on the problem (example: 13 percent × $18,000 per year budgeted equals $2340 per year).

Cost of Quality

Cost of quality consists of all the costs associated with maintaining acceptable quality plus the costs incurred as a result of failure to achieve this quality. The cost-of-quality technique provides managers with cost details often hidden from them. Cost-of-quality analysis could be performed to highlight costs saved by doing the job right the first time.

To conduct a cost-of-quality review, proceed as follows:

- Develop method for collecting data on and reporting on cost of quality.

- Identify quality costs. These are cost of nonconformance and cost of conformance.

- Identify the most significant costs.

- Identify the cause of these major costs.

- Identify the solutions to reduce or eliminate causes.

- Implement solutions.

Customer-Needs Analysis

Customer-needs analysis is a technique for determining the key measurable characteristics that are important to your customer. Customer-needs analysis is a quality management team effort that occurs between you and your customers to answer the following questions:

- What are the *major outputs* of our process?

- Who are the *customers* (both immediate and downstream) for each of these outputs?

- What do our customers say are the *key quality characteristics* that they need in our outputs?

- How can we *measure* our performance on these key characteristics?

- What *goal* would our customers like to see us achieve on these measures?

Possible key quality characteristics are as follows:

• Accuracy	• Completeness	• Flexibility
• Timeliness	• Uniformity	• Understandability
• Relevance	• Consistency	• Reliability

Potential measurements of these characteristics are as follows:

• Physical parameters	• Customer satisfaction
• Time	• Defects and rework
• Cost	• Work output

Customer-Supplier Model

The customer-supplier model depicts the customer-supplier relationship as three triangles in which the center triangle represents the work you do, or your value-added tasks (Figure 10.14). The left triangle represents your supplier(s), the people or organizations who provide you with the input(s) you need to perform your job. The right triangle represents your customer(s), the people or organization(s) who receive your output, or the result of your work.

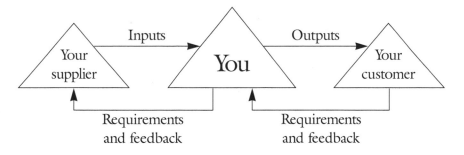

Source: AT&T, *Quality Improvement Process Guidebook* (Baskin Ridge, N.J.: AT&T, 1988), p. 69.

Figure 10.14. Customer-supplier model.

Additional components of the customer-supplier model are requirements and feedback. Requirements are the most critical characteristics of your outputs as defined by your customer. Feedback from your customers communicates the degree to which your output conforms to the negotiated requirements. Analysis of your organization's customer-supplier model is an effective technique to appraise the total impact of quality.

Customer-Supplier Questionnaire
Use this questionnaire as a technique to assess your relations with your customers and suppliers.

Relationship with customers
- What are your primary outputs as a supplier: information, products, and/or services?
- Who are your customers—the primary, direct users or recipients of your outputs?
- What are your customers' requirements for your outputs?
- How do you determine their requirements?
- What are the characteristics of your output that can be measured to determine whether you are meeting your customers' requirements?
- What major quality problems prevent you from meeting your customers' requirements?
- What obstacles stand in your way of resolving these problems?
- What would it take to resolve these problems?

Relationship with suppliers
- Who are your suppliers? Who do you depend on for input—information, products, and/or services—to fulfill your requirements as one who adds value to their inputs?
- What primary inputs do you receive from them?
- What are your requirements for those inputs?

- How do you communicate your requirements to your suppliers?
- How do you provide feedback to suppliers regarding how they are performing?

Shewhart (PDCA) and Deming (PDSA) Cycle

The Shewhart cycle, defined as the plan-do-check-act (PDCA) cycle, has been modified by Deming as the plan-do-study-act (PDSA) cycle, and both are shown in Figure 10.15. Both cycles represent a continuous improvement process for planning and testing improvement activities. When you identify an improvement idea, it is often wise to test it on a small scale before you fully implement it, to validate its benefit. Additionally, by introducing a change on a small scale, employees have time to accept it and are more likely to support it.

To implement these techniques, proceed as follows:

- Plan (P) a change or test.
- Do (D) the change or test, preferably on a small scale.
- Check (C) the effects of the change or test.

(or)

- Study (S) the changes and their impact.
- Act (A) on what you learned.
- Repeat the "plan" step, with new knowledge.
- Repeat the "do" step, and continue onward with process improvement.

Design of Experiments

Design of experiments is a technique in which the analyst chooses factors for study, deliberately varies those factors in a predetermined way, and then studies the effect of these actions. Design of experiments improves the design-to-production transition by quickly optimizing product and process design, reducing costs, stabilizing production processes; and desensitizing production variables.

The following are among the many applications for the design of experiments analysis.

- Compare two machines or methods.
- Study the relative effects of various process variables.

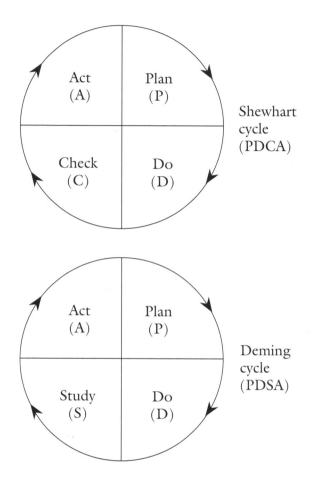

Figure 10.15.   The PDCA and PDSA cycles.

- Determine the optimal values for process variables.
- Evaluate measurement-system errors.
- Determine design tolerances.

To implement the design of experiments technique, proceed as follows:

- Identify the important variables, whether they are product or process parameters, material or components from suppliers, environmental or measuring-equipment factors.

- Break down by key attribute these important variables—generally no more than one to four.

- Reduce the variation on the important variables (including the tight control of interaction effects) through redesign, close tolerancing design, supplier process improvement, and so on.

- Open up the tolerances on the unimportant variables to reduce costs.

Interviewing

Interviewing is a data-gathering process to help quality management teams gain the benefit of others' experience and specialized knowledge.

To use interviewing techniques effectively, proceed as follows:

- Before the interview

  —Gather background information on the topic and interviewee.

  —Outline areas to be covered and major questions to be asked.

  —Meet in a comfortable setting.

  —Tell interviewee the purpose and proposed length of the interview.

- During the interview

  —Help interviewee feel comfortable.

  —Remain analytical and objective.

  —Take notes.

  —Ask open-ended questions to encourage ideas.

  —Ask who, what, where, when, why, and how.

  —Summarize what you learned.

- After the interview

  —Thank the interviewee

  —Review and interpret data as soon as possible (while still fresh in your mind).

Multivoting

Multivoting involves a structured series of votes by a quality management team to help set priorities and thus reduce a list containing a large number of items to a manageable few (usually three to five). This technique may be used throughout the process.

Multivoting steps are as follows:

- First vote: Each person votes for as many items as desired, but only once per item. Circle the items receiving a relatively higher number of votes than the other items. (Example: For team with 10 members, items receiving five or more votes are circled.)

- Second and subsequent votes: Each person votes the number of times equal to one-half the number of circled items. (Example: If six items received five or more votes during the first vote, then each person gets to vote three times during the second vote.)

- Continue multivoting until the list is reduced to three to five items that can be further analyzed. Never multivote down to only one.

Nominal Group Technique

Nominal group technique (NGT) is another method used for reaching consensus. It is a group decision-making process used when priorities or rank order must be established. NGT is similar to brainstorming; however, it is a more structured approach that generates ideas and surveys the opinions of a small (10 to 15 persons) group. NGT is very effective in producing many new ideas or solutions in a short time. It is structured to focus on problems, not people; to open lines of communication; to ensure participation; and to tolerate conflicting ideas. NGT helps build consensus and commitment to the final result.

The basic steps in using NGT are noted here.

- Present issue and instructions.

- Have individuals generate ideas during five to 10 minutes of quiet time, with no discussion.

- Gather ideas one idea at a time, and write them on a flip chart without discussing them.

- Process and clarify ideas by eliminating duplicates and combining like ideas. Discuss the ideas as a group, but only to clarify their meaning, not to argue about them.

- Have individuals set priorities silently.

- Vote to establish the priority or rank of each item.

- Tabulate votes.

- Develop an action plan.

Storyboard

A storyboard is a useful tool for displaying and communicating the big picture. It can be used as an extension of brainstorming exercises or it can integrate ideas, theories, and data generated with different analytical tools and techniques that can be used to improve your processes. To create a storyboard, proceed as follows:

- Clear a large work space or wall to visually collect and display the big picture of the process or problem that is being evaluated.

- Using index cards for new ideas, data plots, problem-solution approaches, and related information, create a visual display of your solution theories and action plan.

- Use your storyboard to integrate the known factors and identify the unknowns that require additional analysis.

Quality Function Deployment

Quality function deployment (QFD) involves the development of a conceptual map that provides the means for cross-functional planning and communications. It is a method for transforming customer wants and needs into quantitative terms. Moreover, QFD, developed in Japan, is a process for ensuring that quality is designed into products and services in an efficient and effective manner.

QFD helps organizations design higher-quality, more competitive, lower-cost products easier and faster and is aimed primarily at the development of new products. The technique is introduced early in new product design efforts and translates customer requirements into design and product characteristics, communicating them in a structured way to influence upstream design decisions and actions. Traditional design organizations have focused more on meeting specifications or technical requirements than on satisfying customer expectations. QFD links customer expectations to the technical considerations of the designer and manufacturer and to the concept of value.

Simply put, QFD helps ensure quality products and processes by detecting and solving problems early. Downstream problems may occur and product quality may suffer when those who work on components and parts have little knowledge of customer requirements or the specifics of the final product and manufacturing processes. The QFD process forces management to analyze broad customer needs and expectations (such as ease of use or comfort) and relate them directly to product characteristics such as weight, strength, speed, and temperature. Those characteristics, in turn, are related to the processes involved in achieving the technical requirements. Specific techniques and tools are employed in the course of QFD. One of the principal quality function deployment tools is the house-of-quality matrix shown in Figure 10.16.

On the matrix, team members identify specific customer requirements, assign priorities to them, and convert them to product attributes and design characteristics through cross-functional team activity. Further, the matrix relates customer needs and expectations to product specifications, such as thickness, strength, and weight, and links those characteristics to the product-related functional area processes. It communicates product-specific requirements, standards, and specifications in a coordinated and consistent way to all the functions that have responsibilities affecting the product. The generation and distribution of quality matrices force early identification of conflicting objectives and potential bottlenecks. Early cross-functional communication should be centered on quality, resolving many potential problems before major investments of time and money have been made.

Of course, products should be designed to meet customer wants and needs so that customers will buy them and continue to buy them. When marketing people, design engineers, manufacturing engineers, and procurement specialists work closely together from the time a

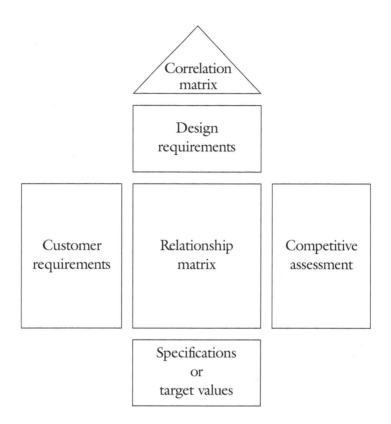

Figure 10.16. House-of-quality matrix for quality function deployment.

product or service is first conceived, they are better able to meet customer requirements. QFD provides a framework within which the cross-functional teams can work.

To begin the QFD process, ask these questions.

- What do customers want (attributes)?

- Are all preferences equally important?

- Will delivering perceived needs yield a competitive advantage?

- What are the characteristics that match customers' attributes?

- How does each characteristic affect each customer attribute?

- How does one change affect other characteristics?

Statistical Process Control

Statistical process control (SPC) is an effective tool for improving performance of any process. It helps identify problems quickly and accurately. It also provides quantifiable data for analysis, provides a reference baseline, and promotes participation and decision making by people doing the job. Statistical process control uses probability theory to control and improve processes and is an excellent technique for determining the cause of variation based on a statistical analysis of the problem.

Statistical process control is a major technique used to implement quality management. Refer to one of the publications noted in Appendix A for substantial how-to information. For a general overview, however, the basic steps involved in statistical process control include the following:

- Identify problems or performance improvement areas. Identify common and special causes. Common causes are random in nature, often minor. Special causes result from an abnormality in the system that prevents the process from becoming stable.

- Do a cause-and-effect analysis.

- Collect data.

- Apply statistical techniques.

- Analyze variations.

- Take corrective action.

This chapter has briefly described the tools and techniques that you may use to improve your quality management. It has provided you with a basic vocabulary and delineation of the application options for each of the basic quality management tools and techniques.

Epilogue

It is time for a new generation of leadership to cope with new problems and new opportunities—for there is a new world to be won.

John Fitzgerald Kennedy
July 4, 1960

Lead Your Quality Management Team

Whoever we are, we can easily fall into the trap of thinking that our organization is too big to be affected by our individual actions. That perception is common and frustrating and, fortunately, it is false. Only through the collective efforts of individual members do organizations change; organizations are incapable of changing themselves.

Whatever your position in your organization, your efforts to perform a job and to improve that performance and productivity directly affect the influence you will have in the organization, the control you will have over your personal situation, and your ability to manage and lead. Combined with the efforts of others, your effectiveness directly influences the organization's overall ability to meet its mission and ultimately affects the perception of good government. Furthermore, how we perform today will affect future generations.

Quality management is a means for improving personal effectiveness and performance and for aligning and focusing all individual quality efforts throughout your organization. It provides a framework within which you may continuously improve everything you do and affect. It is

327

a way of leveraging your individual effort and extending its effect and its importance throughout your organization and beyond.

Make the Decision Today

You have examined in this book the need to adopt a quality management strategy to improve your organization. A guide to the costs and benefits has been presented and shows that your organization should not wait, and that you should act now to improve your level of quality performance. You have read about the different philosophies of quality management improvement from Crosby, Deming, and Juran and found that an amalgam of these principles and practices needs to be created to meet your specific needs. The Federal Quality Awards and related state government quality awards have set the scene for improvement and their winners have shared with you the lessons learned. A series of approximately 200 questions were raised for you to perform an armchair self-assessment of how your organization is doing in terms of quality management. The quality management methodology presented in this book has provided the basic planning and implementation steps needed for you to aggressively and continuously improve your operation. And the basic tools and techniques you and your staff need to use to understand and improve have also been presented.

It is now up to you.

Appendix A: Additional Reading

Albrecht, Karl. *At America's Service: How Corporations Can Revolutionize the Way They Treat Their Customers.* Homewood, Ill.: Dow Jones-Irwin, 1988.

Albrecht, Karl, and Ron Zemke. *Service America: Doing Business in the New Economy.* Milwaukee, Wis.: Publisher's Quality Press, 1985.

Armsdorf, David, and Dan Luria. "A Quality Foundation Beyond Cheerleading." *Modern Michigan* 1, no. 4 (summer 1989).

Aubrey, Charles A., II, and Patricia K. Felkins. *Teamwork: Involving People in Quality and Productivity Improvement.* Milwaukee, Wis.: ASQC Quality Press, 1988.

Ballard, Steven, Timothy Walton, Tracy Torragrossa, and Matt Benner. *High Performance Organizations: Implications for Change in the Public Sector.* Orono, Maine: Margaret Chase Smith Center, University of Maine, November 1991.

Bennis, Warren, and Burt Nanus. *Leaders: The Strategies for Taking Charge.* New York: Harper & Row, 1985.

Carr, K. David, and D. Ian Littman. *Excellence in Government.* Arlington, Va.: Coopers and Lybrand, 1990.

Commission on the Skills of the American Workforce. *America's Choice: High Skills or Low Wages!* Rochester, N.Y.: National Center on Education and the Economy, June 1990.

Creticos, Peter A., Steve Duscha, and Robert G. Sheets. *State-Financed, Customized Training Programs: A Comparative State Survey*. Report submitted to the Office of Technology Assessment, U.S. Congress, September 30, 1990.

Crosby, Philip B. *Quality Is Free: The Art of Making Quality Certain*. New York: McGraw-Hill, 1979.

————. *Quality Without Tears: The Art of Hassle-Free Management*. New York: McGraw-Hill, 1984.

Deming, W. Edwards. *Out of the Crisis*. Cambridge, Mass.: MIT Center for Advanced Engineering Study, 1982.

Ealey, Lance A. *Quality by Design: Taguchi Methods and U.S. Industry*. Dearborn, Mich.: ASI Press, 1988.

Ernst & Young Quality Improvement Consulting Group. *Total Quality: An Executive's Guide for the 1990's*. Homewood, Ill.: Dow Jones-Irwin, 1990.

Garvin, David A. *Managing Quality: The Strategic and Competitive Edge*. New York: Free Press, 1988.

Harrington, H. James. *Excellence—The IBM Way*. Milwaukee, Wis.: ASQC Quality Press, 1988.

————. *The Improvement Process—How America's Leading Companies Improve Quality*. New York: McGraw-Hill, 1987.

Hickman, Craig R., and Michael A. Silva. *Creating Excellence*. New York: New American Library, 1984.

Human Resources Development Institute, AFL-CIO. *Building upon the National Training Trust Model: A Sample of Union-Involved, Joint Training Programs*. Washington, D.C.: AFL-CIO, n.d.

Hunt, V. Daniel. *Quality in America—How to Implement a Competitive Quality Management Program*. Homewood, Ill.: Business One Irwin, 1992.

————. *Reengineering*. Essex Junction, Vt.: Oliver Wight, 1994.

Imai, Masaki. *Kaizen: The Key to Japan's Competitive Success*. New York: Random House, 1986.

Ishikawa, Kaoru. *Guide to Quality Control*. White Plains, N.Y.: Kraus International Publications, 1982.

———. *What Is Total Quality Control? The Japanese Way*. Princeton, N.J.: Prentice Hall, 1985.

Johnston, Kenneth. *Busting Bureaucracy*. Homewood, Ill.: Business One Irwin, 1993.

Juran, Joseph M. *Juran on Leadership for Quality: An Executive Handbook*. New York: Free Press, 1989.

———. *Juran on Planning for Quality*. New York: Free Press, 1988.

———. *Juran's Quality Control Handbook*. New York: McGraw-Hill, 1988.

Kearns, T. David, and A. David Nadler. *Prophets in the Dark*. New York: HarperCollins, 1992.

Kouzes, M. James, and Z. Barry Posner. *The Leadership Challenge*. San Francisco: Jossey-Bass, 1987.

Malcolm Baldrige National Quality Award. *1993 Award Criteria*. Milwaukee, Wis.: American Society for Quality Control, 1993.

McGregor, Douglas. *The Human Side of Enterprise*. New York: McGraw-Hill, 1985.

Michalak, Donald F., and Edwin G. Yager. *Making the Training Process Work*. New York: Harper & Row, 1979.

National Governors' Association. *Excellence at Work: A State Action Agenda*. Washington, D.C.: National Governors' Association, 1991.

———. *Labor Notes*, no. 71. Washington, D.C.: National Governors' Association, March 31, 1992.

Peters, Tom. *Thriving on Chaos*. New York: Alfred A. Knopf, 1987.

Peterson, E. Donald. *A Better Idea*. Boston: Houghton Mifflin, 1991.

Reimann, Curt W. *The Baldrige Award: Leading the Way in Quality Initiatives*. Gaithersburg, Md.: National Institute of Standards and Technology, July 1989.

Scherkenbach, William W. *The Deming Route to Quality and Productivity*. Rockville, Md.: Mercury Press, 1988.

Scholtes, Peter R., et al. *The Team Handbook—How to Use Teams to Improve Quality*. Madison, Wis.: Joiner Associates, 1988.

Secretary's Commission on Achieving Necessary Skills. *Government as a High Performance Employer*. Washington, D.C.: U.S. Department of Labor, February 1992.

U.S. General Accounting Office. *Management Practices: U.S. Companies Improve Performance Through Quality Efforts*. Washington, D.C.: Government Printing Office, May 1991.

U.S. General Accounting Office. *Organizational Culture: Techniques Companies Use to Perpetuate or Change Beliefs and Values*. Washington, D.C.: Government Printing Office, February 1992.

Walter, Jonathan. "The Cult of Total Quality." *Governing* 5, no. 8 (May 1992).

Walton, Mary. *The Deming Management Method*. New York: Dodd, Mead, 1986.

————. *Deming Management at Work*. New York: Putnam, 1990.

Zemke, Ron, and Dick Schaaf. *The Service Edge: 101 Companies that Profit from Customer Care*. New York: New American Library, 1989.

Appendix B: Key Terminology

Appraisal costs—the costs associated with inspecting the product to ensure that it meets the customer's (either internal or external) needs and requirements.

"As-is" process—a description of the current way a product is built or a service is provided, or how a process or methodology is organized or practiced; can be best described in performance metrics. An as-is map shows how specific processes flow and how they intersect with other processes involved in creating a product.

Barrier—anything that impedes progress, extends cycle time, or causes poor quality or failure to meet customer expectations. The goal of continuous process improvement is to remove barriers to performance.

Baselining—obtaining data on the "as-is" process that provide the metrics against which to compare improvements and to use in benchmarking.

Best of class—when overall performance, in terms of effectiveness, efficiency, and adaptability, is superior to all comparables.

Brainstorming—a technique used by a group of people for idea generation. The aim is to elicit as many ideas as possible within a given time frame.

Cause—the established reason for the existence of a result or effect.

Commitment—the open support by management of quality management demonstrated by providing resources, acting as coaches, or serving as facilitators.

Common cause—a source of variation in the process output that is inherent to the process and will affect all the individual results or values of process output.

Conformance—an affirmative indicator or judgment that a product, program, or service has met the agreed-upon requirements of (1) a customer/client/constituent or (2) a relevant specification, contract, or regulation.

Control—the set of activities employed to detect and correct deviation in order to maintain or restore a desired state. A past-oriented approach to quality management.

Correction—the totality of actions to minimize or remove variations and their causes.

Corrective action—the implementation of effective solutions that result in the elimination of identified product, service, and process problems.

Cost-only—steps created because a process does not work or in anticipation of problems in a process. It does not add value to the output of the process.

"Could-be" process—the process as it could be if time and resources were unlimited. The technique is used to break paradigms and encourage creative thinking.

Cross-functional teams—teams with members from several work units that interface with one another. These teams are particularly useful when work units are dependent upon one another for materials, information, and so on.

Culture—a prevailing pattern of activities, interactions, norms, sentiments, beliefs, attitudes, values, and products in an organization.

Customer (external)—a person or organization who receives a product, a service, or information, but who is not part of the organization supplying it. Also called a client or constituent within the public or education sectors.

Customer (internal)—a person or unit who receives output (product, service, or information) from another person or unit within the same unit or from another unit within the larger organization of which it is part.

Customer satisfaction index—a measurement of satisfaction criteria from the customer's perspective as achieved by the supplier interviewing customers. Once criteria are determined, a survey can be taken or some other mutually agreeable measurement can be made. The measurement can then be done by monthly poll or by actually monitoring output on a continuous basis.

Customer-supplier relationship—any formal or informal partnering of customers and suppliers for a long-term relationship.

Data—information or a set of facts presented in descriptive form. There are two basic kinds of data: measured (also known as variable data) and counted (also known as attribute data).

Data management—the process by which the reliability, timeliness, and accessibility of an organization's data base are assured.

Defect—any state of nonconformance to requirements.

Deviation—any departure from a desired or expected value or pattern. The standard deviation is used as the measure of spread for almost all frequency distributions.

Distribution—the population (universe) from which observations are drawn, categorized into cells, and formed into identifiable patterns. Based on the concept of variation, which states that anything measured repeatedly will show different results. These results will fall into statistically predictable patterns. A bell-shaped curve (normal distribution) is an example of a distribution in which the greatest number of observations fall in the center, with fewer observations falling evenly on either side of the average.

Diversity—the characteristics of a work force that result from individual differences between its members. Specific differences may include gender, race, ethnic group, or disabilities. Work force diversity can be a major organizational strength if the knowledge, abilities, and strengths of individual workers are recognized and respected.

Effectiveness—how closely an organization's output meets its goal and/or meets the customer's requirement.

Efficiency—a process characteristic indicating that the process produces the required output at a perceived minimum cost. Ratio of resources expected or planned to be consumed in meeting customer requirements to the resources actually consumed.

Employee involvement—a practice within an organization whereby employees regularly participate in making decisions on how their work is done, including making suggestions for improvements, planning, goal setting, and monitoring performance.

Empowerment—a condition whereby employees have the authority to make decisions and take action in their work areas without prior approval. For example, an operator can stop a production process if he/she detects a problem, or a customer service representative can send out a replacement product if a customer calls with a problem.

Executive steering committee—a system improvement team composed of top management. Its functions include developing statements of values, vision, goals, mission, guiding principles, and policy (strategic plan); identifying customers and evaluating if and how their needs are currently being met; targeting areas for improvement; guiding the quality management implementation plan; providing overall guidance, direction, resources, and support to the quality management's effort; chartering quality management boards and process action teams; and identifying a quality management coordinator.

External failure costs—the costs incurred when an external customer receives a defective product.

Facilitator—a person with extra training in quality management methods and tools who is responsible for assisting teams, keeping meetings moving and focused, and teaching.

Fail-safe techniques—the inclusion in the design and production process of simple automatic checking devices that catch common errors, sometimes called fail-safe production methods.

Fishbone analysis—a diagram that depicts the characteristics of a problem or process and the factors or root causes that contribute to them.

Form-fit-function—part of configuration control; engineering change notices (ECNs) typically support drawing/component changes that do not affect the form, fit, or function of the component in relation to the system in which it is used.

Frequency distribution—
- of a discrete variable. The count of the number of occurrences of individual values over a given range.
- of a continuous variable. The count of cases that lie between certain predetermined limits over the range of values the variable may assume.

Functional organization—an organization responsible for one of the major organizational processes, such as marketing, sales, design, manufacturing, or distribution.

Gain sharing—a reward system that shares productivity gains between owners and employees. Gain sharing is generally used to provide incentives for group efforts toward improvement.

Goal—a statement of attainment/achievement that one proposes to accomplish or attain with an implication of sustained effort and energy directed to it over a longer range.

Guideline—a suggested practice that is not mandatory in programs intended to comply with a standard.

Hypothesis—an assertion made about the value of some parameter of a population.

Input—materials, energy, or information required to complete the activities necessary to produce a specified output (work product).

Installation—a unit with a specifically designated organizational head and/or administrative supervisor who is not subject to on-site supervision by a higher-level installation head and who has been delegated some degree of authority in the performance of personnel management functions.

Internal failure costs—costs generated by defects found within the enterprise, prior to the service or product reaching the external customer.

Key quality characteristics—those attributes that are particularly important with respect to the functioning and performance of products, processes, and services. If a key quality characteristic is defective, then it can seriously affect the performance, function, and reliability of the product, process, and service. Moreover, it may affect customer and user needs, safety, well-being, costs, and productivity.

Labor/work force—the union and nonunion employees of an organization as well as the labor union(s), where applicable. In the education sector, labor also refers to faculty and staff.

Linchpin—a person who provides continuity and unity of effort between executive steering committee, quality management boards, and process action teams. An executive steering committee linchpin is a member of a subordinate quality management board and a quality management board linchpin is a member of a subordinate process action team.

Maintainability—the characteristic of equipment design and/or installation that provides the equipment the ability to be repaired easily and efficiently.

Material review board (MRB)—makes or coordinates the making of decisions at a quality control agency when disposition of nonconforming materials is at issue. This board is composed of a concerned process control engineer, representatives of design engineering, purchasing, and, on material used on products for purchase by government service, the resident government inspector.

Mean time between failures (MTBF)—the average time between successive failures of a given product.

Measurement—the act or process of measuring to compare results to requirements. A quantitative estimate of performance.

Military standards—the (U.S.) government standards of performance for products procured for military systems. These standards include quality standards, performance requirements, statistical-sampling requirements, and component specifications.

Mission—the purpose of the organization; why the organization exists.

Mistake proof—the use of techniques or devices that prevent mistakes or prevent the movement of products with mistakes to the next step in the process. Mistake proofing uses feedback to redesign how work gets done to prevent human error that could be passed on to the customer.

Natural work team—a group of individuals who work within the same function and are involved in a process exclusive to the function.

Need—a lack of something requisite, desired, or useful; a condition requiring provision or relief. Usually expressed by users or customers.

Nonconformities—specific occurrences of a condition that do not conform to specifications or other inspection standards; sometimes called discrepancies or defects. An individual nonconforming unit can have the potential for more than one nonconformity (for example, a door could have several dents and dings; a functional check of a carburetor could reveal any number of discrepancies).

Nominal group technique—a tool for idea generation, problem solving, mission and key-result-area definition, performance-measure definition, and goals/objectives definition.

Normative performance measurement technique—a tool that incorporates structured group processes so that work groups can design measurement systems suited for their own needs. This approach considers behavioral consequences of measurement to foster acceptance of measurement effort.

Objective—a statement of the desired result to be achieved within a specified time. By definition, an objective always has an associated schedule.

Operational definition—communicates consistency in the key quality characteristics to suppliers and customers. Provides (1) a specific method for measuring or testing the key quality characteristic; (2) a criterion for judgment; and (3) a decision whether the criterion has been met in specific cases.

Outputs—materials or information provided to others (internal or external customers).

Paradigm—model or pattern of viewing existing information or methodologies based on history or tradition.

Pareto analysis—used to classify problems or causes by priority; highlights the vital few as opposed to the trivial many; helps to identify which cause or problem is the most significant.

Partnering—the establishment of a long-term relationship between two parties characterized by teamwork and mutual trust, allowing both parties to focus on the needs of a mutual customer or client/constituent. Partners have risks as well as benefits. Partnering arrangements can be made with labor, management, employees, suppliers, government, and educational institutions.

Performance—an attribute of the work product and a general process characteristic. The broad performance characteristics that are of interest to management are quality (effectiveness), cost (efficiency), and schedule. Performance is the highly effective common measurement that links the quality of the work product to efficiency and productivity.

Plan—a specified course of action designed to attain a stated objective.

Policy—a statement of principles and beliefs, or a settled course, adopted to guide the overall management of affairs in support of a stated aim or goal; related primarily to fundamental conduct and usually defines a general framework within which other business and management actions are carried out.

Population—a large collection of items (product observations, data) with certain characteristics about which conclusions and decisions are to be made for purposes of process assessment and quality improvement.

Prevention—a future-oriented approach to quality management that achieves quality improvement through curative action on the process. A strategy that focuses on improving quality by directing analysis and action toward correcting production process defects. Consistent with a philosophy of continuous improvement and "doing it right the first time."

Prevention costs—costs associated with actions taken to plan the product or process to ensure that defects do not occur.

Problem—a question or situation proposed for solution. The result of not conforming to requirements or, in other words, a potential task resulting from the existence of defects.

Process—a system in operation to produce an output of higher value than that of the sum of its inputs. A process is also defined as the logical organization of people, materials, energy, equipment, and procedures into work activities designed to produce a specified end result (work product).

Process action team—a process improvement team composed of individuals selected from among knowledgeable people working in the process. Its functions include identifying barriers to change; collecting data on the process being investigated as directed by the quality management board; solving special causes of variation in those areas under control of the process action team members; recommending solutions to problems discovered within a process beyond process action team's ability to implement; installing measurement systems for process control and feedback to the quality management board.

Process average—the most useful measures of central tendency. It is obtained by dividing the sum of the values in a series of readings by the number of readings.

Process capability—long-term performance level after the process has been brought under control.

Process control—the set of activities employed to detect and remove special causes of variation in order to maintain or restore stability (statistical control).

Process flow analysis—a technique for identification and analysis of key processes. The technique identifies areas and methods of possible improvement. It is particularly useful for roadblock removal.

Process improvement—the set of activities employed to detect and remove common causes of variation in order to improve process capability. Process improvement leads to quality improvement.

Process management—management approach comprising quality management and process optimization.

Process optimization—the major aspect of process management that concerns itself with the efficiency and productivity of the process—that is, with economic factors.

Process owner—a designated person within the process who has authority to manage the process and responsibility for its overall performance.

Process performance—a measure of how effectively and efficiently a process satisfies customer requirements.

Process review—an objective assessment of how well the methodology has been applied to a process. Emphasizes the potential for long-term process results rather than the actual results achieved.

Process/system improvement statement—a statement provided to the executive steering committee by the quality management board that summarizes initial analysis of a key issue/goal and its related processes. Approval of the process/system improvement statement authorizes continued improvement actions by the quality management board.

Productivity—ratio of outputs produced (or service transactions) to inputs required for production/completion. Productivity is an expected outcome of quality and a necessary companion to improving service.

Quality—the extent to which products and services produced conform to customer requirements. Customers can be internal as well as external to the organizational system (for example, products or services may flow to the person at the next desk or work area rather than to people outside the immediate organization). The Federal Quality Institute defines quality as meeting the customer requirements the first time and every time. The Department of Defense (DoD) defines quality as conformance to a set of customer requirements that, if met, result in a product that is fit for its intended use.

Quality circles—a group of workers and their supervisors who voluntarily meet to identify and solve job-related problems. Structured processes are used by the group to accomplish its task.

Quality council—a group composed of top management and/or other staff that provides direction, structure, and oversight to the quality improvement effort. It may also be called an executive steering committee or an executive steering group.

Quality function deployment (QFD)—a disciplined approach to solving quality problems before the design phase of a product. Because the foundation of QFD is the belief that products should be designed to reflect customer desires, marketers, design engineers, and manufacturing personnel work closely together from the beginning to ensure a successful product. The approach involves finding out what features are important to customers, ranking them in importance, identifying conflicts, and translating them into engineering specifications.

Quality management board—a process improvement team composed of individuals with first-hand knowledge and ownership of the processes being investigated. Its functions include identifying and documenting processes in an assigned issue area; prioritizing processes by improvement potential; chartering process action teams to gather data on processes; removing barriers to change; ensuring progress of process action teams; initiating action on problems referred by process action teams; and providing quality management leadership as a group and as individuals.

Quality of work life—the extent to which the organizational culture provides employees with information, knowledge, authority, and rewards to enable them to perform safely and effectively, be compensated equitably, and maintain a sense of human dignity.

Quality performance index—customer satisfaction measurement tool that is often used for a service function where performance requirements vary from month to month. At the end of a specified time period, customers rate supplier performance on a scale of 1 to 100 and provide rationale for the rating. The expected rating of a nominally performing group is 80. Anything below represents an area for improvement; anything above is an area of strength.

Quality teams—teams composed of volunteers who meet regularly to review progress toward goal attainment, plan for changes, decide upon corrective actions, and so on. Members are usually from the same work unit. Also referred to as performance action teams or quality improvement teams.

Quality values—the principles and beliefs that guide an organization and its people toward the accomplishment of its vision, mission, and quality goals.

Range—the difference between the maximum and the minimum value of data in a sample.

Reliability—the probability that a product will perform its specified function under prescribed conditions without failure for a specified period of time. It is a design parameter that can be made part of a requirements statement.

Requirements—what is expected in providing a product or service. The *it* in *do it right the first time*. Specific and measurable customer needs with an associated performance standard.

Roadblock identification analysis—tool that focuses upon identifying roadblocks to performance improvement and/or problems that are causing the group to be less productive than it could be. This tool utilizes the nominal group technique to identify and prioritize performance roadblocks. Action teams are formed to analyze barriers and develop proposals to remove roadblocks. The proposals are implemented, tracked, and evaluated.

Root-cause analysis—an analysis that seeks the root cause, or bottom line, of a problem. Often, problems present themselves only as symptoms. Symptoms do not explain problems; they only point to them. A root cause is the *reason* for the problem or symptom. Root cause analysis, then, is a method used to identify potential root causes of problems, narrow those down to the most significant causes, and analyze them using other quality management tools.

Sample size—a finite number of items taken from a population.

Scanlon committees—committees composed of managers, supervisors, and other employees who work together to implement a philosophy of management/labor cooperation that is believed to enhance productivity. A number of principles and techniques are involved, with employee participation being a major component.

"Should-be" process—the process as it should be, using existing resources and/or some improvements.

Sigma (σ)—the Greek letter used to designate the true standard deviation.

Simulation—the technique of observing and manipulating an artificial mechanism (model) that represents a real-world process which, for technical or economical reasons, is not suitable or available for direct experimentation.

Six Sigma®—quality improvement stretch-goal concept used by Motorola, Inc. It is a statistical term meaning fewer than 3.4 defects per million—allowing for some variation in the mean—or near perfection.

Special cause—a source of variation in the process output that is unpredictable, unstable, or intermittent. Also called assignable cause.

Specification—a document containing a detailed description or enumeration of particulars. Formal description of a work product and the intended manner of providing it. (The provider's view of the work product.)

Standard deviation—a parameter describing the spread of the process output, denoted by the greek letter sigma, σ. The positive square root of the variance.

Statistic—any parameter that can be determined on the basis of the quantitative characteristics of a sample.

- A descriptive statistic is a computed measure of some property of a set of values, making possible a definitive statement about the meaning of the collected data.
- An inferential statistic indicates the confidence that can be placed in any statement regarding its expected accuracy, the range of applicability of the statement, and the probability of its being true. Decisions can be based on inferential statistics.

Statistical control—the status of a process from which all special causes of variation have been removed and only common causes remain. Such a process is also said to be stable.

Statistical estimation—the analysis of a sample parameter in order to predict the values of the corresponding population parameter.

Statistical methods—the application of the theory of probability to problems of variation. There are two groups of statistical methods.

- Basic statistical methods. Relatively simple problem-solving tools and techniques, such as control charts, capability analysis, data summarization and analysis, and statistical inference.

- Advanced statistical methods. More sophisticated specialized techniques of statistical analysis, such as the design of experiments, regression and correlation analysis, and the analysis of variance.

Statistical process control (SPC)—a systematic philosophy of doing business by continually reducing variation around a target value. A disciplined way of identifying and solving problems in order to improve performance. SPC involves use of fishbone diagrams to identify causes and effects of problems. Data are then collected and organized in various ways (graphs, fishbone diagrams, Pareto charts, and/or histograms) to further examine problems. The data may be tracked over time (control charts) to determine variation in the process. The process is then changed in some way, and new data are collected and analyzed to determine whether the process has been improved.

Statistical quality control—a systematic methodology of manufacturing products or services by continually monitoring the state of the product or service based on a target standard of quality.

Strategy—a broad course of action, chosen from a number of alternatives, to accomplish a stated goal in the face of uncertainty.

Stratification—the process of classifying data into subgroups based on characteristics or categories.

Subprocesses—the internal processes that make up a process.

Suppliers—individuals or organizations or firms who provide inputs to the process. Suppliers can be internal or external to a company, firm, or organization.

Supplier development—an organization's efforts to work with a supplier and to certify that the supplier meets all the prescribed quality standards. The process involves rigorous inspection of the supplier's management systems and production processes, education and training in quality improvement criteria, and certification.

Synchronous organization—a process to optimize all resources to produce the right product at the right time, in the right quantities, and based on customer demand. It is a systematic approach to the elimination of waste. The intent is to combine just-in-time principles with other organizational systems to form and integrate the business system. The objective is to improve competitiveness through better organization and process methods by optimizing flow of money, productivity, materials, information, and decisions.

System—a set of well-defined and well-designed processes for meeting the organization's quality and performance requirements.

Taguchi methods—Genichi Taguchi's approach to quality improvement; focused on how to evaluate quality and how to improve and maintain quality in a cost-effective way. Using the Taguchi *loss-function* approach, all quality improvements are measured in terms of cost savings. Cost and quality improvement become one and the same.

Tampering—a condition that exists when management treats all causes of variability as special causes. This condition tends to increase process variability.

Task teams—teams of managers and employees formed to focus on a problem identified by management or another team, to provide recommendations for corrective actions, and to implement those actions. .

Team building—a process of developing and maintaining a group of people who are working toward a common goal. Team building usually focuses on one or more of the following objectives: (1) clarifying role expectations and obligations of team members; (2) improving superior-subordinate or peer relationships; (3) improving problem solving, decision making, resource utilization, or planning activities; (4) reducing conflict; and (5) improving organizational climate.

Timeliness—the promptness with which quality products and services are delivered, relative to customer expectations.

Total employee involvement—a concept based on teamwork, in which employee involvement teams meet regularly to discuss ways to improve the workplace, the production process, and the lines of communication within an organization. Employee involvement flows from the bottom up rather than from the top down of an organization.

Total quality control—a concept originated by Armand V. Feigenbaum; a system for integrating the quality development, quality maintenance, and quality improvement efforts of the groups in an organization so as to enable production and service at the most economical levels that allow for full customer satisfaction.

Total quality management (TQM)—a comprehensive, customer-focused system that many organizations are adopting to improve the quality of their products and services. It is a way of managing the organization at all levels, top management to front line, to achieve customer satisfaction by involving all employees in continuously improving the work process of the organization.

Organizations that have adopted quality management (1) focus on achieving customer satisfaction, (2) seek continuous and long-term improvement in all the organization's processes and outputs, and (3) take steps to assure the full involvement of the entire work force in improving quality. These are TQM's three principles for maximizing customer satisfaction.

Team—any team formed to facilitate the implementation of quality management. These may include functional, cross-functional, task, or process improvement teams and are commonly referred to as process action teams (PATs) or quality improvement teams (QITs).

Transactional analysis—a process that helps people change to be more effective on the job and can also help organizations to change. The process involves several exercises that help identify organizational scripts and games that people may be playing. The results help point the way toward change.

Value-added steps—steps essential for producing the product or service.

Variable—a data item that takes on values within some range with a certain frequency or pattern. Variables may be discrete—that is, limited in value to integer quantities (for example, the number of income tax forms processed). Discrete variables relate to attribute data. Variables may also be continuous—that is, measured to any desired degree of accuracy.

Variance—in quality management terminology, any nonconformance to specifications. In statistics, the square of the standard deviation.

Variation—the inevitable differences between individual inputs and outputs of a process. The sources of variation can be grouped into two major classes: common causes and special causes.

Vision—a brief statement expressing the ideal future state, or what an organization strives to achieve.

Walk the talk—a phrase that describes a person who not only "talks" the quality management philosophy and techniques but also practices them and integrates them into his or her daily work life.

Work in process—that part of raw material, vendor items, or in-house production that is being worked on but not yet completed.

Zero defects—the concept that everyone should do things right the first time, without failures or defects; not a motivation program.

Appendix C: Information Resources

I. National Associations and Centers

American Production and Inventory Control Society (APICS)
500 W. Annandale Rd.
Falls Church, VA 22046
703-237-8344

Focus on just-in-time, capacity management, materials requirements, production activity, and master planning. *Programs and services:* annual conference, seminars/workshops, exhibitions, *Production Inventory Management Journal,* technical publications, professional certification, and local chapter sponsorship.

American Society for Quality Control (ASQC)
611 E. Wisconsin Ave., P.O. Box 3005
Milwaukee, WI 53201-3005
414-272-8575; fax: 414-272-1734

The nation's largest professional society dedicated to the advancement of quality. *Programs and services:* conferences, educational courses, seminars, *Quality Progress* magazine, journals, book publishing, professional certification, technical divisions and committees, and local chapters.

American Society for Training and Development (ASTD)
1630 Duke St.
Alexandria, VA 22313
703-683-8100

Leader in the development of quality training programs. *Programs and services:* professional publications and chapter activities.

Association for Quality and Participation (AQP)
801-B W. 8th St.
Suite 501
Cincinnati, OH 45023
513-381-1959

Focus on quality circles, self-managing teams, union-management committees, sociotechnical analysis, and other aspects of employee involvement. *Programs and services:* conferences, library and research services, *Quality and Participation* journal, newsletter, resource guide, and local chapters.

II.   Community Support

Community Quality Coalition
Ms. Carole Schwinn
c/o Jackson Community College
2111 Emmons Rd.
Jackson, MI 49201
517-787-0800; fax: 517-789-1630

Ms. Jan Partain
c/o Arkansas Industrial Development Commission
One State Capitol Mall
Little Rock, AR 72201
501-682-7327

State Quality Award Network (SQAN)
Mr. John Politi, Chairman
c/o Excellence in Missouri Foundation
P.O. Box 1709
411 Jefferson St.
Jefferson City, MO 65109
314-634-2246; fax: 314-634-4406

III. Federal Government Support

Federal Quality Institute
Federal Quality Institute Information Network
401 F St., NW
Suite 333
Washington, DC 20001

Contact: Jeff Manthos, Information Network Office
202-376-3753

The Federal Quality Institute (FQI) provides a start-up service in quality management for top-level federal government management teams. The FQI serves as a governmentwide focal point for information about quality management through the FQI Information Network, which lends materials such as videotapes, books, and case studies to the federal sector at no cost.

IV. State Government Support

Alabama
Ms. Linda Vincent
Alabama Productivity Center
Farrah Hall, Room 104
P.O. Box 870318
Tuscaloosa, AL 35487-0318
205-348-8956; fax: 205-348-9391

Mr. Edward Kamniker
Department of Finance
State Office of Management Analysis
64 N. Union St., Suite 203
Montgomery, AL 36130-9561
205-242-7931; fax: 205-242-7934

Arizona
Mr. Dennis Sowards
Arizona Quality Alliance
1221 E. Osborn Road, Suite 100
Phoenix, AZ 85014
602-265-6141; fax: 602-265-1262

Ms. Sandy Williams or Mr. Tim Boncoskey
Office for Excellence in Government
1700 W. Washington, Suite 300
Phoenix, AZ 85007
602-542-7546 or 602-542-7569; fax: 602-542-1220

Arkansas
Mr. Shelby McCook
State Quality Coordinator
State of Arkansas
1515 W. 7th St., Suite 600
P.O. Box 2485
Little Rock, AR 72203
501-324-9057; fax: 501-324-9070

Ms. Jan Partain
Quality Management Program
Arkansas Industrial Development Commission
One State Capitol Mall
Little Rock, AR 72201
501-682-7327

Ms. Melanie Kennedy
State of Arkansas
State Quality Management Training Coordinator
Department of Finance
P.O. Box 3278
Little Rock, AR 72203
501-682-7327

California
Ms. Caren Rubin
Department of Planning and Research
Governor's Office
1400 10th St.
Sacramento, CA 95814
916-322-2318

Mr. Peter Brightbill
Governor's Golden State Quality Awards
Department of Consumer Affairs
400 R St., Suite 1040
Sacramento, CA 95814
916-323-3406; fax: 916-323-3968

Mr. Tom Hinton
California Council for Quality and Service
7676 Hazard Center Dr., Suite 500
San Diego, CA 93108
619-497-2599

Colorado
Mr. Jerry Davies
Division of Technical and Consulting Services
Colorado Department of Personnel
1313 Sherman St., Room 115
Denver, CO 80203
303-866-2438; fax: 303-866-2021

Connecticut
Mr. Ernest Nagler
Personnel Development Center
1380 Asylum Ave.
Hartford, CT 06105

Mr. Harry Kenworthy
Connecticut Award for Excellence
c/o Williamantic Division
Rogers Corporation
730 Windham Rd.
South Windham, CT 06266
203-423-6323

District of Columbia
Ms. Marianne K. Clarke or Mr. Eric N. Dobson
National Governors' Association
444 N. Capitol St.
Washington, D.C. 20001
202-624-5300

Delaware
Mr. Gary Smith
Delaware Quality Consortium
State of Delaware Quality Award
Delaware Development Office
99 Kings Highway
P.O. Box 1401
Dover, DE 19901
302-739-4271; fax: 302-739-5749

Mr. Ross Loeser
Du Pont Corporation
Chestnut Run Plaza
Wilmington, DE 19898
302-999-5570

Florida
Mr. John Pieno
Florida Quality Initiative
Governor's Sterling Award for Quality and Productivity
Office of the Governor
The Capitol, Room 209
Tallahassee, FL 32399-0001
904-922-5316

Georgia
Mr. Larry Gess
Division of Strategic Planning
Office of Planning and Budget
254 Washington St., SW
Suite 614
Atlanta, GA 30334
404-656-4311

Mr. John Vinyard
Bekaert Associates, Inc.
2440 Sandy Plains Rd., Bldg. 1
Suite 100
Marietta, GA 30066
404-565-9430; fax: 404-565-9808

Mr. Ned Ellington
Director
Georgia Productivity and Quality Center
Georgia Institute of Technology
151 Sixth St.
Room 221 O'Keefe Building
Atlanta, GA 30332
404-894-4137; fax: 404-853-9172

Hawaii
Ms. Sharon Miyashiro
Department of Personnel Services
830 Punchbowl St., Room 420
Honolulu, HI 96813

Idaho
Idaho Total Quality Institute
Department of Commerce
700 W. State St.
Boise, ID 83720
208-344-0777

Illinois
Ms. Lori Clark
Department of Commerce and Community Affairs
100 W. Randolph, Suite 3-400
Chicago, IL 60601
312-814-2809

Indiana
Mr. Collin Kebo
State Personnel Department
402 W. Washington St., Room W161
Indianapolis, IN 46204
317-232-3006

Mr. Clifford Ong
Indiana Quality Award
1 N. Capitol, Suite 925
Indianapolis, IN 46204
317-635-3058

Mr. Del Schuh
Business Modernization and Technology Corporation
1 N. Capitol, Suite 925
Indianapolis, IN 46204
317-635-3058

Iowa
Mr. Steve Wall
Iowa Department of Management
State Capital, Room 12
Des Moines, IA 50319
515-281-3853; fax: 515-242-5897

Executive Director
Iowa Quality Institute
Iowa Valley Community College
3702 S. Center St., P.O. Box 536
Marshalltown, IA 50158
515-752-8829; fax: 515-752-8829

Kansas
Ms. Bobbi Mariani
Kansas Quality Award
Department of Administration
Division of Personnel
Landon State Office Building
Room 951 South
900 SW Jackson St.
Topeka, KS 66612-1251
913-296-4384; fax: 913-296-6793

Kentucky
Mr. Jerry Pierce
Kentucky State University
Center/Excellence for Quality
Frankfurt, KY 40601

Louisiana
Mr. Raymond Labord
Division of Administration
P.O. Box 94095
State Capitol Annex
Baton Rouge, LA 70804-9095
504-342-7000

Maine
Mr. Brian Warren or Ms. Elaine Trubee
Office of the Governor
State House
Augusta, ME 04333
207-287-3531; fax: 207-287-1034

Maine Quality Center
Margaret Chase Smith Library
P.O. Box 3152
Skowhegan, ME 04976
207-474-0513

Mr. Robert Dalton
Executive Director
Center for Technology Transfer
59 Exeter St.
Portland, ME 04102
207-780-4616; fax: 207-780-4947

Maryland
Ms. Tina Romanowski
Division of Work Force Quality
300 W. Preston St.
Baltimore, MD 21201
410-225-4687

Ms. Alanna Knaus
Maryland Center Quality and Productivity
Maryland Senate Award for Quality and Productivity
College of Business and Management
University of Maryland
College Park, MD 20742-1815
301-405-7099

Massachusetts
Ms. Priscilla Douglas
Commonwealth Quality Improvement Council
Executive Office of Safety
1 Ashburn Pl.
Boston, MA 02108
617-727-7775

Mr. Dave Cohen
Center for Industrial Competitiveness
Armand V. Feigenbaum Massachusetts Quality Award
University of Massachusetts at Lowell
1 University Ave.
Lowell, MA 01854
508-934-2403

Michigan
Mr. Pat Wightman
Department of Commerce
P.O. Box 30004
Lansing, MI 48909
517-373-7466

Ms. Carole Schwinn
Community Quality Coalition
c/o Jackson Community College
2111 Emmons Rd.
Jackson, MI 49201
517-787-0800; fax: 517-789-1630

Minnesota
Department of Administration
Management Analysis Division
50 Sherburne Ave., Room 203
St. Paul, MN 55155
612-297-3904

Mr. Jim Buckman
Ms. Liz Swanson
Minnesota Council for Quality
Minnesota Quality Award
2850 Metro Dr., Suite 300
Bloomington, MN 55425
612-851-3181 or 612-851-3183

Mississippi
Ms. Pamela McCaffrey
Governor's Office
P.O. Box 139
Jackson, MS 39180
601-359-3150; fax: 601-359-3741

Missouri
Mr. John Politi
Excellence in Missouri Foundation
Missouri Quality Award
P.O. Box 1709
411 Jefferson St.
Jefferson City, MO 65109
314-634-2246; fax: 314-634-4406

Montana
Mr. Marc Scow
Professional Development Center
State Personnel
Mitchell Building, Room 130
Helena, MT 59620
406-444-3749; fax: 406-444-2812

Nevada
Mr. Mel Phillips
U.S. Senate Productivity Award for Nevada
Quality and Productivity Institute
P.O. Box 19341
Las Vegas, NV 89193
702-798-7292; fax: 702-798-8653

Ms. Carol Thompson
Nevada Quality and Productivity Institute
2500 Chandler Ave., Suite 1
Las Vegas, NV 89120
702-895-0489

New Hampshire
Mr. Jim Rivers
Press Secretary
Office of the Governor
Governor's Excellence Award
State House
Concord, NH 03301
603-271-2121

New Jersey
New Jersey Quality Achievement Award Office
20 W. State St., CN 827
Trenton, NJ 08625-0827
609-777-0939

New Mexico
Mr. Raymond Cox
Lieutenant Governor's Office
417 State Capitol
Sante Fe, NM 87503
505-827-3050; fax: 505-989-8318

Ms. Karen Martin
Honor Roll Award
Economic Development Department
P.O. Box 549
Mesilla, NM 88046
505-521-3699; fax: 505-521-4099

New York
Quality Through Participation Team
Governor's Office of Employee Relations
Agency Building 2, 11th Floor
Empire State Plaza
Albany, NY 12223
518-474-5255

New York State Department of Labor
The Governor's Excelsior Award
Office of Labor-Management Affairs
Governor W. Averell Harriman
    State Office Building Campus
Albany, NY 12240
518-457-6743

New York State Department of Economic Development
Industrial Effectiveness Program
One Commerce Plaza
Albany, NY 12245
518-474-1131

North Carolina
Ms. Donna Rosefield
Award Administrator
North Carolina Quality Leadership Foundation
North Carolina Quality Leadership Award
P.O. Box 10711
Raleigh, NC 27605
919-733-4856; fax: 919-733-4857

North Dakota
Mr. Brain McClure
Central Personnel Division
Office of Management and Budget
600 E. Boulevard Ave.
Bismark, ND 58505-0120
701-224-4735

Ohio
Mr. Jack Kindler
Office of Total Quality Management
77 S. High St.
Columbus, OH 43266-0601
614-644-5154

Oklahoma
Ms. Paula Land
Office of Personnel Management
2101 N. Lincoln Blvd.
Oklahoma City, OK 73105-4904
405-521-6353; fax: 405-524-6942

Ms. Susan Donchin
Oklahoma State University
900 N. Portland
Oklahoma City, OK 73107
405-947-4421

Oregon
Mr. Keith Menk
Oregon Economic Development Department
Oregon Quality Initiative
775 Summer St. NE
Salem, OR 97310
503-378-6324; fax: 503-581-5115

Pennsylvania
Pennsylvania Quality Leadership Foundation
939 E. Park Dr., MS 210/26
Harrisburg, PA 17111
717-561-6161; fax: 717-561-6179

Rhode Island
Mr. Michael Hughes
Department of Administration
1 Capitol Hill
Providence, RI 02908
401-277-3698

Rhode Island Area Coalition for Excellence
Rhode Island Quality Award
P.O. Box 6766
Providence, RI 02940

South Carolina
Mr. Nathan Strong
Productivity and Quality Services
Division of Human Resource Management
South Carolina Budget and Control Board
1201 Main St.
Suite 1000
Columbia, SC 29201
803-737-0988; fax: 803-737-0968

Mr. Dunk Hale
South Carolina Quality Award
MEMC Electronic Materials, Inc.
P.O. Box 5397
Spartanburg, SC 29304
803-587-3709

Tennessee
Mr. Gary Davis
Department of Economic Community Development
Volunteer Plaza
Suite 660
500 James Robertson Pkwy.
Nashville, TN 37243-0406
615-532-1945; fax: 615-741-0607

Ms. Marie Williams
Tennessee Quality Award Office
National Center for Quality
P.O. Box 246
Blountville, TN 37616
800-453-6474 or 615-323-0224

Texas
Mr. W. C. Enmon
Texas Governor's Office
P.O. Box 12428
Austin, TX 78711
512-463-1903

Ms. Carol Moore, Director
State of Texas
Department of Commerce
Quality Texas Award
P.O. Box 12047
Austin, TX 78711
512-320-9605

Utah
Mr. Conroy Whipple
Human Resource Development
Department of Human Resource Management
2120 State Office Building
Salt Lake City, UT 84114

Mr. Glenn Morris
Utah Quality and Productivity Award
College of Business
Utah State University
Logan, UT 84322
801-750-2279; fax: 801-750-3440

Vermont
Mr. Paul Ohlson
General Services Department
133 State St.
Montpelier, VT 05633
802-828-3331; fax: 802-828-2327

Virginia
Governor's Office of Constituent Affairs
State Capitol
Richmond, VA 23219
804-786-2211

Ms. Elizabeth Ingold or Ms. LeAnn Daugherty
Virginia Productivity Center
Virginia Tech
560 Whittemore
Blacksburg, VA 24061-0118
703-231-6100; fax: 703-231-6925

Washington
Ms. Julia Graham
Washington Department of Personnel
521 Capitol Way South
P.O. Box 47500
Olympia, WA 98504-7500
206-753-5406

West Virginia
Mr. Tom Rice
Governor's Office
State Capitol
Charleston, WV 25311
304-558-2000

Mr. Ron Hutkin
Governor's Award for Quality
West Virginia Community College
College Square
Wheeling, WV 26003
304-233-0272; fax: 304-233-0272

Wisconsin
Mr. Raymond Allen
Department of Employee Relations
137 E. Wilson St.
Madison, WI 53707
608-266-5316

Mr. Tom Mosgaller
Public Sector Quality Network
City of Madison
Room 202
215 Martin Luther King, Jr. Blvd.
Madison, WI 53710
608-266-9037; fax: 608-266-5948

Mr. Michael Williamson
University of Wisconsin
97 Bascom Hall
500 Lincoln Dr.
Madison, WI 53706
608-263-5510; fax: 608-262-8333

Wyoming
Mr. Scott Farris
Governor's Office
State Capitol
Cheyenne, WY 82002
307-777-7434

Ms. Ann Redman
Department of Commerce
Division of Economic and Community Development
Governor's Quality Award
Barrett Building, 4 North
Cheyenne, WY 82002
307-777-7284

Ms. Barbara Stafford
Director of Marketing
Division of Economic and Community Development
Herschler Building
2nd Floor West
122 W. 25th St.
Cheyenne, WY 82002
307-777-7284; fax: 307-777-5840

Appendix D: Abbreviations

DCMDN—Defense Contract Management District Northeast
DCMO—Defense Contract Management Offices
DFAS—Defense Finance and Accounting Services
DLA—Defense Logistics Agency
DOC—Department of Commerce
DoD—Department of Defense
ESC—executive steering committee
FQI—Federal Quality Institute
IRS—Internal Revenue Service
NASA—National Aeronautics and Space Administration
NIST—National Institute of Standards and Technology
NTIS—National Technical Information Service
PAT—process action team
PDCA—plan-do-check-act cycle (Shewhart)
PDSA—plan-do-study-act cycle (Deming)
PQDR—product quality deficiency report
PSR—production system review
QAR—quality assurance representative
QM—quality management
QMB—quality management board
SPC—statistical process control
SQMB—strategic quality management board
TQ—total quality
TQL—total quality leadership
TQM—total quality management
TQO—total quality organization

Index

About the Author

V. Daniel Hunt is president of Technology Research Corporation, located in Springfield, Virginia. He is an internationally known quality consultant, technology analyst, and author in advanced technology fields including productivity (TQM, quality, teamwork), advanced manufacturing technology (CAD, CAM, CIM), and systems engineering (concurrent engineering and product and process improvement). He has almost 30 years of advanced technology analytical and management experience as part of the professional staffs of Johns Hopkins University/Applied Physics Laboratory, TRW, Inc., and Technology Research Corporation.

He has served as a consultant on projects for the Electric Power Research Institute, U.S. Department of Defense, Advanced Research Projects Agency, Drug Enforcement Administration, NOAA, James Martin and Company, Science Applications International Corporation, Professional Services Corporation, the Pymatuning Group, Maxim Technologies, Andersen Consulting, the Dole Foundation, and many other governmental, commercial, and industrial organizations. He has authored many books, including *Quality in America, Reengineering, The Enterprise Integration Sourcebook,* and *Mechatronics: Japan's Newest Threat.*

A holder of degrees in electronics engineering and management, Hunt maintains an active schedule as an author and international lecturer on improving quality and the applications of advanced technology, while serving various industrial companies, government agencies, and other institutions as a consultant.

Technology Research Corporation provides consulting, training, and research service to assist organizations improve their profitability, performance, and survival by applying quality management to their operations. For additional information contact:

Technology Research Corporation
Attn: V. Daniel Hunt
5716 Jonathan Mitchell Road
Fairfax Station, VA 22039
703-764-9432